Arms and Armor
in Colonial America
1526-1783

Plate 1. The French colonists from Fort Caroline find the Indians worshiping a column erected during their first voyage. Jacque Le Moyne, an eye-witness, painted the scene about 1564. It was engraved by Theodore De Bry and published in 1591.

Arms and Armor in Colonial America
1526-1783

by

Harold L. Peterson

BRAMHALL HOUSE: NEW YORK

THE COMPANY OF MILITARY COLLECTORS
    & HISTORIANS

Through its Reviewing Board, takes pride in sponsoring this book and in recommending it as a standard work of reference in the field of American military history.

COLONEL HARRY C. LARTER, USA, Ret.
President

DEDICATION

To my wife
Dorothy
who has helped in this as in all else

Preface

DURING THE PAST FEW DECADES the material culture and social life of the American colonial period have come under close scrutiny from many historians. The belief that a man's thoughts and actions are directly affected and shaped by his physical surroundings has spurred the production of detailed studies of the architecture, furniture, medicine, social customs, and other facets of the era in an effort to gain a better understanding of the men who cleared away the wilderness and brought the United States into being.

Thus far, the emphasis has been placed on social and domestic subjects. Military topics have been almost entirely overlooked. This neglect is the more surprising when one considers the tremendous role that military affairs played in the life of the times. From the very beginning there were battles with the Indians, with colonists of other nations, and even civil wars. For a period of more than 200 years it would be difficult to find more than ten consecutive years during which there were no major wars or threats of wars someplace in the country. Minor skirmishes and encounters with the Indians were almost continuous. For the greater part of the entire period of colonial history in almost every colony, each and every able-bodied man was required to perform some sort of military service. War was a reality to these men, and they lived intimately with it.

In order to understand any military activity, it is necessary to have some knowledge of the types and potentialities of the materiel involved. The supply and capabilities of weapons dictate tactics and frequently decide the outcome of battles and campaigns. They affect the course and progress of explorations through hostile country, and sometimes they even determine the location of towns and cities which must face the possibility of attack or siege.

ARMS AND ARMOR IN COLONIAL AMERICA

It was with the hope of providing this type of data for the colonial period
that the present study has been undertaken. Because of the scope of the subject
and period, a survey form and techniques have been used. This volume traces
only the broad outlines of the development of arms and armor. It is hoped that
future years will produce detailed monographs on the many individual subjects
which warrant such treatment. All forms of arms and armor are touched upon
herein except heavy ordnance. A separate work on that subject is planned
later.

It will soon be noted that Book One deals with all the colonies that later
became part of the continental United States. Book Two, on the other hand,
concerns itself primarily with the English colonies along the Atlantic Seaboard
and secondarily with the French, thus slighting the Spanish colonies in Florida
and the South West. This shift in focus was necessitated by the distribution of
source material. In the eighteenth century, the differentiation between models
of firearms and swords was precise and often based on minor details. Data on
these changes in Spanish arms were not available in the Western Hemisphere,
and therefore it was decided to follow the general trend in most other colonial
histories and concentrate on the area which produced the original thirteen states.

During the twelve years that this work has been in progress many persons
have generously assisted in various ways. Those who have permitted the illustration of specimens from their collections are indicated beneath the respective
pictures and are sincerely thanked herewith. It would be impossible to list all
who have helped, but it is a pleasure to offer public thanks for notable contri-
butions from the following persons.

To Josef Alm of the Kungliga Armémuseum and Dr. Torsten Lenk of the
Kungliga Livrustkammeren, Stockholm; Claude Blair of H. M. Tower of Lon-
don; Javier Cortes of the Real Armería, Madrid; Stephen V. Grancsay and
Leonard A. Heinrich of the Metropolitan Museum of Art, New York; Eleanor
Murray of the Fort Ticonderoga Museum; Mendel L. Peterson, Russell Sirlouis,
and Craddock Goins of the United States National Museum, Washington;
Walter J. Howe, John Harper and Chauncey Stith of the National Rifle Asso-
ciation, Washington; Col. Frederick P. Todd, Gerald C. Stowe and Milton F.
Perry of the West Point Museum, who provided technical information and
placed the vast resources of their institutions at my disposal.

To Dr. Robert L. Brunhouse, Dr. Charles W. Porter, III, and Freeman
Tilden who read the manuscript from an historical and literary standpoint.

PREFACE

To Robert L. Miller and Bluford W. Muir who did much to improve the quality of the illustrations.

To C. O. v. Kienbusch, Joseph Aiken, Col. Harry C. Larter, Jr., H. Charles McBarron, Jr., Detmar H. Finke, Capt. Ross Collins, Herbert A. Sherlock and Tom Parker who contributed freely of their time and talents as well as their technical knowledge in reviewing portions of the manuscript and providing data and pictures from their own researches.

To the Controller of Her Britannic Majesty's Stationery Office for permission to use the Crown copyright illustrations reproduced in Plates 16, 31 and 135.

Arlington, Virginia

Harold L. Peterson

Contents

BOOK I

The Age of Colonization and Exploration

1526-1688

Introduction

THE HISTORY OF ARMOR AND WEAPONS in America from 1526 to 1688 is the fascinating story of the impact of a new environment on the staid military institutions of the Old World and of the remarkable evolution which resulted. The great degree to which a colonist was dependent upon his arms made him extremely careful in selecting the ones he used. In America he found new conditions and new problems which could not be met adequately by standard European methods. Therefore he demanded better weapons and new tactics, and in so doing he pushed the evolution of military material far ahead of contemporary Europe.

The years from 1526 to 1688 in America were years of struggle. The European settlers and explorers continually fought for existence against the wilderness that was America, but there were military conflicts also. A series of bloody Indian wars involved all but a few of the more fortunate settlements. There were bitter conflicts among the colonies of different European nations, and there was civil strife within the individual colonies. In no other comparable period of American history has there been such a large number of armed conflicts actively involving so great a percentage of the population.

Arms and armor were vital necessities. Not only did they serve the explorer or settler in the numerous wars of the period, but they also provided him with much of his food, a good portion of his clothing, and at least a part of the products from which he derived his livelihood.

Aside from the somewhat problematical activities of the Scandinavians, the first Europeans to attempt a permanent settlement in what is now the continental United States were the Spaniards. In 1526 Lucas de Ayllon attempted to establish a colony in what is now northern North Carolina or southern Virginia. He failed, but a few years later other Spaniards founded St. Augustine; and the Spanish domination of Florida had begun.

[3]

The second group of Europeans to undertake a settlement in America were the French, first at Port Royal, South Carolina in 1562, and again at Fort Caroline, in Florida in 1564. The Port Royal colony failed, and Fort Caroline was destroyed by the Spanish in 1565. Defeated in the south, the French turned northward and settled the great St. Lawrence Valley.

Following the French came the English, the Dutch, and the Swedes. After several unsuccessful attempts by Sir Walter Raleigh to found a colony on Roanoke Island, 1585-1589, the English finally established a foothold on Jamestown Island in 1607. After the settlement at Jamestown, the English colonies multiplied rapidly, starting with the New England colonies and then filling in the space between with the exception of the intrusions of the Dutch in New Amsterdam and the Swedes in the lower Delaware Valley, western New Jersey, and eastern Pennsylvania.

At the same time that these settlements were being started on the coast, adventurous explorers were making epic journeys into the uncharted forests. In 1526 Narvaez travelled through the Gulf States in a vain search for gold. In 1539 De Soto surpassed this exploit and discovered and crossed the Mississippi River. At about the same time another Spaniard, Coronado, marched north from Mexico and traversed much of the Southwest. In the north, the French emulated the earlier activities of the Spaniards and sponsored extensive expeditions of their own, including the famous journeys of Champlain in the East, and the great western travels of Marquette, Joliet, and La Salle.

Almost from the very beginning there were hostilities with the Indians. The French and Spanish were more fortunate in their relations with the aborigines and could conserve their strength for struggles with other Europeans. The English, Dutch, and Swedes were not so lucky, however, and years of intermittent warfare resulted. Among the more important conflicts were the famous Virginia Massacre of 1622 when the Indians almost succeeded in annihilating the settlers, the Pequot War and King Philip's War in New England, and Kieft's War in New Netherlands.

From 1565 when the Spanish massacred the Huguenots in Florida until 1763 when England finally defeated France in America, there was strife among the European colonies. The English and Spanish eyed each other warily and fought minor skirmishes in the South. The Dutch conquered the Swedes and seized control of their settlements, only to be conquered in turn by the English a few years later. The really titanic battle between the colonies of England and France for control of the continent, however, did not begin until after the close of the period.

In addition to battles with the Indians and struggles with other colonies, there were also civil wars. The only large-scale outbreak was Bacon's Rebellion in Virginia in 1677, but there were discontented murmurings in many colonies, especially New Netherlands; and almost all English colonies witnessed some violence at the time of the Glorious Revolution in 1688.

The men who came to America to found the colonies and take part in the great events of the period were typical Europeans. The military men among them had received their training on the battlefields of the Continent, and they brought with them the standard military equipment of the day. They wore heavy suits of armor, and every man carried a sword. Their principal projectile weapons were the crossbow and the matchlock musket, and a large percentage of the men were armed with pikes and other pole arms instead of either the bow or the musket.

In Europe where segments of the population fought pitched battles on open fields, usually in good weather, these weapons had served sufficiently well. In America where the whole white population was outnumbered and continually on the defensive, where wars consisted of ambushes, forays, and surprise attacks, at night and in the rain; different and superior weapons were needed. The armor was discarded as too burdensome for the long treks and rapid movements of woodland warfare. Polearms were found to be of little use against an enemy who would neither charge nor stand against a charge. In addition they were too unwieldy for use in rough and forested country. The crossbow and matchlock were too clumsy and slow for use against an enemy who refused to stay in one place long enough for such a weapon to be discharged in his general direction. Better firearms were available in Europe in the form of wheel locks and primitive flint arms. Conditions in America demanded these better arms. The end of the evolution was reached when every soldier answered the muster calls devoid of armor and armed with a sword and a firearm with a flint lock.

In almost every instance the evolution followed the same pattern. The dates of change differed with each colony, but well before the end of the period all had completed the course; and this steady development of military matériel had brought America to a point that was not equalled in Europe for many years.

Chapter One

Firearms

THE PROJECTILE arms of the early explorers and colonists were their most important weapons. The American Indian usually preferred to do battle against Europeans in loose formation and at long range, resorting to hand-to-hand combat only in surprise attacks or when he believed that the enemy had been sufficiently decimated and disorganized by his sniping tactics. Consequently, weapons which could strike at a distance were a prime necessity to the Europeans. In addition to their value in warfare, projectile arms were also important in providing the white man with fresh meat. For these reasons, the evolution of design in such weapons was swifter and more striking than in any other form of military equipment.

The first European projectile arms to appear in this country were the crossbow and the matchlock. Of these, the crossbow was the more important for the first few years. Early journals record distances in terms of "crossbow shots." De Vaca mentioned using the metal pieces from crossbows to make nails when he and his men were building boats in order to get back to civilization in 1528. De Soto had a large number of crossbowmen with him on his expedition across the Mississippi, and in the Southwest crossbows were listed among the effects of both Coronado and Cabrillo.[1]

By the middle of the 16th century, however, the crossbow had been largely superseded as a military weapon in Europe, and its decline was reflected in America. No crossbows are shown in the drawings made in Florida by Jacques Le Moyne in 1564, although many matchlocks are pictured. A few crossbowmen were listed in the Spanish forts of St. Augustine and Santa Elena in Florida in 1570, 1573, but they were distinctly of secondary importance. The last known reference to crossbows for use in America is contained in an inventory of supplies which Don Pedro Ponce de León offered to provide if he were appointed to lead

[7]

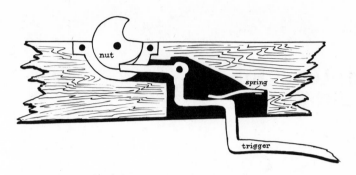

Plate 3. Cross bow mechanism of the simple type found on most military bows.

U. S. National Museum

Plate 4. Sixteenth century crossbow with crannequin in place ready for bending.

an expedition into New Mexico in 1596. The appointment, however, went to Don Juan de Oñate, who mentioned no crossbows.[2]

The military crossbows which came to America with these various expeditions were undoubtedly of the type most popular in Europe at the end of the 15th and the beginning of the 16th centuries. The bow itself was usually made of steel or occasionally horn, and the bow string, of hemp or flax. It was fixed to a stock of some close, straight-grained wood, such as beech. The nut which held the string when the bow was bent was made of steel or of horn reinforced with steel. It pivoted on an axle of iron or heavy cord. The groove in which the arrow or quarrel was placed was usually lined with metal, either brass or iron, or occasionally with horn.[3]

The loading and firing of one of these crossbows required several time-consuming operations. First, the nut was turned until its notch was in position

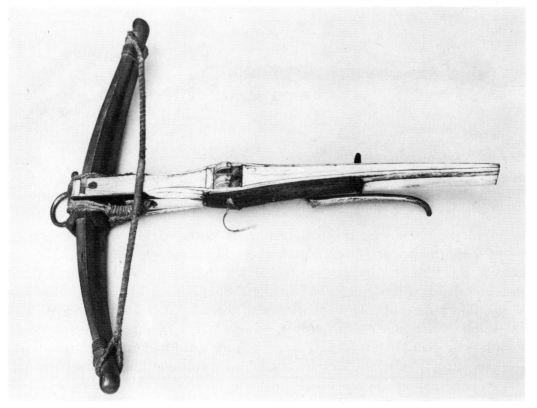

Metropolitan Museum of Art

Plate 5. Early 16th century crossbow without its crannequin.

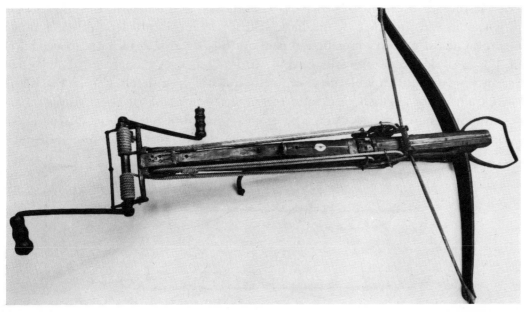

Plate 6. Crossbow with windlass.

Author's Collection

National Park Service

Plate 7. Goat's foot lever from a light 17th century sporting crossbow excavated at Greenspring, Gov. Sir William Berkeley's home near Jamestown.

to receive the bow string. It was automatically locked in this position by the tip of the trigger under pressure from a spring. Next, the bow was bent. Military bows of the 16th century were so heavy that this could not be done without mechanical aid. The devices for bending the bows used by the men on these expeditions were probably the crannequin (a gear and rack arrangement), and the windlass and rope. It is possible, however, that they used a simple lever, known as the goat's foot lever because of the fork that fitted over the stock. After the bow string was drawn back by one of these aids and hooked over the nut, the projectile, known as a bolt or quarrel, was placed in the groove. The bow was then ready for firing, and a pressure on the trigger released the nut which revolved and in turn released the bow string.[4]

Despite its slowness, the crossbow had attained popularity in Europe because of its range and the force of the blow it dealt. The so-called pointblank range of the standard military crossbow was about 60-70 yards, and with an elevation of 45° it could shoot upwards of 350 yards. One heavy siege crossbow tested recently was found capable of sending its quarrel completely through a plank three-quarters of an inch thick at a range of 60 yards. This penetrating power was important in Europe where the enemy was protected by metal armor. In America, however, where the Indian wore little for protection and depended

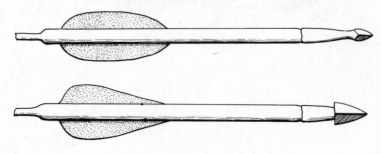

Plate 8. Crossbow quarrels.

on his agility for his safety, the power of the crossbow could not compensate for its lack of speed.[5]

The disadvantages of using the slow-firing crossbow against the swift-moving Indians are well pointed out in the narrative of one of the men who accompanied De Soto. In describing one of their battles with the Indians he complained rather bitterly that:

"They [the Indians] never stand still, but are alwaies running and traversing from one place to another: by reason whereof neither crossebow nor arcubuse can aime at them: and before one crossebowman can make one shot, an Indian will discharge three or foure arrowes; and he seldome misseth what he shooteth at." [6]

Continuing his comparison, the writer adds that:

"An [Indian] arrow, where it findeth no armour, pierceth as deeply as a crossebow. Their bowes are very long, and their arrowes are made of certaine cane like reedes, very heavy & so strong, that a sharpe cane passeth thorow a Target: . . . For the most part when they light upon an armour, they breake at the place where they are bound together. Those of cane do split and pierce a coate of maile, and are more hurtful than the other." [7]

Before leaving the subject of bows entirely, it might be well to examine what part, if any, the long bow played in the early colonial history of America. By the time that European exploration and colonization of the New World had begun, the long bow had all but disappeared. Only in England was the traditional weapon retained, and even there it had lost much of its importance by the end of the 16th century. Thus, only in the English colonies would one expect to find traces of the long bow. There is no direct evidence proving that long bows actually were used on the American continent, but there are strong indications that they may have been. The first such indication is found in an anonymous document advising Sir Walter Raleigh on the military and civil technicalities involved in founding a colony. In this document, the writer advised Raleigh to arm 150 of his 800 men with long bows. It will never be known whether Raleigh accepted this advice and sent some bowmen with the other settlers to Roanoke Island, but there is at least a possibility that he did.[8]

A second reference to long bows in America is found in a list of arms sent to Virginia following the disastrous Indian massacre of 1622. At that time the Tower of London and other government arsenals were examined, and a shipload of arms and armor, some new, but mostly obsolete, was sent to help the surviving colonists rearm. Included among the stores sent were 400 long bows and 800 sheaves of arrows. When the Virginians learned of the inclusion of these items

Plate 9. The French from Fort Caroline help Chief Outina defeat his enemies. Engraved by De Bry from Le Moyne's original painting. Note that De Bry forgot to show the match in the men's arquebusses and that the apical peaks on the cabassets are pointing front instead of back.

in the shipment, they promptly requested that they be unloaded in Bermuda and kept in storage there. They stated as their reason that in Bermuda the bows and arrows would be near enough to be readily procured in time of need; and in the meantime they would not be where the Indians could observe them closely and perhaps learn how to improve their own weapons by studying the British manufacturing techniques. These two instances constitute the only known direct references to the European long bow in Colonial America.[9]

In addition to the crossbow and possibly the long bow, the European explorers and settlers brought with them some firearms. During the first part of the 16th century, these arms were all matchlocks. That is, they were fired by bringing a lighted slow-match into contact with the priming powder.

The matchlocks carried by the early European adventurers were variously described by participants as arquebuses, calivers, and muskets. Unfortunately, there was a great confusion of terms, and it is necessary to infer from the indi-

[12]

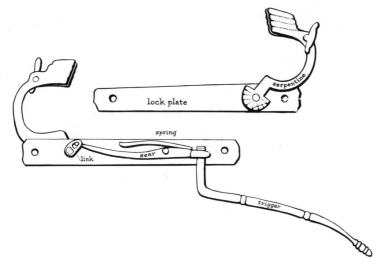

Plate 10. Early matchlock mechanism with lever trigger.

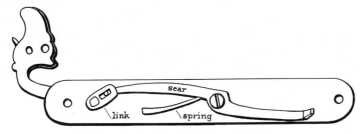

Plate 11. Matchlock with sear trigger.

vidual author's comments exactly what kind of gun he is referring to. This is particularly true in regard to the word "arquebus." Some authors applied it indiscriminately to any firearm. Other and more careful writers used it to designate a gun which was lighter than a musket and fired without a rest, thus making it for a short period synonymous with "caliver." Still later, toward the beginning of the 17th century, it began to be used to designate a wheel lock as opposed to a matchlock.[10]

The term "caliver" has a somewhat hazy history, but its use was for the most part more precise than "arquebus." Many authorities state that the word was derived from the same source as the modern word "caliber," meaning the diameter of the bore of a gun, and that it was applied to the arms of certain regiments whose guns were all of the same size. However this may be, the word as employed by the 16th and 17th century authors signified a firearm lighter than the musket and fired without a rest. It was in this sense that its meaning was synonymous with the most frequent connotation given the word "arquebus" during the middle two decades of the 16th century. An illustration of the type

Plate 12. Late 16th century Italian matchlock musket believed to have been used at Plymouth.

of gun referred to at that time by these two terms may be seen in the pictures of Jacques Le Moyne [See cut].

The term "musket" has always referred to a heavy military gun. In the 16th and early 17th century it was a matchlock, so heavy that a forked rest was required to hold the barrel steady in firing. At this time, its lighter companion, as noted above, was designated "caliver," but toward the middle of the 17th century the word "fusil" or, corruptly, "fuzee" superseded the earlier term. It is generally believed that the word "musket" [mosquete] was first used by the Spanish to denote a heavy military firearm which they developed about the middle of the 16th century, and which was introduced into the Spanish military service by the Duke of Alba. This weapon weighed about 20 pounds, and possessed a bore of 8 or 10 gauge. It is frequently stated by early writers that the heavy charge of powder fired from these arms (up to 2 ounces per charge) led the Spanish to develop the technique of firing with the butt braced against the shoulder in the modern manner rather than holding it in front of the chest as was the usual practice at that time.

As the years passed, the weight of the musket was reduced until by the middle of the 17th century the usual English musket weighed about 16 pounds. The caliber of the arm in England also was sufficiently standardized at 10 gauge. so that "musket bore" became a standard term of measure. Despite the fact that the bore of the gun was 10 gauge, it is interesting to note that the standard musket ball was 12 gauge. This difference in size was calculated to minimize the effects of powder fouling and permit a musketeer to load with ease after many discharges without cleaning the barrel.[11]

The matchlocks which the earliest European brought with them were operated by a very simple mechanism. On the outside of the lock was a forked holder for the match, known as the serpentine. This was attached on the inside of the lock to a lever, known as the sear, by a simple link arrangement. The sear was pivoted in the center on the inside of the lock plate. The trigger, which greatly resembled its counterpart on the contemporary crossbow, was attached directly to the end of the sear opposite the serpentine. With this arrangement, an upward pressure on the trigger acted through the sear and the link to depress the serpentine holding the lighted match in a sweeping arc toward the flash pan with its priming powder. The match thus ignited the powder in the pan which in turn set off the charge in the barrel through a small touch hole drilled from the pan to the interior of the barrel. A light spring fastened to the lock plate and exerting a force on the sear counter to that of the trigger served to hold the serpentine up and away from the pan when pressure was not being applied.

Additional protection against accidental discharge was provided by placing a hinged cover on the pan which could be closed when it was not desired to fire the gun. In most matchlocks, the pan was forged as a part of the barrel and not as a part of the lock. The match itself consisted of a loosely braided cord which had been soaked in a solution of salt peter so that it would maintain an even fire and burn at the rate of about 4 or 5 inches an hour.[12]

Although the mechanism was simple, the loading of a matchlock was a long and complicated procedure. After having fired his musket, the first task of the soldier was to remove his match (which according to regulations was lighted at both ends) so that he would not accidentally ignite any of his powder. To do this, he loosened the thumb screw which clamped the match in the fork of the serpentine and grasped the cord with his left hand, holding one of the lighted

Folger Shakespeare Library
Plate 13. Musketeer ready to aim and fire. From De Gheyn.

Folger Shakespeare Library
Plate 14. Musketeer reloading. Here the match has been removed, and he is blowing in the pan to clean it before priming with the flask in his right hand. From De Gheyn.

[15]

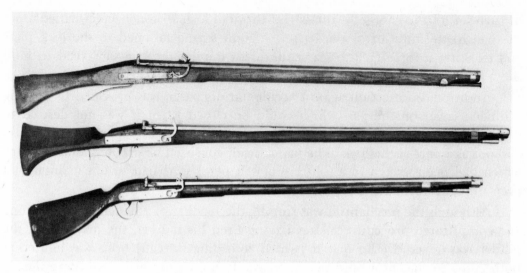

Author's Collection

Plate 15. Matchlock muskets. Top, Italian c. 1580-1610 with restored stock; middle, German, c, 1600-1630; bottom, German, c. 1640-1670.

ends between his second and third fingers and the other end between his third and fourth fingers. Then, seizing the barrel of the gun with the thumb and fore-finger of the same hand, he would hold it while he loaded. Having thus prepared the piece to receive the charge, he would use his right hand to open one of the wooden cylinders on his bandolier, each of which contained a single charge of powder, and pour the contents down the barrel. Next came a ball from its pouch, or from his mouth if it was during an action, and, finally, a wad of tow or paper. All this was forced home with the rammer. Then he would prime the piece by filling the flash pan with fine-grained powder from a little flask which was sus-pended from his belt, close the pan cover, and carefully blow away any loose powder.

The piece was then loaded, but several actions were still necessary before it could be fired. The match had to be returned to the serpentine and adjusted. The coal on its end had to be blown into activity. If the gunner was forced to wait any length of time before firing, he had to change the adjustment of the

H. M. Tower of London

Plate 16. Matchlock in its most highly developed form, c. 1670-1690.

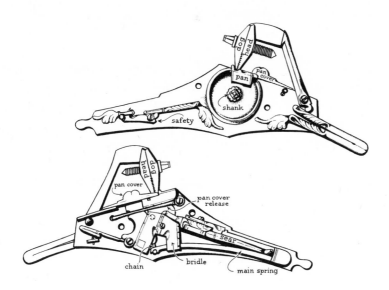

Plate 17. German wheel lock mechanism c. 1565.

match continually to insure that it would strike the pan and also to prevent it from burning down to the serpentine and going out. If it did go out, he re-lighted it from the coal at the other end of the match, which was kept burning for that purpose.[13]

It was this long procedure that the author of the martial laws of Virginia had in mind when he prescribed the appearance and duties of a sentinel in 1611:

"... he shall shoulder his piece, both ends of his match being alight, and his piece charged, and prined, and bullets in his mouth, there to stand with a careful and waking eye, untill such time as his Corporall shall relieve him." [14]

Over the course of the years the appearance of the matchlock underwent considerable alteration. By the latter part of the 17th century, it had acquired many of the features of the later flintlock arms. The pan was no longer forged as part of the barrel, but was attached to the lock plate as a separate piece. The trigger was no longer screwed directly into the sear, but operated against it in much the manner of a modern arm. The trigger also had attained a more modern appearance and was supplied with a guard. The shape of the lock plate began to achieve a form similar to the flint lock; and finally the stock began to be fashioned in more of what is now considered a conventional form.

These changes did not take place all at once, nor did they follow a definite evolutionary series. In England, the standard military musket of the middle of the 17th century had completed the evolution. In France, however, the military matchlock of 1700 still retained the old trigger and trigger mechanism although the lock plate, pan attachment and stock shape had reached the final stage of development. Within countries, also, there was a wide variation in the fabrication of these arms due primarily to the individual preference and abilities of the different makers and also to the thrifty practice of utilizing old parts when they were available. Thus, one frequently finds a highly developed trigger mechanism on early lock plates, and sometimes even with lock plates of the latest design one finds the pan attached to the barrel. Consequently, it is necessary to take all features of such a gun into consideration when assigning it a date. Reliance on any one feature in dating a piece will lead more often to error than to accuracy.[15]

As was noted above, some matchlocks were brought to America with the very first expeditions. In the earliest accounts these guns were almost always referred to as arquebuses; undoubtedly these were fairly light weapons with sharply curved stocks. Jacques Le Moyne illustrates this type of gun excellently in his drawings of the French in Florida in 1564. [See cut] [16]

The first use of the term "musket" in connection with America appears in the accounts of the Coronado expedition of 1540. Whether or not it definitely indicated a musket in the generally accepted meaning of that term, it is impossible now to determine. Allowing for the fact that Coronado must have purchased the arms quite some time before the actual year in which they are mentioned, it places the date somewhat early for the appearance of the true musket. Nevertheless, since the musket was supposedly a Spanish innovation and since it was adopted into the Spanish military service about 1550, it is well within the realm of possibility that Coronado's men actually had them. By 1578, there is no longer any question that the musket as it is known today was in use in Florida. Returns of the military supplies in the Spanish forts of Santa Elena and St.

National Park Service

Plate 18. Wheel lock excavated at Jamestown.

Plate 19. Wheel lock musket c. 1600-1625.

Jac Weller Collection

U. S. National Museum

Plate 20. Wheel lock musket c. 1620-1650.

Augustine made in that year sharply differentiate between the musket and its lighter companion, the arquebus or caliver.[17]

Although the matchlock was used in America for approximately 150 years, its service as the principal projectile weapon lasted less than half that period. In the beginning, it was definitely a subsidiary of the crossbow. By 1550 it had supplanted the crossbow, and its period of greatest importance had begun. It reigned supreme without serious challenge until the second decade of the 17th century when its many drawbacks finally caused it to be set aside in favor of better arms. The retirement of the matchlock was gradual, but by the beginning of the fourth quarter of the 17th century it had practically disappeared as a military arm in America.

The faults which caused the abandonment of the matchlock were many. As was noted above, it was slow. It could not compete either in speed of firing or in accuracy with the Indian's arrow. Its only physical advantage over the arrow was that when it did hit its mark the result was fearful. It did, however, possess considerable psychological advantages in its noise, flame, and smoke.

In addition to its slowness and clumsiness, the fact that it was necessary to have a lighted match was a great liability. A lighted match was a constant hazard in the presence of powder. Not only was an accidental discharge likely if the pan cover happened to be open, but there was also the danger of setting off loose powder carried upon the person. Just such an accident happened to Capt. John Smith in 1609 when a lighted match ignited some powder in his pocket and burned him severely. He was still laid up from this accident when his enemies seized upon him and deported him to England to stand trial for alleged misconduct.[18]

The necessity of a lighted match was also a liability in other ways. It was almost impossible to maintain a live coal on a windy or rainy day, and on these occasions the gun was useless. Henry Hudson's men were badly cut up in a

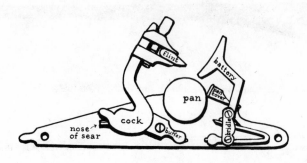

Plate 21. Snaphaunce lock.

fight with the Indians in 1609 when rain put their matches out. A glowing match in the dark immediately indicated the presence of a soldier and hence made him particularly liable to an ambush while making it next to impossible for him to surprise anyone else.[19]

Finally, unless the match were kept burning all the time, it was necessary for the soldier to have a fire close at hand in order to relight it. This led to many dangerous situations. In 1620, a surprise attack at dawn caught a party of the Pilgrims with their matches out, and it was only the presence of a few men equipped with flint arms that enabled them to hold off the Indians until the rest had lighted their matches.[20]

The significance of the lighted match was not lost on the Indian, and he soon made use of his knowledge. The following adventure which happened to Captain Raleigh Gilbert on the Coast of Maine in 1607 is one example of the Indians' attempt to strike the matchlock at its weak point:

"... the Salvadges perceiving so much, subtilely devised how they might put out the fier in the shallop, by which meanes they sawe they should be free from the danger of our men's pieces, and to performe the

National Park Service
Plate 22. Snaphaunce lock excavated at Jamestown.

same, one of the salvadges came into the shallop and taking the fier brand which one of our company held in his hand thereby to light the matches, as if he would light a pipe of tobacco, as sone as he had gotten yt into his hand he presently threw it into the water and leapt out of the shallop. Captain Gilbert seeing that, suddenly commanded his men to their musketts and the targettiers too, from the head of the boat, and bad one of the men before, with his targett on his arme, to stepp on the shore for more fier; the salvages resisted him and would not suffer him to take any, and some others holding fast the boat roap that the shallop could not pott off. Captain Gilbert caused the musquettiers to present their peeces, the which, the salvages seeing presently let go the boatroap, . . ." [21]

In this instance, the psychological effect of pointing the muskets apparently was sufficient to overawe the Indians even though they knew that the guns could not be fired. Such luck, however, could not be counted on to hold good in every instance.

Despite the many and obvious drawbacks of the matchlock, it retained its ascendancy for many years even though better arms were available. As early as 1520, a much swifter and surer ignition system, known as the wheel lock, had been developed in Germany. Less than 50 years later, the snaphaunce appeared, first in the Low Countries, and very shortly after 1600 a primitive form of flintlock was in use in England. The greater complexity of these locks and the resulting greater expense, however, delayed their general acceptance as military arms. It was not until the second decade of the 17th century that they began to

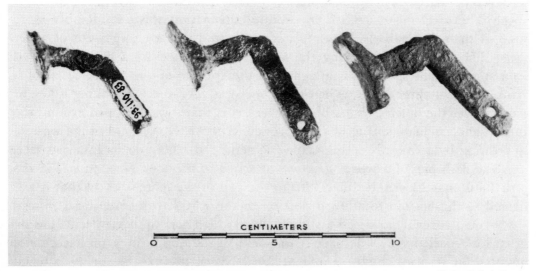

CENTIMETERS

0   5   10

National Park Service

Plate 23. Snaphaunce batteries excavated at Jamestown.

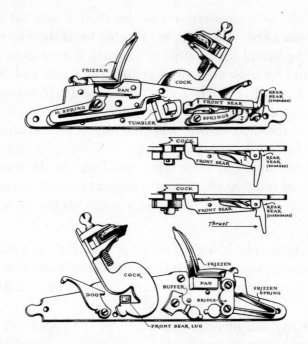

National Rifle Association

Plate 24. Early dog lock. Note the double sear similar to a wheel lock which does not touch the tumbler. Drawing by Robert L. Miller.

supplant the matchlock in America, and it was almost a hundred years later that they ousted the matchlock in Europe.[22]

The wheel lock, chronologically the first of the improved ignition systems, was based on the same principle as the modern cigarette lighter. That is, the spark was produced by holding a piece of pyrites against a revolving rough-edged wheel. The mechanism devised to produce this action was considerably more complex than the matchlock, yet it was sturdy and not apt to get out of order easily. The power for revolving the wheel was supplied by a heavy V-shaped main spring. This spring was attached to the spindle of the wheel by a short chain of two or three links. When the wheel was revolved by hooking a key or spanner over the outside shank of the wheel, this chain was wrapped around the spindle, and the main spring was compressed. The wheel was held in the wound-up position by a laterally acting sear which engaged a hole on its inner surface.

The flash pan of a wheel lock was attached to the lock plate just as it was in the later matchlocks. It differed from the pan of the matchlock in that it was pierced in the bottom to allow a portion of the wheel to intrude; and instead of a pivoted cover it possessed a sliding cover which was connected with the internal lock mechanism. The pyrites was held in the dog head, a miniature vise mounted on an arm which pivoted just in front of the pan. A spring fastened on the outside of the lock plate just below the arm of the dog head acted upon the arm in such a way that when the head was placed against the pan cover in firing position, a constant downward pressure was maintained.

The loading and firing of a wheel lock was a comparatively simple and sure process. First, the wheel was wound. Then, the charge was placed in the barrel in the normal manner. Next, the pan was filled with priming powder, the cover was slid shut, and the dog head pushed down against it. The trigger was then pulled. The pressure on the trigger released the sear from its lodging in the hole in the wheel. The wheel thus freed began to turn, and as it did so a cam which was attached to it struck against a bar connected to the pan cover and automatically opened the pan. The dog head with the pyrites which had been held against the pan cover by its spring was thus forced against that part of the revolving wheel which intruded through the slot in the pan. The resultant contact produced a strong series of sparks and ignited the priming powder.[23]

Less is known about the role played by the wheel lock in America than of almost any other weapon. This is true because the early writers were seldom specific about the types of weapons which they used. It is thus often necessary to rely on incidental comment or description to learn exactly what ignition system was referred to. With the matchlock, this was relatively simple because of the constant references to match, the need for fire and the presence of rests.

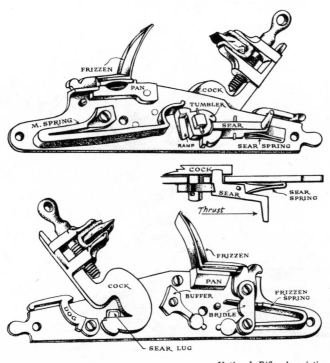

National Rifle Association
Plate 25. Early dog lock with the more common sear which slides down a ramp on the tumbler. Drawing by Robert L. Miller.

When the wheel lock first began to appear on the scene the contemporary accounts often used the term "firelock" to differentiate between the wheel lock and the matchlock. This term, however, was also soon applied to flint arms when they appeared, and hence the accurate distinction was lost.

Despite these difficulties, however, it is still possible to obtain some knowledge of the wheel lock in America. The first recorded event which definitely indicates the presence of a wheel lock occurred at the ill-fated English settlements on Roanoke Island. There, in 1586, Governor Ralph Lane reported that an Indian had accidentally been shot with a petronel, a light firearm falling in a class between a pistol and a caliver. In the same report he also referred to some pistols. At this date, both of these classes of firearms would almost undoubtedly have been wheel locks. In 1597, there occurs one of the few specific references to wheel locks as such. In that year, Don Luís de Velasco had a sworn inventory made of all the personal equipment which he was taking on the expedition of Don Juan de Oñate into New Mexico. Included in this list were three wheel lock arquebuses *(Arcabusses De rrueda)* with large and small powder horns, "bullet screws,

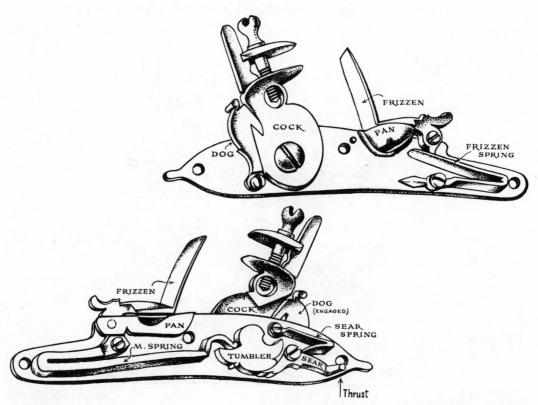

National Rifle Association

Plate 26. Late dog lock with vertically acting sear but no halfcock notch on the tumbler. Drawing by Robert L. Miller.

National Park Service

Plate 27. Early dog lock excavated at the site of a 17th century outpost. Yorktown, Va.

moulds, and all the rest that pertains to each one." On that same expedition it was also noted in an inspection report that among the firearms provided by Oñate, there were 15 wheel locks and 19 matchlocks.[24]

It has long been the fashion to dismiss the subject of the wheel lock in the English colonies with the statement that since the wheel lock was an expensive weapon and since the English colonies were generally poor, very few of these arms came to America except as the private guns of the wealthy. It would seem, however, that this traditional statement would bear some question and that perhaps the situation should be re-evaluated. It is true that wheel locks were considerably more expensive than matchlocks, but this does not automatically preclude the possibility of their being purchased as colony arms by the English settlers. Even though they were poor, the colonists were not always inclined to economize on matters which affected their life expectancy as closely as their weapons did. Two complete and several fragmentary wheel locks and six military spanners were uncovered in recent excavations on the site of old Jamestown by National Park Service archeologists. This large number of military wheel lock parts found in the excavation of only a small part of the site of the original town seems to indicate that these arms were more widely used than has hitherto been supposed.[25]

In order fully to understand the development of the flint lock in America, it is necessary first of all to obtain a clear understanding of the terminology involved. Modern collectors recognize at least six distinct types of flint locks: the snaphaunce, English lock, dog lock, Scandinavian "snaplock," miquelet lock, and the "true" flint lock. These terms denote both different evolutionary stages in the development of the flint lock and different regional aberrations. Seventeenth century writers, however, did not recognize these modern distinctions as such. They accepted the Dutch word *snaphaan* or snaphaunce at its literal meaning, "snapping cock." To them, any firearm in which the ignition spark was produced by striking a piece of flint held in the jaws of a cock *(hahn, haan)* sharply against a piece of steel was a "snaphaunce." It is most important for all students of early firearms to remember that in the vast majority of instances in which an early writer uses the term snaphaunce, he is not referring to the specific type of ignition system which is designated by that name today.

The first form of flint lock to appear on the European scene was probably that type which is now designated the snaphaunce. It is generally believed that this ignition system was developed in Scandinavia and the Low Countries about the middle of the 16th century. From there it quickly spread to England and the rest of western Europe.

The basic theory of the snaphaunce and, in fact, of all flint arms, was the idea of duplicating mechanically the contemporary method of lighting fires by striking a piece of flint against a bar of steel. In this mechanical version, the flint was held in a vise on one end of an arm, known as the cock. The other end of the arm was pivoted on the lock plate so that the flint-bearing end could be swung in an arc in the direction of the steel. The steel which was also called the battery, was mounted on another pivoted arm and placed in a position opposing the cock. The flashpan, equipped with a sliding cover, was placed directly below the battery.

The internal mechanism of the snaphaunce was relatively simple. A heavy V-shaped mainspring supplied the force which activated the cock. It acted upon the cock through the medium of a lug, known as the tumbler, which was attached by a pin to the spindle on which the cock pivoted. As the cock was drawn back, the tumbler rotated and compressed the mainspring. When a certain position was reached, the end of the sear, which operated in much the same way as its counterpart on the wheel lock, was allowed to pass through a hole in the lock plate and engage a projection on the tail of the cock, thus holding the spring in a compressed position. When the trigger was pulled, the end of the sear was withdrawn. The spring, thus released, impelled the cock forward in a short arc. The flint in the jaws of the cock struck the steel a glancing blow, producing a shower of sparks which dropped into the priming powder in the flash-pan below. The forward progress of the cock was finally stopped by a small metal block, called the buffer, screwed to the outside of the lock plate. On some locks an arm attached to the tumbler automatically opened the pan cover as the

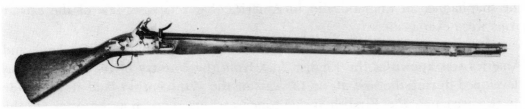

Plate 28. Early dog lock musket c. 1630-1650.

Plate 29. Middle dog lock musket, c. 1650, used in the capture of Sir Edmund Andros in 1689.

cock moved forward. On others, the opening and closing of the pan were purely manual operations.[26]

As a general rule, no half-cock or "safety" position was provided for on snaphaunce locks as it was on later flint locks. Such a device would have been superfluous on the snaphaunce, for even with the cock "set," the arm could be rendered safe from accidental discharge by withdrawing the battery from its position over the flash pan.[27]

It was formerly the generally accepted theory that the type of flint lock which is now known as the snaphaunce was very widely used in Colonial America. This misconception was largely caused by the failure to understand the generic sense in which "snaphaunce" was used by the 17th century authors. If, indeed, the early writers had meant a flint arm in which the steel and pan cover were separate units every time they used the word "snaphaunce," it would have indicated the presence in this country of many thousands of these arms, and it would be logical to assume that a fair number of surviving examples could be found today. Actually, the only existing fragments of snaphaunces definitely known to have been used in America consist of one lock (lacking the battery), one lock plate, and three separate batteries found in the National Park Service excavations at Jamestown, and one separate battery found during the excavation of an Indian site in central New York State. There are, in fact, fewer remnants of snaphaunces than of any other type of firearm used in Colonial America. The same condition is true in England and to a lesser degree on the Continent. Putting all the evidence together, modern students have reached the conclusion that the second form of flintlock, the English lock, so quickly superseded the snaphaunce in England and in America that relatively few of the earlier arms were ever made.

The improved lock which supplanted the snaphaunce in England and America was known as the English lock from the country of its origin. It was developed during the first 10 or 15 years of the 17th century, and it was made in two varieties, the English lock proper and its more popular variant, the dog lock.[29]

In most respects, the mechanism of the English lock was like that of the snaphaunce. The principal innovation consisted in forging the steel and pan cover in one piece, known technically as the hammer. In recent years the term "hammer" has come to be applied so universally to what was then known as the cock that the contemporary word "battery" or the 19th century term "frizzen" will be used here to avoid confusion. The combined steel and pan cover were pivoted on the lockplate and held in position by a light V-shaped spring, known as the feather spring or frizzen spring. When the battery was struck a glancing blow by the flint in the cock, it was automatically knocked backward, and the pan was thus uncovered. This single improvement over the snaphaunce made the English lock a faster device by eliminating one motion and a simpler mechanism by eliminating the sliding cover machinery.[30]

Another innovation of the English lock was the provision for a half-cock or "safety" position. This intermediate position was rendered necessary by the combining of the steel and pan cover, for the gun could no longer be carried safely at the full-cock position. In the English lock proper, this half-cock position was provided for by cutting a notch in the tumbler which the lateral-acting sear could engage. In the most popular form of the English lock, how-

National Park Service
Plate 30. Middle dog lock excavated at Jamestown. In this specimen the sear still acts laterally.

H. M. Tower of London

Plate 31. Late dog lock musket c. 1680-1690.

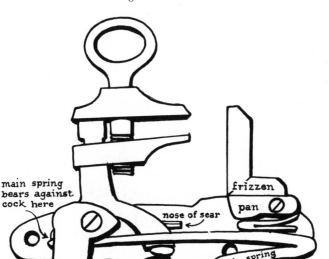

Plate 32. Spanish miquelet lock.

ever, this position was achieved by hooking a small dog catch to the back of the cock. It was this catch which gave the type of lock using it the name of dog lock.[31]

The English lock and/or the dog lock underwent a long evolutionary development, and the number of minor variations in the internal mechanism is legion. In some, the sear held the cock in the full or set position by engaging a notch in the tumbler instead of projecting through the lock plate. In some there was a double sear reminiscent of the wheel lock. In some, there were notches on the tumbler for both full and half-cock positions—and a dog catch on the outside in addition. In others, especially the very early types, the sear did not touch the tumbler at all. Later, the sear was modified to act vertically instead of laterally as it had ever since the development of the wheel lock. Still other minor mechanical variations resulting from individual imagination and craftsmanship are continually met with.[32]

The outward design of the dog lock also underwent an evolution. At the beginning of the 17th century, the lock plate was long and slender. The

[29]

bottom edge was a straight line while the top edge followed a series of angular steps. Usually the back end of the plate terminated in a ball finial. The cock was an elongated "S" shape, more angular than curved; and the pan was square and box-like. As the century progressed, however, the shapes changed until by the middle of the 1600's the lock plate had attained lines generally similar to those of the later flint lock. The long tail disappeared from the cock, and the dog catch hooked into a small notch on the back, just below the neck. Finally, the pan achieved generally softer lines, sometimes through a rounding of the edges and sometimes through the filing of several flat faces which gave it a hexagonal or octagonal feeling.

English gunsmiths apparently stopped making dog locks with lateral acting

St. Augustine Historical Society
Plate 33B. Miquelet cock excavated in Florida.

National Park Service
Plate 33A. Miquelet lock excavated at Jamestown.

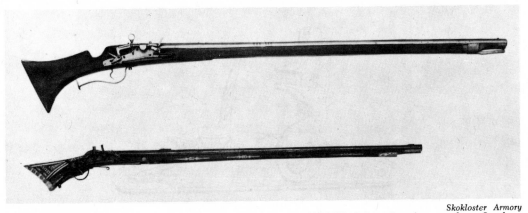

Skokloster Armory

Plate 34. *Above:* Swedish musket with "Snaplock" about 1620-1630. *Below:* Sporting gun from Southern Sweden, 1625-1650.

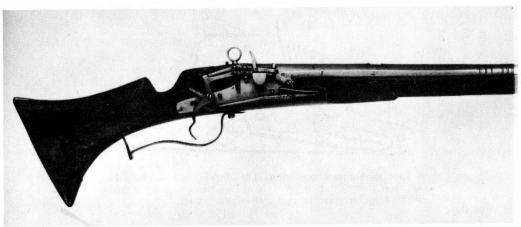

Skokloster Armory

Plate 35. Lock detail of Swedish musket.

sears shortly after the middle of the 17th century. Dog locks were used by the British army, however, until after 1700. These later dog locks had vertically acting sears, and often the tumbler had notches for both the half and full-cock positions.[33]

Judging from the number of dog locks used in Colonial America that are still extant today, it would appear that that type of lock was more widely used than any other from about 1625-1675. Dog locks and parts of dog locks have been found in quantity in the excavations of 17th century sites, and several well-preserved and well-authenticated specimens exist in public and private collections throughout the country. The number of these existing dog lock specimens is more than three times that of all the other ignition systems of the period combined. Two complete locks, one early and one late, and numerous cocks were excavated at Jamestown. A beautifully preserved early dog lock was excavated at Yorktown. Several complete locks were found

[31]

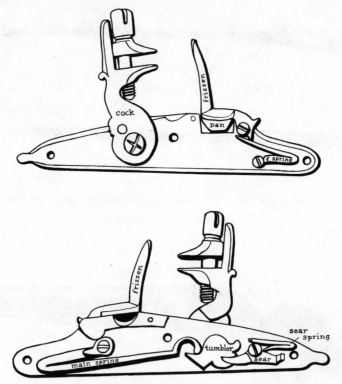

Author's Collection
Plate 36. Flintlock mechanism. This drawing is based on a lock
of about 1660-1670. It is probably of Dutch origin and was found
in an Iroquois grave in central New York State.

in Indian sites in central New York State. A very early and most interesting
dog lock was found at the site of the Jireh Bull garrison house in Rhode Island.
Two of the remaining guns of the Plymouth colonists are dog locks. The
lock of the "old style musket" with which King Philip was killed in 1676 is
a dog lock. The latter is now preserved in the collections of the Massachusetts
Historical Society. These are but a few of the important specimens which still
exist for students to examine. Twenty-two authentic specimens used in America
were studied in the preparation of this work, and there are undoubtedly others
which were overlooked or unavailable.[34]

In addition to the English lock and the dog lock, there were two other
primitive types of flint arms which also saw service in America. These were
the miquelet and the Scandinavian "snaplock."

The miquelet lock was developed on the Iberian peninsula, and the type
spread along the northern shores of the Mediterranean from Spain to Italy
during the middle years of the 16th century. Apparently, almost all miquelet
locks were made with the steel and pan cover in one piece from the very begin-

ning. The outstanding characteristic of the miquelet is found in the action of the mainspring on the cock. In all these locks the mainspring is on the outside of the lock plate and one end bears directly upon a projection on the bottom of the cock.

In Spanish locks, the pressure of the spring is upwards against the rear of the cock. A half-cock position is provided by a bolt which passes through the lock plate and protrudes in front of the cock, holding it in place. When the cock is pulled back to the full position, the end of the sear passes through another hole higher up in the lock plate and engages the cock. When the trigger is pulled, both the sear and the half-cock bolt are withdrawn simultaneously, leaving the cock free to move with the impulse of the spring.[35]

The only direct evidence indicating that miquelet locks were used in America consists of two excavated locks, one found at Jamestown and one in Massachusetts, and a very early cock dug up in Florida. There is every reason

National Park Service

Plate 37. Early cocks excavated at Jamestown.

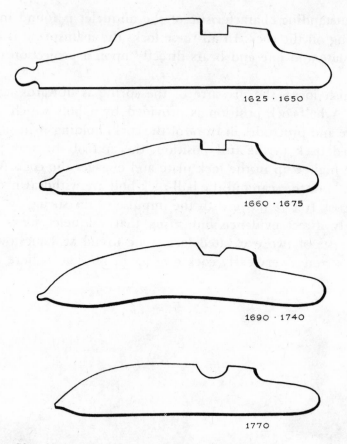

1625 · 1650

1660 · 1675

1690 · 1740

1770

Plate 38. Some flintlock lock plates indicating the general trend
in the evolution of the plate.

to believe, however, that they were widely used by the Spanish in Florida and in the Southwest. There is one reference to flint locks (arcobuces de pedernal) in the "Indies" in 1596, and these could well have been miquelets.[36]

The other regional type of flint lock, the Scandinavian "snaplock," was made both with separate steel and pan cover and with the combined frizzen. In both its main forms, the Swedish and the Norwegian, the Scandinavian lock is readily identifiable by the unusual shape of the cock and by the fact that like the miquelet the mainspring on the early locks is on the outside. Also the mainspring usually serves both the cock and the battery. In those instances in which the battery is separate, the pan cover is almost always pivoted instead of sliding.[37]

The service of the Scandinavian "snaplocks" in America must have been very brief, and they were probably never brought over in large numbers. They would have been used only in the Swedish settlements along the Delaware River which were begun in 1638 and were conquered by the Dutch in 1655.

[34]

Even there, they were subordinate first to the matchlock and then, shortly after 1650, to the "French fusil," which became popular with the Swedish settlers about that time.[38]

The final stage in the development of flint and steel arms, the "true" flintlock, was developed in France about 1610-1615. From there it spread throughout Western Europe. By the third quarter of the century, it had supplanted the dog lock as the chief flint arm in England. Even allowing for a normal time lag, it is safe to esimate that the new flintlocks were reaching America in considerable quantity by 1660.[39]

There are two main characteristics by which the true flintlock can be distinguished from the preceding primitive flint actions. The sear moves vertically in engaging the notches in the tumbler. There are notches for both half- and full-cock positions.

Despite the fact that the basic flintlock mechanism was used on a wide scale for over 200 years after its first appearance in the 1630's, there are certain minor variations in manufacture and design which are useful in identifying a 17th century specimen. In the mechanism of the lock, the most important feature is the presence or absence of a reinforcing bridle on the tumbler. Most 17th century flintlocks were made without these reinforcing bridles. It is true that a few of the better locks were equipped with bridles as early as 1670, but the bridle did not become standard until about 1700. It should be noted however, that some cheap locks were manufactured without bridles well into the 18th century.

Shortly after 1700, another bridle, this time extending forward from the pan and providing support for the pivot of the battery, began to put in its appearance. The presence of this latter bridle on the lock of a gun would almost automatically preclude the possibility of 17th century manufacture. A third important mechanical feature is the method of attaching the cock. A cock and shank forged in one piece is as certain an evidence of 17th century production as any single feature could be. Early in the dog lock period some makers had begun to forge cocks separately and attach them to the shank by a screw on the outside. The practice became increasingly popular, but there were a few conservatives who continued to forge cock and shank in the old way almost into the last quarter of the century. Consequently, the absence of this structure is of little significance, but its presence is of the utmost importance.

Two other mechanical features are worthy of attention. One is the attachment of the lock, and the other, the placement of the barrel tang screw. In many 17th century guns the lock was attached to the barrel by 3 screws instead of the 2 screws which later were deemed sufficient. A number of 17th century locks fitted for only 2 screws are to be found, but extremely few 18th century pieces

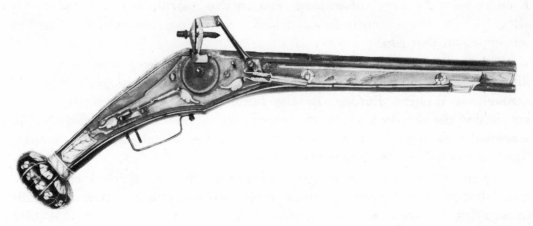

Author's Collection

Plate 39. German wheel lock pistol, c. 1575.

fitted for 3 screws are known. The tang screws of a large number of 17th century firearms attach to the tang from underneath. That is, the head of the screw is usually contained within the trigger guard, and the threads are joined in the barrel tang. Many European and American pieces of the 17th century are found with the tang screw in the normal position, but the inverted tang screw is practically never found on the 18th century guns.

Stylistic variations are much harder to define and date than mechanical changes. Nevertheless, there are a few features which should always be noted for the corrobative evidence which they supply to the mechanical data. On the lock, the two most important structures to observe are the cock and the lock plate. The cock underwent a long evolution from the angular and attenuated "S" of the early dog locks to the goose neck of the late 17th century and the entire 18th century. After the absorption of the tail on the "S", the early cocks were usually characterized by a relatively straight back. The definition of the neck and the graceful curves developed slowly. Also, the jaws of the flint were usually wide and flat, the so-called duck bill shape, and the jaw screws frequently had cylindrical heads. In this connection it should be noted that the reinforcing arm from the body of the cock to the lower jaw of the flint vise, a structure popularly associated with French muskets of the middle of the 18th century, is frequently encountered in 17th century locks.

Like the cock, the lock plate also underwent an evolution before reaching the conventional shape. After attaining the standard form, the 17th and early 18th century lock plates were often characterized by a sharp downward curve at the back of the plate.

On the barrel, the most important thing to notice is that the breach of a 17th century flintlock was almost always sharply differentiated from the rest

[36]

of the barrel, or the "chase." Often it was octagonal or hexagonal while the chase was round, and there was an ornamental moulding where the two joined. Later, the flats were allowed to blend with the round without notable demarcation. In other instances, when both the breech and chase were round, a distinction was achieved by engraving or chiseling a band around the barrel. This practice was carried over into the 18th century to a slight degree. The differentiation was not so distinct, however, and the feature disappeared almost entirely during the second quarter of the century.

There are a few characteristics in the furniture of mountings which are easily recognizable and which have some significance. First of all, the key plate or screw plate, which is not usually encountered until after 1650, is often pierced for 3 screws. Also, it is frequently elaborately cast with open work designs in the form of monsters or foliage. These elaborate screw plates with cast openwork designs are seldom found on 18th century muskets. The one major exception to the above statement is found in the Indian trade fusil, and even in these there is a decidedly different "feeling" in the design. On some 17th and early 18th century flintlocks there are found distinctive fluted ramroad thimbles. Except for an occasional Dutch piece, these fluted thimbles disappear before 1725.

There are many more slight variations and nuances in design and construction which will assist the student in dating an early flintlock. These characteristics, unfortunately, are even more impossible to describe on paper than those given in the last few paragraphs. The features listed above are intended only as a guide to point out what an interested individual may look for. Real familiarity with 17th century arms can come only through viewing and handling many actual specimens.

As a word of warning, it cannot be stated too often that no single charac-

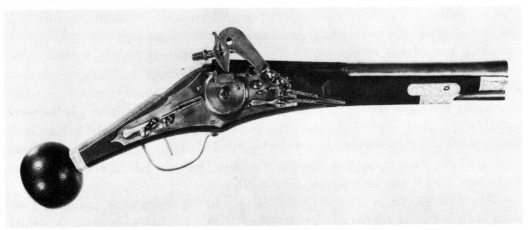

U. S. National Museum

Plate 40. German wheel lock pistol dated 1588.

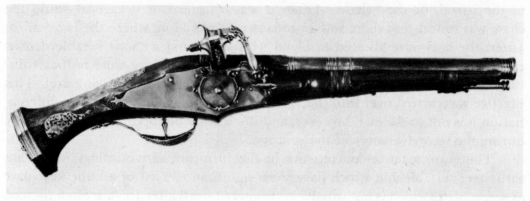

U. S. *National Museum*

Plate 41. Italian wheel lock pistol, early 17th century.

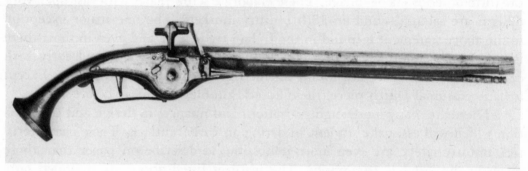

Hermann W. Williams, Jr. Collection

Plate 42. German wheel lock pistol, c. 1620-1640.

teristic is sufficient evidence for dating a specimen. As is the case wherever individual craftsmanship is encountered, there are wide variations caused by the preferences and abilities of the men concerned. Every feature of the gun must be considered and the evidence it presents critically evaluated before it is possible to reach any reasonable conclusion regarding its age.

With the advent of the wheel lock and the various forms of flint locks, several new classes of arms appeared. These new classes included the pistol, petronel, carbine, musketoon, fusil, blunderbuss and long fowler. The pistol apparently first appeared in Europe during the 1520's. The first pistols were probably the wheel lock dags, the long heavy pistols with straight grips much in vogue with the 16th century cavalry. This dag design was carried over into the era of the flint arms, but shortly after the beginning of the 17th century the curved grip began to supersede the earlier form.[40]

The first specific reference to pistols in colonial America is found in Governor Ralph Lane's report of the progress of the English colony on Roanoke Island in 1586. Thereafter, the references multiply rapidly. Captain John Smith used a French pistol, apparently a snaphaunce, in the famous fight with the

Indians in 1607 which led to his capture by Powhatan and subsequent rescue by Pocahontas. In the martial laws of Virginia for 1611, all targeteers were ordered to carry either flint or wheel lock pistols in addition to their swords and targets, and in 1624-1625, the military census of Virginia revealed the presence of 55 pistols of all sorts in that colony.

A most interesting early dog lock pistol belonging to John Thompson who settled at Plymouth in 1622 is still preserved in Pilgrim Hall at Plymouth. In 1643. Maryn Adrianzen attempted to assassinate Director Kieft of New Amsterdam with a flint pistol, but the plot was foiled when one of Kieft's councilors thrust his thumb between the cock and frizzen of the assassin's gun. These and many other references indicate the growing popularity of the pistol in America as a weapon for targeteers and cavalry and as a personal arm.[41]

The petronel was a type of firearm halfway between the pistol and the arquebus of the early 16th century. It was longer and of a larger caliber than the pistol; and it possessed a sharply curved butt terminating in a flat surface which could be held against the chest in firing. Almost all petronels were wheel locks.[42]

Pilgrim Hall, Plymouth

Plate 43. Brass-barrelled dog lock pistol owned by John Thompson.

Memorial Hall, Deerfield

Plate 44. Photograph made about 1900 of a middle dog lock pistol used in the defense of the "Indian House" at Deerfield, Mass. The whereabouts of the pistol itself are unknown.

[39]

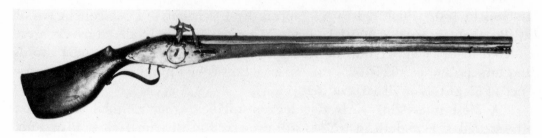

National Rifle Association

Plate 45. Italian wheel lock carbine found in a 17th century house in Boston and believed to have been restocked in America.

Benjamin F. Hubbell Collection

Plate 46. Long fowler owned by John Forbes of East Hartford.

As a weapon, the petronel was never very popular in Europe, and it was perhaps even less popular in America. References to them in this country are particularly scarce. Ralph Lane mentioned one in reporting an accidental shooting on Roanoke Island in 1586; and the military census of Virginia in 1624-1625 gave a clear indication of their popularity at that time when it listed only 6 petronels in a total of 1,089 firearms.[43]

The fusil was a light military arm patterned after the heavier musket. It was developed during the first half of the 17th century and was always a flint arm. For many years, the term was used to distinguish a flint musket from a matchlock. This was particularly true in France and the Low Countries. Thus, one finds in France the so-called *fusil-mousquet,* a firearm having a combination match and flint lock. Later, especially during the 18th century, the term fusil was used to designate a very light form of flint musket carried by officers and light troops.[44]

The carbine and musketoon were short firearms usually carried by cavalry. Of the two, the term carbine is probably the older. The first carbines were wheel locks, but by the middle of the 17th century they were usually flint. Some carbines were rifled, but others were not. The musketoon was apparently always flint and never rifled. Thus, in some cases, it could be used synonymously with carbine, but the beginning of the modern differentiation between musketoon and carbine based on the question of rifling was already apparent.[45]

The carbine was a popular weapon in 17th century America. References to it are numerous, particularly toward the middle of the century. It was used in the wilderness by both cavalry and infantry. Although it could never compete with the full-size musket or fusil, it was the next most popular firearm. An indication of the prevalence of the carbine is found in the listing of public arms in the various counties of Maryland, made in 1678. A total count of the firearms listed reveals a proportion of 177 carbines to 613 muskets, slightly less than 1 to 3.[46]

The blunderbuss was a short gun of large caliber with a wide flaring muzzle. This weapon was developed on the continent of Europe and introduced into England about the middle of the 17th century. A few wheel lock specimens are known, but it was almost always a flint arm during the 17th and 18th centuries. The blunderbuss was designed to deliver a deadly spray of slugs at close quarters, hence, its main uses were defending streets and houses and repelling boarding parties in naval warfare. Coach guards also liked the arm and used it much as the 19th century guard used his short double-barreled shot gun.[47]

The blunderbuss has always been associated with 17th century America in the popular mind. Actually, however, the weapon was little used in this country before the 18th century. It was too specialized an arm for widespread use, and the particular conditions under which it was most useful were seldom encountered. An idea of its popularity may be obtained from the 1678 military inventory of Maryland arms referred to above. In that list, there is only one blunderbuss listed out of a total of 791 arms. As late as 1694, Maryland listed only "one old Iron Blunderbuss w[th]out a Lock" and "one fixt Brass blunderbuss." It was not until the 18th century brought greater urbanization and increased naval activity that the blunderbuss achieved any prominence among American weapons.[48]

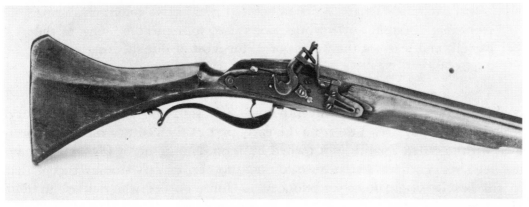

Benjamin F. Hubbell Collection

Plate 47. Lock of the Forbes fowler.

Old Colony Historical Society, Taunton
Plate 48. Long fowler owned by John Thompson of Plymouth and restocked in American oak.

Herb Glass Collection
Plate 49. Hudson Valley long fowler, c. 1670-1680, stocked in curly maple and brass mounted.

The long fowler, the last of the types listed above, was a very important and interesting arm. As its name implies, it was primarily a hunting gun rather than a military weapon. Nevertheless all firearms were subject to warlike use during an emergency, and the long fowler was no exception. Its great length and heavy breech, in fact, gave it a longer range than the standard musket, and thus it was most useful in defending a fixed position where the disadvantage of its unwieldiness was at a minimum.

References to these long fowlers appear early. The settlers of Massachusetts Bay brought with them:

"6 long ffowlinge peeces wᵗʰ muskett boare, 6 foote long ½" and "4 longe ffowling peeces wᵗʰ bastard muskett boare 5-½ foote longe."

In Plymouth, Edward Winslow advised prospective colonists: "Bring every man a musket or fowling piece. Let your piece be long in the barrell; and fear not the weight of it, for most of our shooting is from stands."[49]

These long guns, ranging in length up to seven and one-half feet, remained popular throughout the seventeenth and well into the eighteenth century. A number still survive. Two from the early part of the century include a specimen with so-called English lock owned by John Thompson of Plymouth which has been restocked in American oak, and another, exactly similar except that it still has its original stock, belonged to John Forbes who settled in East Hartford, Connecticut in 1640. The greatest number of these arms, however, are found in the Hudson Valley of New York, where the settlers made good use of them during the heavy migrations of geese and ducks which followed that fly-way each year. These latter guns were frequently assembled in America using barrels and locks made in Holland or England and stocks of American curly maple.

The transition from matchlock to flintlock varied somewhat from colony to colony, but the over-all pattern was remarkably uniform. A brief history of this evolution in some of the major colonies will illustrate the general trend.

When the English settlers first landed at Jamestown in 1607, they brought mostly matchlocks. Even from the first, however, there were some wheel locks and snaphaunces. When Capt. John Smith left the colony in October, 1609, he reported that there were "300 muskets [matchlocks] snapchanches and fire lockes, shot powder and match sufficient." William Strachey's *Martial Lavves* of 1611 further illuminate the situation by stating that musketeers were to be armed with matchlocks; and officers, including sergeants and corporals, were to carry snaphaunces or fire locks. Targeteers were to carry, in addition to their swords and targets, either a pistol or "scuppet." The word "scuppet" as used by Strachey was probably a corruption of esclopette (a short wheel lock with a hinged stock which was carried in a holster like a long pistol) rather than a version of the French "scoppette" (a form of the hand cannon which had gone out of use many years before). In both the Smith and Strachey statements, it is safe to translate fire lock as wheel lock since they both differentiate between it and the snaphaunce.[50]

By 1624-1625, however, a sharp change had occurred, and the matchlock was on the way out. The military census of those years showed that the matchlock had slipped from its position as the most popular arm and had almost vanished. There were, in fact, only 47 matchlocks listed out of a total of 1,089 firearms. Thus, the matchlock had all but disappeared. In a few years it was gone entirely and Thomas Matthew could write in describing Bacon's Rebel-

Herb Glass Collection

Plate 50. Lock detail of the long fowler, 1670-1680.

Plate 51. Hudson Valley long fowler, 1688-1700, stocked in curly maple and mounted in brass. The barrel bears the Amsterdam proof mark.

lion of 1675-1676 that Bacon's men had flint arms since matchlocks were not used in Virginia.[51]

In the English colonies in New England, the story was much the same. When the Pilgrims landed at Plymouth in 1620, their principal firearm was the matchlock, but they also had some flint weapons and possibly some wheel locks. For the first ten years the supremacy of the matchlock was unchallenged. With the coming of the settlers to Massachusetts Bay in 1630, however, the transition began in earnest. The common arms supply of the Massachusetts Bay Company contained:

> 80 bastard musketts, wth snaphances,
>   4 ffoote in the barrill wth out rests;
> 6 longe ffowlinge peeces wth muskett boare,
>   6 foote longe, ½;
> 4 longe ffowlinge peeces wth bastard muskett boare,
>   5-½ foote longe;
> 10 ffull musketts, 4 foote barril, wth matchlocks
>   and rests;[52]

A definite superiority of flint arms is this indicated in the public stores.[53]

From 1630 until the outbreak of King Philip's War in 1675, the change is plainly visible. There are more references to matches than to flints in inventories and court records until the beginning of the Pequot War in 1637, but the tales of snap-shooting increase and during the war the stories of ambushes and surprise attacks indicate that flint arms were becoming more plentiful. In 1643, the Plymouth General Court ordered that every soldier should be supplied with either a matchlock or a flint arm. By 1645, Governor William Bradford could report that the Plymouth troops had been sent to a muster at Seacunk "well armed all with snaphance peeces." In the same year, the Massachusetts General Court passed the following law:

"It being requisite y[t] all inhabitants wth in y[s] jurisdiction should endeavo[r] after such armes as may be most usefull for their owne & y[e] countryes defence, it is y[r] fore ordered y[t] no pieces shalbe allowed for serviceable, in o[r] trained bands, but such as are ether full musket boare, or basterd musket at y[e] least, & that none should be under three foote 9 inches, nor any above foure foote 3 inches in length, & y[t] ev[r]y man have also a priming wyer, a worme, & scourer, fit for y[e] boare of his muskett, w[ch] we find not required in any former order."[54]

In 1646, while matchlocks were still permitted for private arms, the Plymouth General Court allowed only flint or wheel lock arms for town property. In 1673, the number of improved arms was greatly increased when the Massachusetts General Court ordered Hezekiah Usher to purchase five hundred "new snaphances or fire lock musketts" in England for the use of the colony.[55]

With the coming of King Philip's War, the era of the matchlock in Massachusetts was definitely past. The campaign of that war, forays into the wilderness, night attacks, ambushes, battles in the rain, and the encounters between individuals which required snap-shooting, indicate clearly that a form of flint arm was the principal weapon. In 1677, toward the end of the war, the final blow was administered when the Plymouth General Court outlawed the matchlock completely as an acceptable weapon.[56]

In Connecticut, when the colony of New Haven was organized in 1643, the General Court allowed either matchlocks or flint arms. By 1649, only flint guns were allowed for public arms, and a program for converting matchlocks to flint was underway. Then, in 1676, Connecticut, which had united with New Haven in 1664-1665, passed a law recognizing only flint arms as serviceable

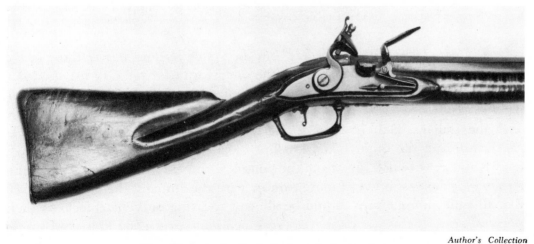

Author's Collection

Plate 52. Lock detail of the long fowler. 1688-1700.

weapons. In taking this action in 1676, Connecticut was one year ahead of Plymouth.[57]

Among the non-English colonies, the records of the Dutch in New Netherlands provide perhaps the fullest account of the development of firearms. The first Dutch settlers arrived in America in 1624, bringing with them mostly matchlocks but including some wheel locks and flint arms. The flint arms rapidly

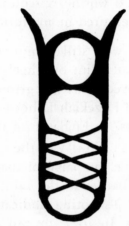

Plate 53. Amsterdam proof mark.

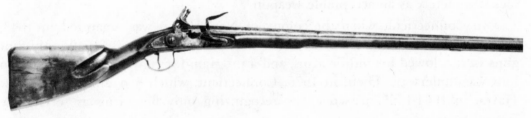

Henry J. Kauffman Collection

Plate 54. New England long fowler of the late 17th century. This particular butt shape, which is found only on New England guns, was used by some makers as late as the early 19th century.

gained in popularity with the people, but the Dutch leaders, unlike those in the English colonies, clung tenaciously to the older forms for military use. In 1655, the government in New Amsterdam requested the Dutch West India Company to send over 3,000 to 4,000 soldiers to help meet the threat of trouble with the Indians. Half of these soldiers were to be armed with wheel locks (*vuerroers*) and the other half with flint locks (*snaphaan-roers*) with 3½ foot barrels and a caliber of 16 balls to the pound. The next year (1656), still frightened about the possibility of more trouble with the Indians, the Dutch resolved that all future immigrants should be allowed to bring only matchlocks as their personal arms. If this was done, they reasoned that fewer good flint arms would reach the Indians.

[46]

Whether this resolution was ever put into effect is not known. In the same year an estimate of the necessary arms for a party of 150 men to found a colony on the Delaware revealed the proportion of the different systems of firearms which the Dutch leaders believed most desirable. They suggested that half the men be armed with matchlocks and the other half with either wheel locks or flint arms.[58]

Ensign   *Fusiliers, winter garrison dress and winter campaign dress*

The French Regiment of Carignan — Sallieres, Canada, 1665-1668

Company of Military Collectors & Historians

Plate 55. When the Carrignan-Sallières Regiment was sent to Canada, it was armed with flintlocks and so became the first regiment in the French army to be so equipped. Drawing by Col. Harry C. Larter, Jr.

Despite the fact that the Dutch leaders usually asked for either wheel locks or flint arms, it is apparent that relatively few wheel locks ever reached the colony. Direct references to the use of wheel locks are extremely rare, while references to flint arms are common. The key to the situation, however, is contained in a request for arms by the magistrates of Wiltwyck after the Indian massacre of 1663. They asked for a number of arms and concluded:

". . . we request that the carabines may be snaphaunce, as the people here are but little conversant with the use of the wheel lock."[59]

In 1664, New Netherlands was conquered by the English. By the terms of the surrender, the Dutch garrison marched out of New Amsterdam with their matches lighted, and were replaced by the English. Thereafter, the evolution of firearms in New York followed the same pattern as the other English colonies.[60]

Despite their conservatism and their reluctance to depart entirely from older methods, the Dutch pioneered in two phases of military armament. They devised a more rigid system for the inspection of arms, and when necessary they supplied arms to the inhabitants for their defense. Such arms as were submitted by the individual or provided by the West India Company for military purposes were stamped with the company mark (see cut) and could not be sold or traded. In 1650, the gun inspections were ordered every three months. It was this rigid control which permitted the Dutch to standardize calibers (their

Plate 56. West India Company Mark.

second military contribution). Apparently, there were two calibers allowed, regular musket bore (12 gauge) for the matchlocks, and 16 gauge for the wheel lock and flint arms.[61]

The evidence presented by the records of these six colonies gives a relatively clear picture of firearms in Colonial America. The surviving records of the other colonies, although they are not nearly so complete from the standpoint of armament, corroborate the conclusions suggested by these detailed histories.

[48]

Thus, it would seem that all the colonies founded during the first half of the 17th century the matchlock was at first a popular or, at least, a tolerated weapon. Soon, however, the conditions of warfare in America made its weaknesses apparent; and the great dependence of the colonists on their weapons caused them to seek the best arms available. Even poor colonies overlooked the greater cost of the better guns, so great was their need. Thus, the change was rapid. In Virginia, the matchlock had all but disappeared by 1625. In the New England colonies, which were founded later, the matchlock was relegated to a minor role before 1650 and completely abandoned by 1677. Even in New Netherlands and New Sweden, where the conservative authorities clung to a certain percentage of matchlocks for military use, the civilian population early indicated its preference for flint arms; and when both these colonies came under English rule in 1664, the matchlock was soon discarded there, too. In completing this evolution as it did, America was years in advance of Europe where the clumsy matchlock persisted in military use well into the early years of the next century.

NOTES—CHAPTER ONE

1. Alvar Nuñez Cabeça de Vaca, *The Narrative of Cabeza de Vaca*, Frederick W. Hodge and Theodore H. Lewis, editors, *Spanish Explorers in the Southern United States, 1528-1543*, New York, 1907, 35. The Gentleman of Elvas, *The Narrative of the Expedition of Hernando de Soto, by the Gentleman of Elvas*, ibid., 148, 159, *et passim*. Pedro de Castañeda, *The Narrative of the Expedition of Coronado*, ibid., 295, 319. Juan Rodriguez Cabrillo, *Relation of the Voyage of Juan Rodriguez de Cabrillo, 1542-1543*, Herbert E. Bolton, editor, *Spanish Exploration in the South West*, New York, 1916, 19. 23.

2. Testimony of Baltasar Lopez, "Investigation Made in Madrid by Licentiate Gamboa on Matters Concerning Florida, February 4, 1573," Jeanette T. Connor, editor, *Colonial Records of Spanish Florida*, 2 vols., Deland, Florida, 1925, 1930, I, 97. "Investigation of the Return from Florida of Esteban de las Alas," December 22, 1570, ibid., 303. "Statement of What Don Juan de Oñate and Don Pedro Ponce de León offer for the exploration, pacification and settlement of New Mexico," Charles W. Hackett, editor, *Historical Documents Relating to New Mexico, Nueva Vizcaya, and Approaches Thereto, to 1773*, 3 vols., Washington, 1923-1937, I, 280-283.

3. There are several good studies of the crossbow. The best historical sketch is J. Alm, "Europeiska Armborst," *Vaabenhistoriske Aarbger*, Vb, (1947),

105-255. The most thorough analysis in English is Sir Ralph Payne-Gallwey, *The Crossbow*, London, 1903. Also useful is John Metschl, *The Rudolph J. Nunnemacher Collection of Projectile Arms*, Bulletin no. 9 of the Milwaukee Public Museum, 2 vols., Milwaukee, 1928, I, 24-43.

4. Alm, "Europeiska Armborst," 143-175, 190-199, *et passim*. Payne-Gallwey, *Crossbow*, 90-128.

5. Payne-Gallwey, *Crossbow*, 15. Francis Grose, *Military Antiquities*, 2 vols. London, 1801, I, 149, 150.

6. [Gentleman of Elvas], *Virginia Richly Valued*, translated by Richard Hackluyt, London, 1609, Peter Force, compiler, *Tracts and Other Papers*, 4 vols., Washington, 1836-1846, IV, no. 1, 22. In this instance the Hackluyt translation is considered preferable for quotation. Another rendering of the same passage can be found in Elvas, *Narrative*, 148.

7. *Ibid*.

8. *For Mr Rauleys Viage*, ms., County Record Office, Chelmsford, Essex, D/DRh, M1. Copy in author's possession supplied by Dr. David B. Quinn. David B. Quinn, "Preparations for the 1585 Virginia Voyage," *William and Mary Quarterly*, 3rd Series, VI, no. 2, (April 1949), 208-236, 212.

9. Warrant to the Lord Treasurer, September 1622, Susan M. Kingsbury, editor, *The Records of the Virginia Company of London*, 4 vols., Wash-

ington, 1906-1935, III, 676. Minutes of a Court held for Virginia, August 14, 1622, *ibid*, II, 99, 100.

10. For a representative sampling of attempts to determine the meaning of arquebus, caliver, and musket, see Grose, *Military Antiquities*, I, 152n, 153n, 154n, 156, 156n, II, 292. George C. Stone, *A Glossary of the Construction, Decoration and Use of Arms and Armor*, Portland, Maine, 1934, 71, 158, 461. John N. George, *English Guns and Rifles*, Onslow County, North Carolina, 1947, 7, 19-21.

11. George, *Guns and Rifles*, 19-21.

12. Excellent studies of the matchlock mechanism may be found in Morritz Thierbach, *Die Geschichtliche Entwickelung der Handfeuerwaffen*, Dresden, 1899, 7-19; and J. Alm *Eldhandvapen*, 2 vols., Stockholm, 1933, I, 9-160. For a study of the development of the matchlock before 1500, see Robert C. Clephan, *An Outline of the History and Development of Hand Firearms, from the Earliest Period to about the End of the Fifteenth Century*, reprint edition, Huntingdon, West Virginia, 194.

13. There are several excellent contemporary drill manuals which give the matchlock manual in detail. Perhaps the best is Jacques de Gheyn, *Maniement d'Armes, d'Arquebuses, Musquetz, et Piques*, Amsterdam, 1608. Good directions in English are found in Henry Hexham, *The First Part of the Principles of the Art Military*, Delft, 1642; and Robert Ward, *Animadversions of Warre*, London 1639.

14. William Stratchey [Strachey], *For the Colony in Virginea Brittannia. Lavves Diuine, Morall and Martiall, &c.*, London, 1612, Force *Tracts*, III, no. 2, 60.

15. George, *Guns and Rifles*, 37-39. Pierre Surirey de Saint Remy, *Memoires D'Artillerie*, 2nd edition, 2 vols., Paris, 1707, I, 321, 322. Alm. *Eldhandvapen*, I, 9-160. Thierbach, *Handfeuerwaffen*, 7-19.

16. Elvas, *Narrative*, 148, 159, *et passim*.

17. Castañeda, *Coronado*, 305, 319, 334, 336, 362. The Visitation Made by Alvaro Flores of the Forts of Florida, 1578. Connor, *Records of Florida*, II, 117-203.

18. George Percy, "A Trewe Relacyon," *Tyler's Quarterly Historical and Genealogical Magazine*, III (April, 1922), 264. Roger, Earl of Orrery, warned about this hazard and listed many other disadvantages of the matchlock in his *Treatise on the Art of War*, London, 1677, 30, 31.

19. Robert Juet, *The Third Voyage of Master Henry Hudson*, J. Franklin Jameson, editor, *Narratives of New Netherlands, 1609-1664*, New York, 1909, 19.

20. [William Bradford and Edward Winslow], *A Relation or Journal of the Beginning and Proceedings of the English Plantation*, Edward Arber, editor, *The Story of the Pilgrim Fathers, 1606-1623 A.D., As Told by Themselves, Their Friends, and Their Enemies*, London, 1897, 432.

21. William Strachey, *Historie of Travaile into Virginia*, Henry S. Burrage, editor, *Early English and French Voyages, Chiefly from Hakluyt, 1534-*

1608, New York, 1906, 416, 417.

22. See below pages 43-49. For the abandonment of the matchlock in Europe, see Grose, *Military Antiquities*, passim; and Saint Remy, *Memoires D'Artillerie*, I, 321, 322.

23. Excellent descriptions and drawings of various wheel lock mechanisms can be found in Thierbach, *Handfeuerwaffen*, 27-49 and related plates; and Alm, *Eldhandvapen*, I, 9-160. See also Herbert J. Jackson, *European Hand Firearms of the Sixteenth, Seventeenth & Eighteenth Centuries*, London, 1922, 1-10.

24. Ralph Lane, *Account of the Particularities of the Imployments of the Englishmen Left in Virginia, 1585-1586*, Burrage, *English and French Voyages*, 267. Manifest made by Captain Don Luis de Velasco of the goods, arms, and horses which he is taking to serve his Majesty in the expedition to New Mexico, of which Don Juan de Oñate goes as Governor and Captain General, May 19, 1597, Hackett, *Historical Documents*, I, 428-433. Grose, *Military Antiquities*, I, 105, 106n, 152n, 153n, 154n. Stone, *Glossary*, 495. Hammond and Rey, *Oñate*, I, 137.

25. Harold L. Peterson, "New Evidence on Colonial Firearms from Jamestown Excavations," *The Gun Collector*, June, 1949, 313-316. For a comparison of the cost of wheel locks, matchlocks, and snaphaunces in the early 17th century, see George, *Guns and Rifles*, 36, 37.

26. Excellent descriptions and drawings of the snaphaunce mechanism can be found in Thierbach, *Handfeuerwaffen*, 50-64 and related plates; and Jackson, *Hand Firearms*, 11-14.

27. *Ibid.*

28. Peterson, "Jamestown Excavations," 313-316. Joseph R. Mayer, *Flintlocks of the Iroquois, 1620-1687*, *Research Records* of the Rochester Museum of Arts and Sciences, No. 6, Rochester, New York, 1943, 31. Charles W. Sawyer, *Firearms in American History, 1600-1800*, Boston, 1910, 7. George, *Guns and Rifles*, 30, 31, 41, 42.

29. George, *Guns and Rifles*, 31-34.

30. For additional discussions and pictures of the English lock and dog lock, see George, *Guns and Rifles*, 31-34, 48, 49; R. H. Walton, *Early Civil War Firearms in the Curtis Museum, Alton*, Alton, Hampshire, 1948, *passim*; Joseph R. Mayer, *Early Virginia Gunlocks*, Rochester Museum *Occasional Papers and Reprints*, Rochester, New York, 1939, 1-6; Jackson *Hand Firearms*, 23-26.

31. *Ibid.*

32. *Ibid.*

33. George, *Guns and Rifles*, 62, 63, 75. Alm, *Eldhandvapen*, I, 219-326.

34. Public collections containing important colonial dog locks include Colonial National Historical Park, Yorktown, Virginia; the Massachusetts Historical Society, Boston, Massachusetts; Memorial Hall, Deerfield, Massachusetts; Pilgrim Hall, Plymouth, Massachusetts; Rhode Island Historical Soci-

ety, Providence, Rhode Island. Some of these locks have been illustrated in Ralph H. Gabriel, editor, *The Pageant of America*, 15 vols., New Haven, 1925-1929, VI, 20; Howard M. Chapin and Charles D. Cook, "Colonial Firearms," *Antiques Magazine*, XI, No. 2 (February, 1927), 113-118, and No. 6 (June, 1927), 466-469; Peterson, "Jamestown Excavations," 313-316; Mayer, *Early Virginia Gunlocks, passim;* and Mayer, *Flintlocks of the Iroquois, passim.*

35. Jackson, *Hand Firearms*, 23-26.

36. Peterson, "Jamestown Excavations," 313-316. Petition of Don Pedro Ponce de León to the President of the Council of the Indies, April 23, 1566, Hackett, *Historical Documents*, I, 294-297.

37. Alm, *Eldhandvapen*, 69-215. Torsten Lenk, "Nordiska Snapplåsvapen," *Svenska Vapenhistoriska Sällskapets Skrifter*, Nya Serien II, 15-45.

38. Report of Gov. Rising, 1654, Myers, *Narratives of Pennsylvania, West New Jersey and Delaware*, 147.

39. J. Margerand, *Armament et Équipment de L'Infanterie Française du XVIe au XXe Siècle*, Paris, n. d., 19. George, *Guns and Rifles*, 42.

40. Stone, *Glossary*, 503-509. Sir James G. Mann, *European Arms and Armour*, Wallace Collection Catalogues, part III, London, 1945, 620. John N. George, *English Pistols and Revolvers*, Onslow County, North Carolina, 1938, 3. 4.

41. Lane, *Account*, 267, John Smith, *A True Relation of such occurrences and accidents of noate as hath happened in Virginia since the first planting of that Collony, which is now resident in the South part thereof, till the last return from thence*, Lyon Gardiner Tyler, editor, *Narratives of Early Virginia, 1606-1625*, New York, 1907, 43, 47. William Simmonds, *Proceedings of the English Colonies in Virginia, ibid*, 172. Strachey, *Lavves*, 32. "Military Census of Virginia," *Virginia Magazine of History and Biography*, VII (April 1910), 364-367; also Alexander Brown, *The First Republic in America*, Boston, 1898, 610-627. "Journal of New Netherlands," Edmund B. O'Callaghan and others, editors, *Documents Relative to the Colonial History of New York*, 15 vols., Albany, 1853-1887, I, 184. "Interrogatories to be proposed to Secretary van Tienhoven," *ibid.*, I, 413.

42. Stone, *Glossary*, 495. Grose, *Military Antiquities*, I, 105. Mann, *Arms and Armour*, III, 635.

43. Lane, *Account*, 267. "Military Census of Virginia," 635. Brown, *First Republic*, 610-627.

44. Stone, *Glossary*, 242. Louis de Gaya, *Gaya's Traité des Armes, 1678*, Charles ffoulkes, editor, London, 1911, 21-31, Saint Remy, *Memoires D'Artillerie*, I, 319-330. Margerand, *Armement*, 14-23.

45. Gaya, *Traité*, 26-31. Saint Remy. *Memoires D'Artillerie*, I, 327, 328. Margerand, *Armement*, 15-20, George, *Guns and Rifles*, 72, 73.

46. Proceedings of the General Assembly, Lower House, October 31, 1678, William H. Browne and others, editors, *Archives of Maryland*, Baltimore, 1884—, VII, 30.

47. George, *Guns and Rifles*, 59-61.

48. Proceedings of the General Assembly, Lower House, October 31, 1678, Browne, *Archives of Maryland*, VII, 30. "An Accot of Publick Ammunition," *ibid.*, XX, 207.

49. Shurtleff, *Massachusetts Records*, I, 25, 26. Bradford and Winslow, *Relation*, 493.

50. Smith, *True Relation*, 43, 58, 67. Simmonds, *Proceedings*, 168, 197. Strachey, *Lavves*, 32, 59-61. "Report of the Voyage to Virginia . . .," November 13, 1611, Alexander Brown, editor, *The Genesis of the United States*, 2 vols., Boston, 1890, 1897, I, 516. Stone, *Glossary*, 222. Commandant Guillaume, *Les Premières Armes à Feu de l'Infanterie*, Fribourg, n.d., 14, 15.

51. Military Census of Virginia," 364-367. "Meeting of a Committee for Smythes Hundred," May 18, 1618, Kingsbury, *Records*, III, 96. Thomas Matthew, *Bacon's Rebellion*, Force, *Tracts*, I, No. 8, 16, 17.

52. Nathaniel B. Shurtleff, editor. *Records of the Governor and Company of Massachusetts Bay in New England*, 5 vols., Boston, 1853, 1854, I, 25, 26.

53. Bradford and Williams, *Relation*, 415, 416, 420, 423, 426, 493. Harold L. Peterson, "The Military Equipment of the Plymouth and Bay Colonies, 1620-1690," *The New England Quarterly*, XX, No. 2 (June 1947), 203, 204.

54. Shurtleff, *Massachusetts Records*, II, 134, 135.

55. *Ibid.*, IV, pt. 2, 562; V, 22; I, 125, 207, 208; II, 72, 73, 134, 135, 222. John Noble, editor, *Records of the Court of Assistants in the Colony of the Massachusetts Bay, 1630-1692*, 3 vols., Boston, 1904, II, 13. William Bradford, *History of Plimoth Plantation*, Boston, 1899, 351, 518. Nathaniel B. Shurtleff and David Pulsifer, editors, *Records of the Colony of New Plymouth in New England*, 12 vols., Boston, 1855-1861, II, 65; XI, 51, 105. Cotton Mather, *Magnalia Christi Americana*, 2 vols., Hartford, 1833, II, 561, 562. John Winthrop, *The History of New England from 1630 to 1649*, James Savage, editor, 2 vols., Boston, 1853, I, 475. William Hubbard, *The History of the Indian Wars in New England from the First Settlement to the Termination of the War with King Philip, in 1677*, Samuel Drake, editor, 2 vols., Roxbury, 1845, *passim*. Thomas Church [and Benjamin Church], *The History of Philip's War, Commonly Called the Great Indian War of 1675 and 1676, Also of the French and Indian Wars at the Eastward, in 1689, 1690, 1692, 1696, and 1704*, Exeter, New Hampshire, 1829, *passim*.

56. Shurtleff, *Massachusetts Records*, V. 63. Shurtleff, *Plymouth Records*, XI, 244. Mather, *Magnalia*, II, 564, 565, 569-571, 575. Church, *Philip's War, passim*. Hubbard, *Indian Wars, passim*. Samuel Drake, editor, *The Old Indian Chronicle*, Boston, 1836, *passim*.

57. Charles J. Hoadly, editor, *Records of the*

Colony and Plantation of New Haven from 1638 to 1649, Hartford, 1857, 25, 26, 96, 97, 131, 503. Charles J. Hoadly, editor, *The Public Records of the Colony of Connecticut*, 15 vols., Hartford, 1850-1890, II, 285.

58. "Journal of New Netherlands," O'Callaghan, *Documents*, I, 182, 184. "Interrogatories to be Pro-posed to Secretary Van Tienhoven," *ibid.*, 413. Also, *ibid.*, 645; II, 89, 185, 191, 252, 507; XIII, 51, 64.

59. *Ibid.*, XIII, 257.

60. *Ibid.*, II, 252.

61. *Ibid.*, I, 123, 342, 382, 383, 389; III, 342; XIII, 47.

Chapter Two

Ammunition and Equipment

THE EARLY EXPLORER and colonist needed several distinct forms of ammunition and many separate pieces of equipment in order to discharge and care for his firearms. As the guns themselves passed through an evolution from the slow and awkward matchlock to the faster, handier flintlock, the ammunition and equipment developed along similar lines. Articles such as rests for matchlocks and spanners for wheel locks were discarded when flint arms were used. Other pieces of equipment which remained necessary no matter what ignition system was used changed form and became more adaptable and more compact. Finally, improved manufacturing methods brought changes to still other essential goods.

The ammunition was, of course, the prime necessity for all types of firearms. The components of this essential were, at the beginning, the powder, match, and bullets. Of these three elements, the latter was the only one which served through the entire period without any change in material or design. The round ball of lead used by De Soto's men was exactly the same, except perhaps for size, as the ball used by the United States Army until 1855.

Gun powder developed slowly throughout the whole period. From the time of its discovery in Europe, sometime during the 13th century, until the appearance of smokeless powder late in the 19th century, all gun powder was composed of three essential ingredients—saltpeter, charcoal, and sulphur. The earliest method of making powder was to grind these three ingredients and mix them together. This resulted in a dusty black substance of about the texture and consistency of fine coal dirt. This form of powder was known as "meal" or "serpentine" powder. It was explosive, but it had many distinct disadvantages. It was unstable. It was hygroscopic, and when it was stored in a damp place it formed lumps which would burn slowly but would not explode. If the powder were rammed in to the barrel with too great a pressure, it would form a lump and lose much, if not all, of its explosive force. Even when the complete charge remained in its mealy form, it did not all burn, and a gummy residue quickly fouled the gun barrel.[1]

Plate 57. Match case. After Wallhausen and Ward.

Plate 58. Flint profiles.

There were other disadvantages, too, which related primarily to shipping and storing serpentine powder. Because of the dusty nature of its contents, a quantity of highly explosive dust was given off every time a container of the powder was shifted or jarred, which created a distinct safety hazard. Also, since the mixture of the three ingredients was purely a mechanical alignment, there was a tendency for these materials to settle out according to their specific densities if the powder were allowed to stand undisturbed for any period of time. Consequently, the periodic inverting of powder kegs was an important part of the ritual of every well-run magazine.[2]

Despite these obvious drawbacks, serpentine powder continued in use as the main propelling charge in firearms until about the middle of the 16th century, when "corned" powder began to supersede it. Corned or granulated powder was made by adding 2 or 3 percent of water to the mixture and squeezing the resultant mass through sieves under considerable pressure. Corned powder overcame almost all the disadvantages of the serpentine powder, and in addition it burned much more rapidly and thus added considerable force to the explosion. For these reasons, corned powder quickly supplanted the earlier variety as the main propellant for firearms. Serpentine powder, however, remained as the principal material for priming.[3]

The third element in the ammunition necessary for the matchlock was the match. This match was usually made of lightly twisted strands of hemp or cotton which had been soaked in saltpeter or some similar substance to enhance its burning qualities. Match prepared in this way burned comparatively slowly and maintained a steady coal until the end. The rate of burning, of course, varied according to the exact composition of the match itself and the nature of the treatment it had undergone. Thus, one finds rates of burning listed that vary from a foot in 2 hours and 20 minutes to three-quarters of a foot an hour. Taking these burning rates into consideration, it is easy to understand why early colonial ordnances required each owner of a matchlock to maintain a considerable quantity of match (up to 24 feet in New Haven) ready for use at all times.[4]

Match was carried by the soldier in many ways. The most common way was to loop it over the belt or bandolier. In wet weather it was often coiled around the body under the jacket or around the head under the hat or in the pocket. Lighted match was usually carried in the left hand. Shortly before 1600, however, an invention attributed to the Walloons permitted lighted match to be carried apart from the gun, thus lessening the danger of an accidental discharge. This device, known as a "match box" or "match case" consisted of a metal tube pierced with many holes for ventilation. The lighted end of the match was inserted into the tube and fastened in place so that it could burn with little danger to the soldier and at the same time be somewhat protected from the elements. These match boxes were usually about a foot long and were worn suspended from the belt. Later these match boxes degenerated into the small appendages worn on the cross belt by grenadiers and used by them to hold the match for lighting their grenades.[5]

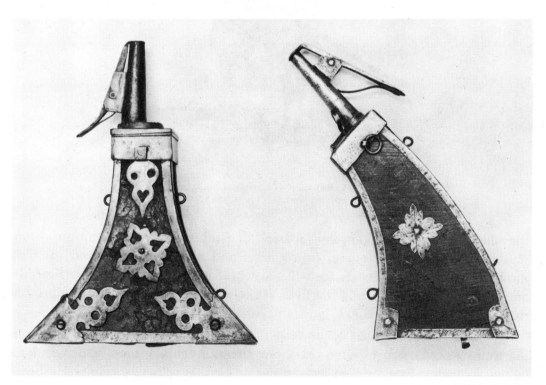

Author's Collection

Plate 59. Powder flasks, late 16th—early 17th centuries.

When the matchlock was superseded by the wheel lock and the snaphaunce, the match was no longer necessary. The spark for igniting the powder was generated by striking a piece of stone sharply against a piece of steel. This effect was achieved either by placing the stone in position and striking it many times with the individual facets of a serrated wheel or by striking the stone in a long scrap-

Folger Shakespeare Library
Plate 60. Caliverman with regular flask worn on a carrier and priming flask suspended on cords. From De Gheyn.

ing motion against a single plate of steel, depending on which ignition system was used. Two types of stone, iron pyrites and flint were employed in these mechanisms. Iron pyrites was used in the wheel locks. A few of the earlier flint arms also made use of pyrites, but flint soon entirely superseded it and impressed its name on the whole generic ignition system.

The pieces of flint used in the early flint arms differed slightly in shape from the well-known design of later years. Seventeenth century locks which still retained their flints have been excavated in this country. These specimens indicate that in the first half of the century flints were often much thinner than the later ones, sometimes barely $\frac{3}{16}$ of an inch thick. Also, the bevel was often evenly cut on both the top and bottom so that the sharp striking edge was in the center of the front instead of being either at the top or bottom of the flint, as was customary later. Lock specimens dating from the second half of the 17th century are usually found with flints of the more conventional design.[6]

Folger Shakespeare Library
Plate 61. · Caliverman loading his piece. Note the carrier and the hook on the back of the flask for attaching to it. The cord served merely to prevent loss of the flask. From De Gheyn.

The greatest evolution connected with ammunition, however, is to be found in the methods of carrying it and using it. In this aspect is found the transition from flask to bandolier to cartridge box and the evolution from loose to semi-fixed to fixed ammunition.

In the early 16th century, when De Soto's men came to America, the powder flask and bullet bag were the principal means of carrying ammunition. These powder flasks were usually made of wood, covered with leather and bound with iron. The earliest flasks had nozzles closed by a simple stopper, but probably during De Soto's time and certainly by 1550 three varieties of spring closures had been developed which were to remain popular for nearly 200 years. In one type the nozzle was closed by a cap at its distal end. In another the nozzle was closed by a pivoted gate at its base; and in a third variety both closures were employed. It is impossible to assign an evolutionary sequence to these develop-

Folger Shakespeare Library
Plate 62. Musketeer wearing bandolier and carrying a
gun fork or rest. From De Gheyn.

ments except to state that the third one undoubtedly came last. All of them developed apparently within a few years and all were used as long as flasks were made.[7]

The first type, a spring operated cap at the distal end of the nozzle, was just one step better than the stopper. Its advantages, however, were several. First, it was fastened to the flask and could not be lost. Second, since it required only the pressure of the thumb to open it, it avoided the complexities of removing a stopper and could be used much more swiftly and easily. Finally, it closed the flask automatically and immediately when the thumb was removed, thus relieving the operator from the worry of replacing the stopper or losing his powder.

The second type of closure, the pivoted gate at the base of the nozzle, was a vast improvement. It possessed all the virtues of the cap and it also allowed the operator to measure the charge of powder he was putting in his gun To use this measure, the operator tilted his flask, placed a finger over the end of the nozzle, and opened the gate. When the nozzle had filled with powder he released the spring and allowed the gate to close. Then he righted the flask and

Folger Shakespeare Library
Plate 63. Musketeer pouring the contents of one of the bandolier cylinders into his piece. The rest has been shifted to his left hand and trails by its thong. From De Gheyn.

removed his finger. In this manner he obtained a quantity of powder exactly determined by the capacity of the nozzle, which was generally contrived to be the amount necessary for a charge.

The third type of closure, the combination of both the previous types, actually had little if any advantage over the second type. It may possibly have been easier to use, but by increasing the complexity of the mechanism it increased the possibility for error. If the excited soldier pushed the wrong spring, either

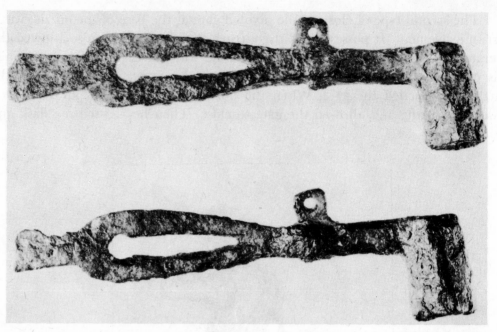

National Park Service

Plate 64. Military spanners excavated at Jamestown.

when he was filling the nozzle or putting the charge in the barrel, he got no powder whatsoever and was likely to be none the wiser unil he tried to fire the piece. For these reasons this type of closure, though very popular for a hundred years or so after its development, dropped from use before either of its two predecessors.

There were, of course, many other types of flask in addition to the usual military variety. Many materials, including horn, shell, ivory, leather, and metal were utilized, and many designs and mechanisms were employed, especially on elaborate and expensive flasks. Throughout the entire period, simple horns with the large end closed and a stopper in the small end found favor with the poorer classes and with those who experienced difficulty in obtaining the manufactured varieties. It was this latter type, commonly referred to now as a "powder horn," rather than the powder flask that found increasing favor among individuals in America, beginning really toward the middle of the 17th century and reaching its height of popularity during the 18th century. When manufactured flasks became both cheaper and more readily available during the 19th century, the popuarity of the horn declined correspondingly.[8]

During the very early 1500's, when serpentine powder was used for both the propelling and the priming charges, only one flask was used. Later, two flasks were often carried, a large one containing the corned powder for the propellant and a small one holding the serpentine powder for priming. Thus, Don Luís de

Velasco speaks of his "three wheel lock arquebuses with their large and small powder horns," which he took with him to New Mexico in 1597. A majority of the population, however, probably continued to carry only one flask or horn, using corned powder for both charge and priming.[9]

In addition to their flasks or horns, the early settlers often carried a pouch for bullets. This bag, usually of soft leather, was customarily worn suspended from the waist belt on the right side. Sometimes the pouch and flask were hung together on a leather strap known variously as a flask carrier or *porte tache*. Those carriers designed for use with a wheel lock also provided an attachment for holding the spanner. When going into action or when standing watch, the soldier took a few balls from the pouch and placed them in his mouth for more rapid loading in the event of an emergency.[10]

Another means of carrying ammunition which was popular for a time in America was the bandolier. This device consisted of a leather strap or baldrick from which were suspended a number of cylinders, each of which contained sufficient powder for one charge. These cylinders varied in number, although twelve was about average, and they were made of several different materials. Wood was probably most popular, but copper, tin, pewter, and jacked leather were also used. The bandolier is generally believed to have been developed in the Low Countries during the first half of the 16th century. From there it spread rapidly throughout western Europe except in Spain, where it apparently was viewed with little favor. With the bandolier, it was customary to carry a priming flask and a bullet pouch.[11]

References to the bandolier in America do not appear until the 17th century. There is no reference to them in the unusually complete inventories of the Spanish forts in Florida for the 16th century or in the available records of the Spanish expeditions in the Southwest. Apparently, the Spanish antipathy toward the device which was noted by some contemporary writers was widespread

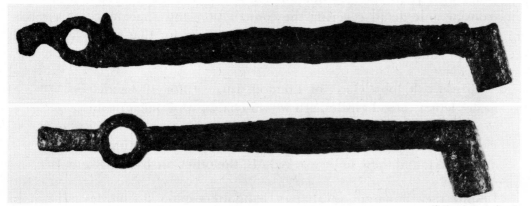

National Park Service

Plate 65. Military spanners excavated at Jamestown.

enough to prevent them from reaching the Spanish colonies in any quantity. The records of the French colony in Florida are equally silent, and Le Moyne's pictures illustrate flasks only. With the arrival of the English settlers at James-

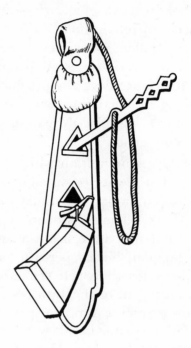

Plate 66. *Porte tache* or flask carrier. After Wallhausen.

town and the Dutch and Swedish settlements along the coast, the listings of bandoliers become ever more frequent.

Before they left England, the settlers of the Massachusetts Bay Colony wrote a contract with John Gace of London for forty bandoliers. This contract contains considerable detail covering the construction and appearance of the bandoliers which these colonists brought with them, and for that reason it is worth repeating in full.

Agreed wth John Gace, of London, turner, ffor 40 bandeleers,*** neates lether, broad girdles, ech wth 12 charg^s, w^rof one a priming bx x of wood, covered wth black lether, at 2 s a peece, to bee dd next [weeke]; the boxes to bee for bastard muskett sise, excepting 10 for full mus[ketts], and these to be marked M., the other for bas^t musketts B.[12]

Despite their apparent advantages, bandoliers suffered from several serious defects which did much to undermine their popularity and make their period of popularity relatively short. Lord Orrery, one of the outstanding military writers of the 17th century, analyzed these shortcomings in detail:

> Besides, I have often seen much prejudice in the use of bandeleers, which being worn in the belts for them, above the soldiers' coats, are often apt to take fire, especially if the matchlock musket be used; and when they take fire, they commonly wound and often kill him that wears them, and those near him: for likely if one bandeleer take fire, all the rest do in that collar: they often tangle those which use them on service, when they have fired, and on falling off by the flanks of the files of the intervals, to get into the rear to charge again. To which I shall add, that in secret attempts in the night, their rattling often discovers the design, and enables the enemy to prevent it; and in the day time on service, especially if the weather be windy, their rattling also too frequently hinders the soldiers from hearing, and consequently obeying the officer's word of command, which must be fatal when it happens . . .[13]

The device that appeared to supplant the bandolier in America after less than half a century of popularity was the paper cartridge. This innovation was

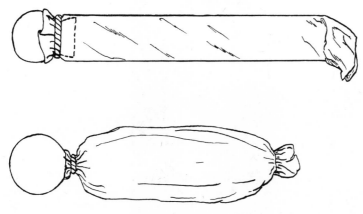

Plate 67. Late 16th century paper cartridge with ball attached by flange. Seventeenth century paper cartridge with ball attached by sprue. After Saint Remy.

developed in Europe sometime during the second half of the 16th century. The first cartridges were simply individual charges of powder rolled in paper tubes. The balls were still carried in the pouch. They were, thus, a true form of semi-fixed ammunition. By the end of the century, however, a means of attaching the ball had been devised. This was done by tying one end of the paper tube to the sprue which was left when the ball was cast or to a special flange which was sometimes added to the ball. In neither of these instances was the ball covered by the paper, but now a form or fixed ammunition had been developed. It is not known just when the completely wrapped cartridge was developed, but as late as 1697 Saint Remy illustrated a cartridge with the ball attached by its sprue as the latest type.[14]

Cartridges were normally carried in a box or pouch specifically designed for that purpose. The earliest boxes were usually comparatively small, designed

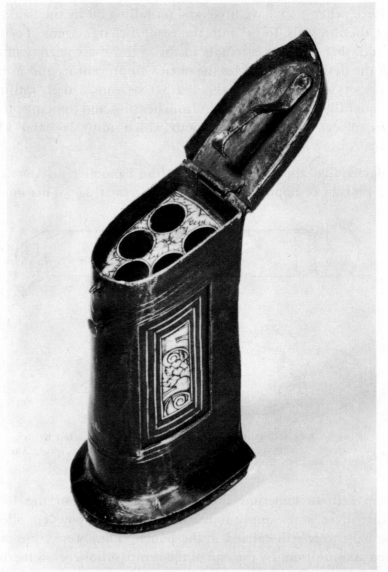

Plate 68. Patron with blued iron frame and wooden insert inlaid with bone, second half of the 16th century.

to hold pistol cartridges, and were used primarily by cavalry. These early boxes are known today by the name of patrons, from the German and Scandinavian word meaning cartridge. Usually they were made of wood or bone, often with elaborately etched and engraved iron mountings. Some, made entirely of sculptured iron or steel, are also known. The lid was usually hinged at the back and held shut by a spring latch at the front. Three rectangular metal staples provided the means of attachment to belt or sling.[15]

Later, when the use of cartridges spread from the cavalry to the infantry, cartridge boxes of the more conventional form began to develop. Gustavus Adolphus of Sweden is often credited with being the first European monarch to equip his infantry with cartridges, and indeed his action early in the 17th century certainly places him as one of the first, well ahead of England and France. The Swedes brought their fondness for cartridge boxes with them to America, and the earliest actual description of a cartridge box in America is found in the report of Governor Rising of the Swedish settlements in 1654. In his report he asked specifically for:

"... bags of leather with three or four compartments, in which one could place cartridges; these are many times better in the woods than bandoliers...."[16]

The exact date at which cartridges were first brought to America will never be known, but most of the references to them are found about the middle of the 17th century. The Dutch in New Amsterdam used bandoliers for their matchlocks but ordered cartridge boxes for their wheel locks and flint arms. In New England, Captain Church frequently referred to the use of cartridges in King Philip's War, 1675-1677, and inventories of arms of that period in various individual colonies included cartridge boxes. It is safe, then, to assume that the cartridge was in widespread use in America by the third quarter of the 17th century.[17]

It should not be supposed from the above comments that the bandolier completely superseded the flask and that the cartridge completely superseded the bandolier in the period under consideration. The flask and horn retained considerable popularity, especially for non-military use, throughout the entire period and indeed until the metallic cartridge made the muzzle loader completely obsolete. The bandolier enjoyed only a short period of popularity, but a few survived until almost 1700.

And then there were a few individuals who threw all caution aside and carried powder loose in their pockets. No less a soldier than Captain John Smith himself resorted to this practice at least once and was so badly burned when the powder accidentally took fire that he was forced to return to England. All of these means of carrying powder were popular during the 17th century, and the newest development by no means excluded the earlier methods.[18]

In addition to the necessary containers for his ammunition, there were several other items of equipment which were necessary for proper operation of colonial firearms. First among these was the rest, which was required when a heavy matchlock musket was used. These rests were simple staves, about four

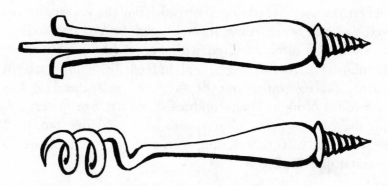

Plate 69. Seventeenth century cleaner and worm. After Wallhausen.

feet long, with a fork on one end in which the barrel of the musket could be laid. The usual material for these implements was wood with iron tips, but an occasional specimen with brass tips is found.

Toward the end of their period of use, one branch of the fork was sometimes lengthened and sharpened for use in defense against cavalry. Also, a sharp blade was sometimes concealed within the staff and activated by a spring so that it could be ejected by the touch of a lever. This last type was known as the swine s feather or sometimes as the Swedish feather. These rests were usually attached to the left wrist by a thong and carried it in the left hand on the march.[19]

In order to keep his piece clean and in working order, the colonist also needed a variety of small tools. These included a scourer, a worm, a priming iron, and a brush. Edward Davies described these items and their use in 1619:

> . . . neither must he [a soldier] want his necessarie tooles, as a scowrer, tirebale [ball screw] and worme, having every one a vice to turne into the end of the scouring sticke, so that if thorough wet weather, or any other accident, his peece will not be discharged, the skilful souldier may with his tirebale pull out his bullet with the worme, the paper, and wet powder, and with his scourer make his peece cleane within. His scourer must be trimmed on the end with a linen cloth of sufficient substance, therewith to make cleane the cannon [bore] of his peece

within. The one end of his scouring stick ought to have a round end of bone of just bigness with the mouth of his peece, therewithall at his pleasure, to ramme in powder and paper, or instead of paper, suche softe haire as they stuff saddles withall, the danger whereof is not like; but this the soldier must use when time permits. During the time of his service let him ever have a dilligent care to keepe his peece cleane and bright within, and once a fortnight, or at least once a month, take out the breech, and thoroughly view and wash the barrel within, to see whether it hath any flawes, brackes, chambers, frettings, or ruptures, which would endanger the breaking thereof, especially if beforehand the end of his bare scourer hath given him any cause to suspect such faults, to the intent he may change the same for a new for feare of spoiling himselfe.[20]

The priming iron and brush, which Davies did not explain in this paragraph, were used to clean the touch hole and pan.

In addition to the above items, two devices for carrying arms were in comparatively widespread use. The mounted trooper hung long leather holsters for his pistols in front of his saddle. These holsters differed little from those used for the next two hundred years except that, since the pistols were generally longer, the holsters, too, were longer. Usually, there was a cap of leather or fur to keep out moisture, and sometimes there was a pocket for cartridges. Wheel

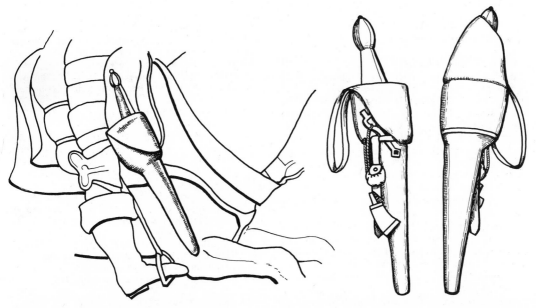

Plate 70. Wheel lock pistol holsters. At left a sketch of the holster in position, after Wallhausen; at right, a reconstruction of a pair of holsters, the obverse indicating the *porte tache* in place, the reverse showing the flap raised. Based primarily on Wallhausen.

[67]

lock holsters frequently provided a means for carrying the spanner. Also, although the sling was not generally used for the foot soldier's gun, carbines were usually carried on a sling. These slings were worn over one shoulder and across the body. The carbine was attached to them by a snap and swivel on a sliding ring.

These were the forms of ammunition and principal pieces of equipment for firearms used by the American colonist from 1526 to 1688. Compared to the frequent and rapid changes in ignition systems, the evolution of these articles was slow. The special influence of the American environment is not so apparent here as in some other phases of the subject. Only in the rapid adoption of the paper cartridges for military use can one find America in the vanguard of munitions progress. Even in this, America was behind some nations, such as Sweden, but almost fifty years ahead of others, such as France, where the cartridge was not officially adopted for military use until 1702.

NOTES—CHAPTER TWO

1. Henry W. L. Hime, *The Origin of Artillery*, London, 1915, 11-25, 102, 121, 149, 159. Albert C. Manucy, *Artillery Through The Ages*, Washington, 1949, 23-25. J. Scoffern, *Projectile Weapons of War and Explosive Compounds*, London, 1858, 103-108. Metschl, *Nunnemacher Catalog*, I, 56-59.

2. *Ibid.*

3. *Ibid.* Gaya, *Traité*, 68.

4. Edward Davies, "England's Trainings," 1619, reprinted in Grose, *Military Antiquities*, II, 125. Gaya, *Traité*, 72. Metschl, *Nunnemacher Catalog*, I, 55. Manucy, *Artillery*, 26. Minutes of the General Court, July 6, 1643, April 3, 1644, Hoadly, *New Haven Records*, 96, 97, 131.

5. Davies, "England's Trainings," 122. Grose, *Military Antiquities*, II, 129n, Alm, *Eldhandvapen*, I, 245, 246. Metschl, *Nunnemacher Catalog*, I, 56. Orrery, *Art of War*, 30, 31.

6. Mayer, *Flintlocks of the Iroquois*, passim. Peterson, "Jamestown Excavations," 314.

7. Davies, "England's Trainings," 124, 125. Alm, *Eldhandvapen*, I, 99-103. Stone, *Glossary*, 230-232. Mann, *Wallace Collection*, III, 396, 418. Harold L. Peterson, "The Flask Through the Ages," Ray Riling, *The Powder Flask Book*, New Hope, Pennsylvania, 1953, 1-13.

8. *Ibid.* Stephen V. Grancsay, *American Engraved Powder Horns*, New York, 1945, *passim.*

9. *Ibid.* Manifest made by Captain Don Luís de Velasco, Hackett, *Historical Documents*, I, 428-433.

The Visitation Made by Alvaro Flores to the Forts of Florida, 1578, Connor, *Records of Florida*, II, 137-203.

10. Strachey, *Lavves*, 32. Minutes of the General Court, November 29, 1649, Hoadly, *New Haven Records*, 503. Church, *History*, 23-25. Alm, *Eldhandvapen*, I, 99-103. Orrery, *Art of War*, 131, 132. See also Ward, Hexham, and de Gheyn.

11. Grose, *Military Antiquities*, II, 124, 128n. Alm, *Eldhanvdapen*, I, 104, 105. Margerand, *Armement*, 58, 59.

12. Shurtleff, *Massachusetts Records*, I, 31.

13. Orrery, *Art of War*, 31, 32.

14. Thierbach, *Handfeuerwaffen*, 22, 23. Alm, *Eldhandvapen*, I, 103, 104, Saint Remy, *Memoires D'Artillerie*, I, 141-147.

15. Alm, *Eldhandvapen*, I, 116-118. Thierbach, *Handfeuerwaffen*, 22, 23.

16. *Ibid.* Report of Governor Rising, 1654, Albert C. Myers, editor, *Narratives of Early Pennsylvania, West New Jersey and Delaware*, New York, 1912, 147.

17. O'Callaghan, *Documents*, I, 645; II, 185, 191, 507; XIII, 236. Church, *History*, 60. "Records of the United Colonies," Hoadly, *Connecticut Records*, III, 499. Minutes of the Court of Election, May 9, 1678, *ibid*, 12.

18. Percy, "Trewe Relacyon," 264.

19. Grose, *Military Antiquities*, I, 156, 157, 157n.

20. Edward Davies, "England's Trainings," 122, 123.

Chapter Three

Edged Weapons

IT WAS STATED previously that the early colonist's firearm was his most important single weapon. It should not be deduced from this, however, that he could have carried on with that weapon alone. Edged weapons were also absolutely necessary. Firearms were needed to engage an enemy at a distance, but once the conflict became hand-to-hand, they were useless because of the length of time required to load them. The bayonet with which the modern soldier converts his gun to a polearm did not come into general use in America until after the close of the period under consideration, and so the explorers and settlers were forced to carry separate weapons. Also, during the early years there were certain groups, notably the Spanish lancers, the pikemen, and some of the targeteers who carried no firearms at all. These groups, however, gradually disappeared as they were found to be impractical in woodland warfare. Finally, there were some specialized edged weapons such as arms emblematic of rank or justice, hatchets, and the like designed and used for specific purposes.

Of all the various forms of edged weapons, the one in most widespread usage throughout the whole period was the sword. All men on military duty whether they carried a firearm or not were required to have a sword. Since all able-bodied men in a colony were normally called upon for such duty, this meant that all had to be familiar with the use of that weapon. Consequently, it is not surprising frequently to find more swords than guns listed in inventories and estates, or to learn that more have survived the ravages of time. It is interesting to note also that when Captain John Smith left Virginia in 1608 he reported that there were on hand in the colony more swords than men and that in 1618 a Committee for Smythes Hundred in Virginia recommended that 40 swords and daggers be provided for 35 men expecting to come from England.[1]

[69]

Examples of almost every type of sword in use in contemporary Europe probably found their way to America during the early colonial period. Even a "Japanese cutlass" was listed in a New Amsterdam estate inventory of 1643. The men who used these weapons, however, normally referred to them only in generic terms, seldom specifically identifying a type. Consequently, it is impossible to determine as accurately as one would like the exact form of sword used in every instance. Nevertheless, certain generalizations can be made for each period and locality, and in a few instances exact data may be given.[2]

The swords which the early Spanish explorers brought with them and which were the dominant types throughout the 16th century fall into two main types.

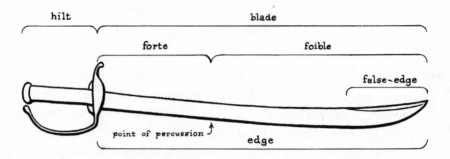

hilt · blade · forte · foible · false-edge · point of percussion · edge

The sword is always described in this position. The side toward the viewer is the obverse side. The other is the reverse

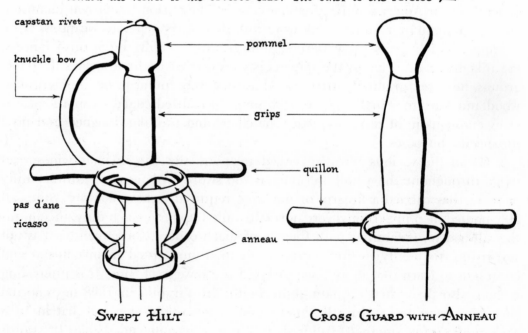

capstan rivet · pommel · knuckle bow · grips · quillon · pas d'ane · ricasso · anneau

SWEPT HILT   CROSS GUARD WITH ANNEAU

Plate 71. The terminology of the sword.

First was the double-edged cutting sword developed from the knightly sword of earlier centuries, and second was the rapier. At first the sword was used partially for thrusting as well as cutting, and the edge of the rapier was used as well as the point. At this stage of development it is often difficult to distinguish one from the other. Later, as the art of fencing developed, the rapier came to be used almost exclusively for thrusting. As its functions became more specialized,

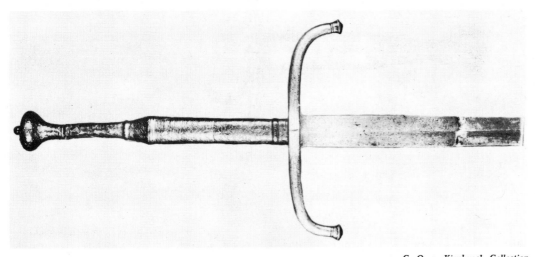

Plate 72. Italian hand-and-a-half sword with cross quillons curving forward over the blade, c. 1500.

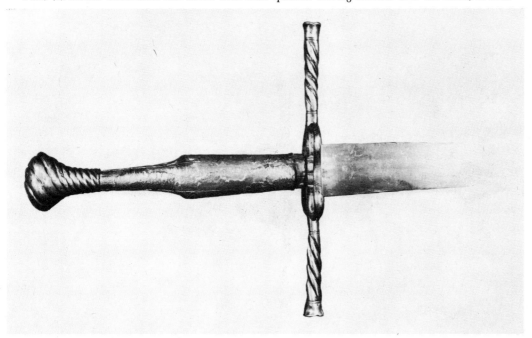

Plate 73. German sword with straight cross quillons and simple *anneaux* on either side, early 16th century.

C. O. v. Kienbusch Collection

Plate 74. German sword with a branch on either side of the quillons and a rudimentary *pas d'ane* below the blade, early 16th century.

C. O. v. Kienbusch Collection

Plate 75. German sword with two anneaux on either side joined by *pas d'anes*, early 16th century.

the design of the rapier blade changed too. It became longer, narrorer, more rigid, and what edge it possessed was purely rudimentary.[3]

The hilts of both types developed along roughly parallel lines. The long straight quillons of the knightly sword were bent and augmented. Sometimes small rings (pas d'anes) were added in front of the quillons. A branch was attached to the lower quillon and curved upward toward the pommel forming the prototype of the later knuckle bow. Counterguards of rings (anneaux) at right angles to the blade were built up. Finally, the quillons themselves were bent in a double curve resembling the letter "S" laid on its side with the upward curve below the knuckles and the downward curve above the blade. The final development of this type of hilt with the branches sweeping around the hand from below the knuckles and recurving above the blade has been denoted in modern parlance a swept hilt.[4]

The hilt development described above began late in the 15th century and continued into the opening years of the 17th century. Generalizations linking

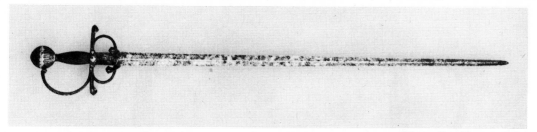

Metropolitan Museum of Art
Plate 76. Swept-hilted rapier, Italian c. 1550. The wire wrapping of the grips is missing.

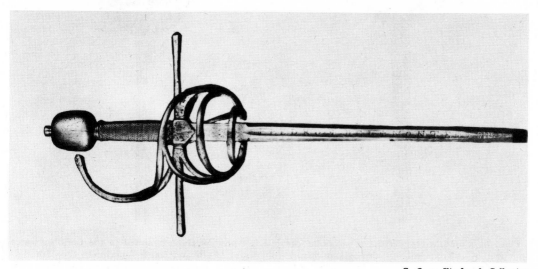

C. O. v. Kienbusch Collection
Plate 77. Swept-hilted rapier with Spanish blade and probably an Italian hilt, c. 1590.

[73]

design and date are always dangerous, and there are many exceptions. Nevertheless, it may be ventured that as a general rule the simpler the guard, the larger the pommel, and the shorter the grip, the earlier the type of hilt.

During the 17th century the hilt of the rapier underwent a further change as the cup hilt was developed. In this evolution the complex counterguard of separate rings was replaced by a solid cup, frequently beautifully chiselled and pierced. The *pas d'anes* were often retained inside the cup, and the quillons stretched across the open top. The transition to the cup hilt was gradual, and design varied considerably, apparently, according to national preference. The full deep cup with wide-spreading quillons which one immediately calls to mind when the term cup hilt is mentioned was developed in Italy and Spain and never achieved widespread popularity outside those southern European countries.

In France and England the cups normally remained shallow and were supplemented by branches from the knuckle bow and sometimes by *anneaux*. One particular form of this shallow cup-hilted sword has been denoted in modern

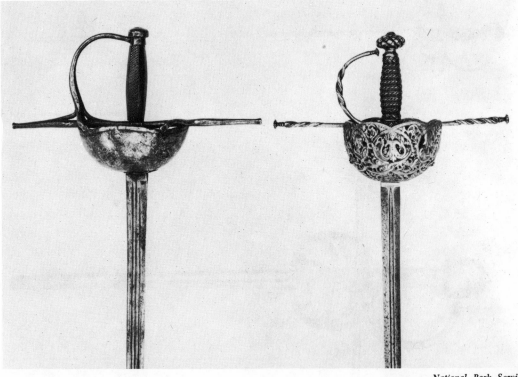

National Park Service

Plate 78. Cup-hilted rapiers. The sword at the left is typical of those mounted in the Caribbean area and used by common soldiers throughout Spain's colonies in North and South America in the 17th century. The grips are usually either hard wood or horn. The other rapier is an example of the finest type of cup hilt with chiseled steel mounts.

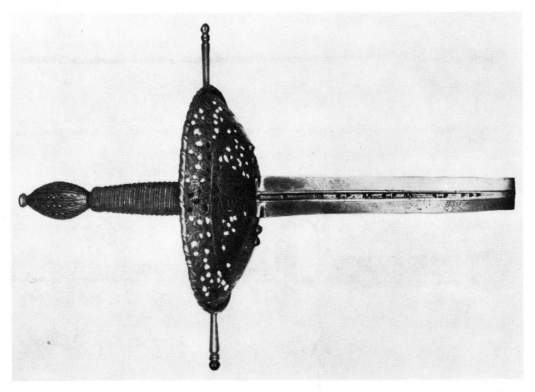

Plate 79. Spanish flamberge, c. 1660.

C. O. v. Kienbusch Collection

parlance the flamberge. It was characterized by a narrow quadrangular blade and a simple hilt, usually without knuckle bow and often without *pas d'ane,* the guard consisting only of the shallow cup and short straight quillons. The flamberge was in reality the transition between the true rapier and the small sword.[5]

The small sword, that excellent weapon which became so popular in the 18th century, was developed in France about the middle of the 17th century. It is reported to have been introduced into England by King Charles II at the time of his restoration. In all probability a limited number of these arms reached America before 1688, the terminal date of the period under consideration.[6]

The small sword was essentially a light weapon for civilian use. It placed its emphasis on speed and dexterity rather than on the ponderous thrusts and parries of the rapier. It was entirely a thrusting weapon. The light blade was usually hexagonal in section at first. Soon, however, a triangular shape with all three sides concave was developed, giving the effect of a three-edged blade. This triangular design increased the strength and the rigidity of the blade without adding unwanted weight.[7]

A further development of the small sword blade took place about 1680.

[75]

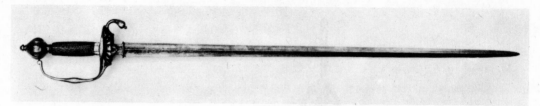

Hermann W. Williams, Jr. Collection

Plate 80. Sword of the transitional type between rapier and small sword believed to have been used by a sheriff of New Jersey. c. 1675.

Plate 81. Dutch small sword c. 1685.

Metropolitan Museum of Art

This new design comprised a blade with a wide forte narrowing suddenly to a slender foible. The wide section normally ran about one-quarter the length of the blade. This had the advantage of increasing the strength of the part of the blade near the hilt where the parries were made and lightening the section used in the attack. The earliest blades of this design look as if they had been ground down from larger hexagonal blades. Later ones are usually found with the triangular blade. Small swords of this type are known today as colichemardes. Tradition states that the word colichemarde is a French corruption of Königsmark, the name of the Swedish soldier of fortune who rose to be a Marshal of France and who supposedly originated the design. Recent researches, however, have indicated that there is little evidence to support the legend.[8]

The earliest small-sword hilts were essentially the same as the flamberge. Gradually the cup became bilobate and smaller. A baluster knuckle-bow and *pas d'anes* were added, and the quillon on the side of the knuckle-bow disappeared. The normal metals for the hilt were silver or bright, blackened or russeted steel. Few, if any, of this fully developed small sword reached America before the end of the period.[9]

Some of the types included in this first category which comprises the development of the thrusting sword, can be linked definitely to certain persons and events in American history through data supplied by documents and surviving specimens. The earliest known specific evidence is found in the paintings of Jacques Le Moyne of the French in Florida in 1564. In his picture of the battle with the Indians [see plate], Le Moyne clearly indicates two of the early forms. The officer with the target holds in his right hand a straight double-edged sword. The quillons are straight but enlarged at the ends, and there is an anneau. The pommel is pear-shaped with a button. This sword could quite correctly be described as a lineal descendant of the knightly sword. Immediately behind the officer is a calliverman, whose sword, in a scabbard on his left side, is partially concealed. Nevertheless, enough is visible to indicate that here is an early form of the swept hilt. The pommel end of the recurving branch which serves as a knuckle-bow is plainly visible. This same type of sword hilt is also visible in Le Moyne's drawing of the Indians worshipping a column, [see plate].

Two other pieces of documentary evidence from widely separated areas are also of interest. In 1597, Captain Don Luís de Velasco, who accompanied Don Juan de Oñate into New Mexico, took with him "A sword and a gilded dagger with their waist belts stitched with purple, yellow, and white silk." Velasco did not specify the type of sword, but from the date and its association with the dagger one would expect a rapier. This guess is supported by the fact that he also listed "One broadsword with shoulder belt . . ." The combination would have given him one of each type. Twelve years later, in 1609, Samuel de Champlain had his famous fight with the Indians. His own drawing of that event is small and indistinct, (see plate), but it is quite definitely a swept-hilted sword that he wears on a waist belt.[10]

National Park Service

Plate 82. Swept-hilted rapier c. 1600 by Johannes Wundes of Solingen excavated at Jamestown.

Some supporting evidence is also supplied by archeologists. Not nearly so many sword fragments as gun parts have been excavated thus far, but the National Park Service has to date uncovered one complete swept hilt rapier and several other swept hilts in the partial excavations at Jamestown. Also the entire guard of a swept hilt rapier was recently excavated at the site of an outpost of Jamestown and is now in the Smithsonian Institution.

Two important swords of this first category survive in good condition from

U. S. National Museum
Plate 83. Guard from a swept-hilted rapier.
c. 1590, excavated at the site of Kecoughtan, an
early outpost of Jamestown.

the colonial period. The earliest of these belonged to Captain John Mason, the Connecticut soldier famous for his exploits in the Pequot War, and is preserved by the New London County Historical Society. It has a 32-inch straight double-edged blade, 1¾ inches wide at the hilt, and diamond-shaped in cross section. There is an inscription on the blade which is now illegible but which has been recorded as "Veni Vidi Vici." The quillons are "S" shaped, but in a plane at right angles to the blade instead of with the blade as was more common. The pas d'anes are large, and the counter-guard consists of a large ring on the obverse with a shell guard inside it. The original grips and pommel are missing. The second sword is a rapier which belonged to Captain Miles Standish of

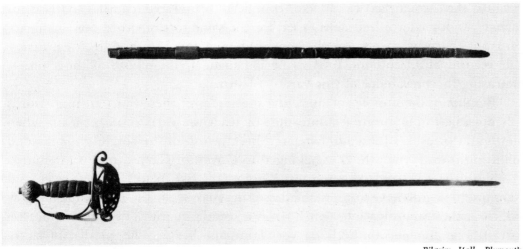

Pilgrim Hall, Plymouth

Plate 84A. Miles Standish's rapier and scabbard. Note that the throat of the scabbard has slipped down the body somewhat.

Plate 84B. Detail of hilt of Standish rapier.

Plymouth. It is an interesting example of the English type of cup-hilted rapier which has survived in remarkably good condition along with its original scabbard.[11]

Another category of swords which saw widespread use in Colonial America was the short, single-edged, cutting sword. The term most commonly used by contemporary writers to describe these weapons was "cutlass" or one of its variants, such as cutilax, curtle axe, coutelace, coutel axe, coutilas, cutlash, or cutlace. Another term frequently used for the same sort of sword was "hanger." This was the usual sword for the foot soldier of the 17th and 18th centuries. The records of all colonies for this period made frequent use of these terms, indicating the prevalence of this variety of sword.[12]

Because of the number of surviving specimens of these short cutting swords it is possible to obtain an accurate idea of what the early writers meant when they used the terms cutlass and hanger. Three swords of this sort survive in good condition from Plymouth. One belonged to Governor Carver, one is attributed to Elder Brewster, and one to John Thompson (see plate). The Carver and Thompson swords have straight blades. The guards consist of a knuckle bow with branches on either side which form a counterguard. The quillons are re-curved. The pommels on both are very large and heavy. The guards and pommels are of iron, and all the surfaces are covered with raised floral decorations.

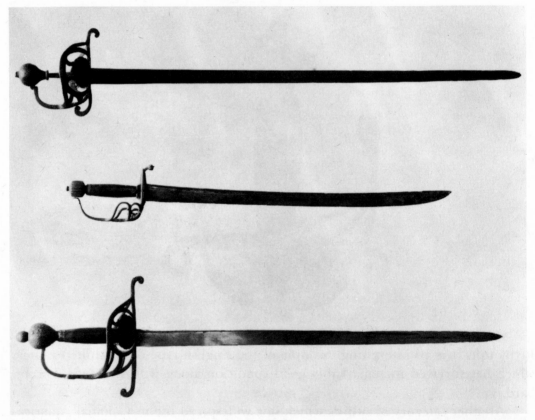

Pilgrim Hall, Plymouth

Plate 85. Cutting swords of the Pilgrims. Top, Governor Carver's double-edged broadsword; middle, short cutting sword attributed to Elder Brewster; bottom, John Thompson's single-edged cutting sword.

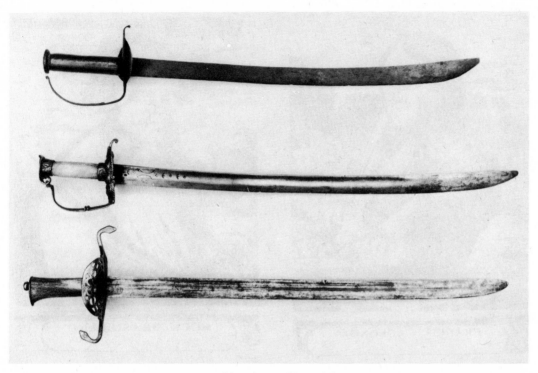

Plate 86. Short cutting swords or "cutlasses." Top: sword of Capt. Benjamin Church, mid 17th century. Middle: English cutting sword of about 1660 used in New England. Bottom: Early 17th century cutting sword used by Sergeant William Hayden.

The hilts from several similar swords have been excavated at Jamestown by the National Park Service. The Brewster sword is somewhat lighter than the others in both blade and guard, and the blade is slightly curved. It has a generally more "modern" appearance. All three of these swords are preserved at Pilgrim Hall, Plymouth, Massachusetts.

Another surviving sword of this general type is one which belonged to Captain Benjamin Church, famous Indian fighter of King Philip's War (1675-78). It is owned by the Massachusetts Historical Society in Boston. The sword is so simply and crudely made that it could well have been manufactured in this country. The blade is short and slightly curved. The grip is a simple cylinder of wood. The counterguard and knuckle bow (which does not join the pommel) are forged from a single piece of iron.

Still another specimen of a somewhat different type is preserved in the Connecticut Historical Society. It has stag horn grips and no knuckle-bow. The guard consists on broad quillons and a pierced iron plate. This sword belonged to Sergeant William Hayden of Windsor, Connecticut and was carried by him in the Pequot War, 1635-1637, when he served under Captain John Mason

FRANCIS LOLONOIS.

ROCK BRASILIANO

Plate 87. Portraits of Lolonois and Brasiliano from Esquemeling.

and is indeed credited with having saved Mason's life by using this sword to cut the bow string of an Indian who was taking aim at the Captain.

A second type of cutlass used in America during the latter half of the 17th century and into the early 18th century is also represented by pictures and surviving specimens. This form of cutlass was characterized by a huge shell guard on the obverse side of the hilt and a ring for the thumb on the reverse. The quillons were sometimes straight and sometimes recurved with the lower quillon reaching almost to the pommel and thus serving as a knuckle bow. The shell counterguard and the quillons were normally forged in one piece. The blades were usually sharply curved, but some straight ones are known. Clipped points were common. John Esquemeling in his *Buccaniers of America*, published in 1684, illustrates this weapon very precisely in a number of his plates, especially in the portraits of Brasiliano and Lolonois. (See plate). The pommel and counterguard from one of these cutlasses were excavated at the site of a 17th century Indian village in central New York State and are now preserved by the Rochester Museum of Arts and Sciences.[13]

One other specific form of single-edged cutting sword, the falchion, is mentioned in two separate instances. The falchion was a short cutting sword with a broad heavy blade, often with a clipped point. Usually there was only a simple cross guard formed by recurved quillons. It is, of course, impossible to determine if the contemporary writers were using the word in its pure sense, but since the term appears only twice, and each writer who used it never applied it again, it is a strong indication of an unusual type of sword, quite possibly the one still denoted by the term. The first man to use the term was William Simmonds who stated that Captain John Smith carried a falchion in his fight with Paspaheigh on Glass House Point in 1609.

The other reference to a falchion is found in a description by John Winthrop of the execution of an Indian in 1644. Despite the fact that the poor Indian in question had to suffer eight strokes before his head was severed, it should be noted that a falchion would have been a logical choice for a beheading sword because of its weight and wide blade. Hence, this is another reason for the belief that the writers may have been using the term in the generally accepted sense.[14]

Rochester Museum of Arts and Sciences
Plate 88. Pommel and shell guard of a late 17th century cutlass excavated in New York State.

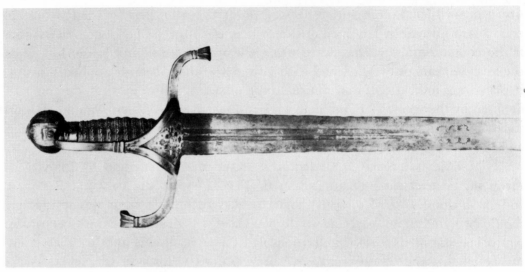

Plate 89. Infantry sword with S-curved quillons and side knuckle-bow, c. 1630.

Although most of the military forces of the 17th century American Colonies were infantry, there were also some mounted troops. Neither the rapier nor the short, single-edged cutting sword were the optimum weapon for combat on horseback, consequently one finds frequent references to "horsemen's swords." These swords were long, straight, normally double-edged and often basket-hilted. The basket hilts were of many designs. Some were made of an interlacing network of rods welded together where they joined. Others were made from a single sheet which was cut out in an openwork pattern. Much depended on the originality and ability of the individual swordsmith. In the Spanish colonies particularly, the cup hilt was often used on this type of sword as well as on the rapier.[15]

One complete horseman's sword and about ten hilts which were used in America are available as specimens of the types carried here after about 1650. The complete horseman's sword which has survived belonged to a member of the Winslow family. It is owned today by a descendant. All the hilts were excavated by the National Park Service, all but one at Jamestown and the other from the grave of an Indian buried about the turn of the 18th century near Macon, Georgia. All are basket hilted swords. Most of them are of the form commonly associated with the Scottish by the layman today. Actually, this form of broadsword made its appearance in England as early as the Civil War (1642-1649). There it quickly gained popularity and became the standard British dragoon sword of the first three-quarters of the 18th century.[16]

As a general comment on all the forms of swords described thus far, it should be noted that blades were a popular commodity in international trade. The great

Mary Van Renssalear Thayer Collection

Plate 90. Seventeenth century basket-hilted broadsword with German blade used in Massachusetts by a member of the Winslow family.

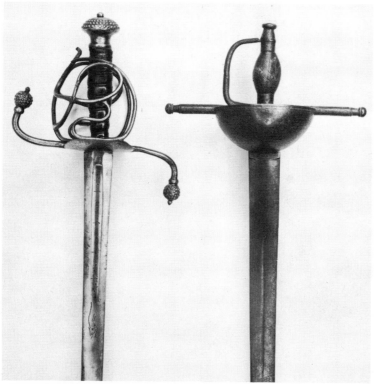

Author's Collection

Plate 91. Seventeenth century broadswords. Left: German basket-hilted sword; right: Caribbean cup-hilted sword.

majority of blades were made in one of the large manufacturing centers on the Continent. From there they were shipped to destinations all over Europe where they were equipped with hilts by local artisans. The greatest manufacturing center of the times was the German city of Solingen, but Munich, Passau, Amsterdam, Toledo, Valencia, Milan, Bologna, Brescia, and many other cities were also noted for sword production. Spanish and Italian blades, especially those made in Toledo, Valencia, and Milan, enjoyed a distinguished reputation for quality, and the premium that such names brought soon led the German and other north European makers to copy Spanish and Italian marks, even adding

[85]

Plate 92. Basket-hilted broadsword excavated at Jamestown.

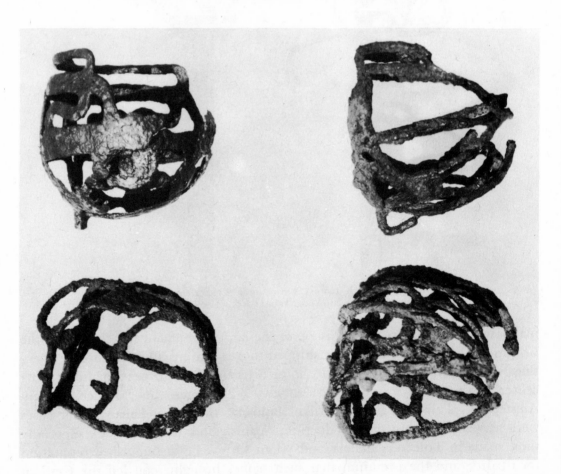

Plate 93. Various forms of basket hilts excavated at Jamestown.

Plate 94. Detail of a Le Moyne picture of the French
in Florida illustrating a mid 16th century sword frog.

the names of famous bladesmiths and cities. The forging of these names and
marks became so blatant that one frequently finds blades bearing both the running wolf mark of Solingen and Passau and also the marks of a Spanish blade-
smith and the word Toledo or Valencia.[17]

In 1675, Connecticut issued an order that:

> "Ten good and serviceable hatchets be provided in each county for
> the use of the army, and ten soldiers to carry them instead of swords."

This is the first known indication of a trend that was to become much more
popular in the next century. The hatchet was originally adopted for use in clear-
ing away obstructions, and the ten soldiers for each county would thus act as
pioneers for the rest of the force. As the American colonists became more used
to the fighting techniques of the hatchet, however, many grew to prefer them
to swords. Also when the individual had to provide his own weapons, it was

much more practical to have a hatchet since it could also be used for domestic purposes. Thus, as will be noted in more detail later, the hatchet became an increasingly popular substitute for the sword.[18]

Before leaving the subject of swords, it might be well to review briefly the suspensory equipment which accompanied them. Unfortunately, such equipment was normally made of quite perishable materials, such as leather or textiles, and consequently few have survived the ravages of time. Nevertheless, it is pos-

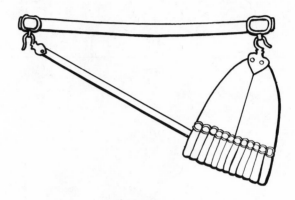

Plate 95. Sword carrier.

sible to make some generalizations based upon the few surviving specimens and upon contemporary pictures.

The long double-edged swords, the prototypes of the rapier, were normally carried in a frog-like arrangement suspended from the waist belt by two relatively long straps. This frog attached to the throat of the scabbard usually either by a stud or clip. Some shoulder belts are known, but the waist belt was more common.

The rapier proper and later examples of the double-edged sword were customarily hung in a carrier, an arrangement of from two to a dozen loops suspended from either a waist belt or a baldric. The scabbard was thrust through these loops and held in place partly by gravity and partly by a clip at the throat of the scabbard. Toward the end of the period an adjustable spring tackle carrier was developed. This carrier usually consisted of a pivoted semicircular loop of metal which could be set at any angle it was desired that the rapier should hang and locked in position by a spring catch. The scabbard was attached to the hanger by passing a tubular holder fastened to its throat over a split bar catch on the semicircular loop. A socket joint between the carrier and the buckle or plate which attached to the belt allowed the sword and carrier to swing from side to side.

Cutting swords were normally carried with a frog. Short ones were occasionally attached to the waist belt, but more often to a shoulder belt. The long broadswords of the mounted troops were almost always carried on a shoulder belt. A few scabbards with the two-ring arrangement common on 19th century specimens are known as early as the 16th century, but they are exceptional.

A constant companion of the sword in the 16th and 17th centuries was the dagger. Unfortunately, although there are many references to daggers in the Colonial records, none are specific as to the particular form of the weapon.

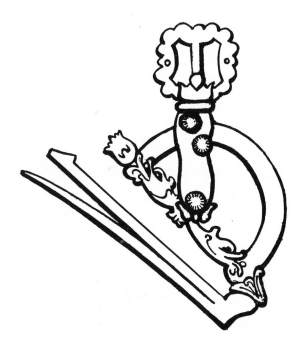

Plate 96. Spring tackle carrier.

Velasco mentioned his "gilded dagger" on his 1597 trip to New Mexico. Forty daggers were requested as part of the arms for 35 men who were to be sent to Smythes Hundred in 1678. Miles Standish and his men relied on the dagger alone to liquidate the troublemakers in a locked room in Wessagusset. These and many general references indicate that, as would be expected, the dagger was a popular weapon in Colonial America.[19]

Although no known specimen with positive American association exists, there is one specific piece of evidence on daggers in Colonial America. Jacques Le Moyne, in his painting of the Indians worshiping a column, has shown Réné de Laudonnière, the leader of the party, wearing a left hand dagger of the type called a poignard (see frontispiece). This and other Le Moyne pictures are the only direct and specific evidence known on the subject of the daggers worn by the early colonists, but certain inferences are probably justifiable. One of the popular styles of fencing in Europe during the late 16th and early 17th centuries involved the use of the rapier and dagger. The dagger designed for this practice was known as the left hand dagger, and of these there were two principal types, the poignard and the main gauche. The poignard was a form of the generic type known as quillon daggers because of their cross guard. These left hand daggers had simple guards, consisting usually of curved quillons with supplementary *anneaux*. Later, especially in southern Europe, a type developed with straight quillons and wide triangular knuckle bows, and this type is generally called today the main gauche.

Because of the quantity of rapiers brought to America, it is probable that

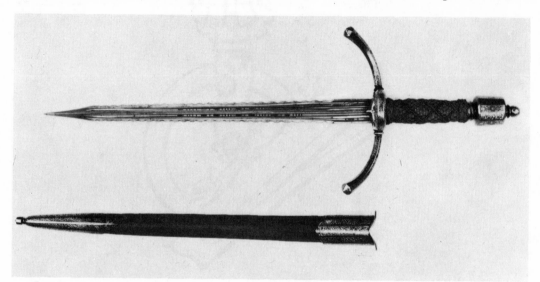

National Park Service

Plate 97. Left hand dagger of the mid 16th century with gold damascened decoration. The scabbard is covered with green velvet.

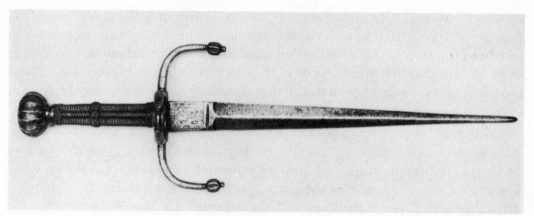

Plate 98. Plain left hand dagger, second half of the 16th century. *Author's Collection*

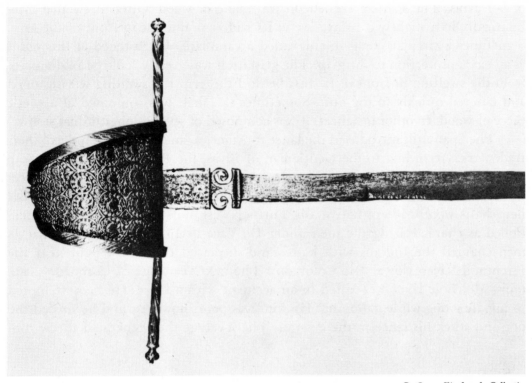

Plate 99. Spanish or Italian main gauche, c. 1650.

a number of these poignards and mains gauches accompanied them. Judging from the popularity of the various styles of dagger in Europe, it is probable that the poignard and main gauche and possibly also the stiletto, a light thrusting weapon with a triangular or quadrangular blade, were the standard types in America.[20]

In addition to the sword, dagger, and hatchet, there was another large category of edged weapons which saw widespread service in Colonial America— the polearm. Fortunately, the founding fathers were usually specific when they referred to these weapons, and consequently it is possible to determine the exact form of weapon mentioned in almost any given instance. This happy situation cannot be matched with any other arm.

The forms of polearms to which the early writers referred were the lance, the halberd, the partizan, the bill, the pike, and the half-pike. The first of these arms in importance chronologically was the lance. In the 16th century, the lance was a horseman's spear, usually between 10 and 14 feet in length. The steel head was normally leaf-shaped and attached to the shaft either by a socket or by a tang which was driven into the wood. Ordinarily, there were no iron straps or langets to protect the shaft from sword strokes such as were common on other forms

[91]

of polearms. The shaft or truncheon was made of wood. Often it swelled symmetrically in a slightly conclave arc to its widest point just in front of the grip. Sometimes a circular metal shield, called a vamplate, was fastened at this point as an extra protection to the grip. The grip itself was greatly reduced in diameter from the swelling in front of it. Just behind the grip the swelling was resumed and tapered quickly to the butt. Sometimes the shaft was composed of a single piece of wood. In other instances, it was composed of several longitudinal strips.[21]

The Spaniards introduced the lance to America, and it became, indeed, their trademark. According to the Gentleman of Elvas, the Portuguese with De Soto were well armed, but the Castilians had "very bad lances." Later, these lances were burned in the disastrous fire at Chicaca, but the heads were retempered, and new shafts were made of native ash. Further west, horses and lances were mentioned as characterizing the men under De Vaca in 1536. In 1540, Coronado's men charged the Indians with lances and dispersed them in a fight near the Firebrand River (lower Rio Colorado). The next year, one of Coronado's captains, Melchoir Diaz, was killed in an accident with a lance. He had attempted to impale a dog while galloping. His aim was poor, however, and he missed the dog and stuck his lance in the ground. The leverage thus generated threw him

C. O. v. Kienbusch Collection

Plate 100. Italian main gauche, c. 1650.

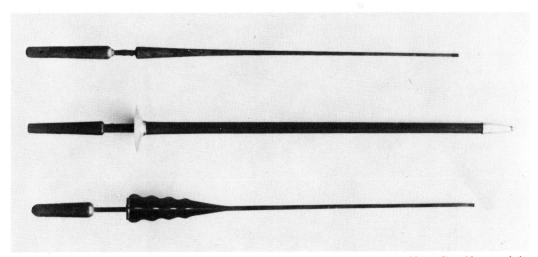

Metropolitan Museum of Art

Plate 101. Tournament lances. The center lance dates from the first half of the 16th century. Those on either side are late 16th or early 17th century specimens. Military lances differed from these primarily in the type of point.

out of the saddle and killed him. Although the lance was a favorite weapon with the Spanish at least until 1600, it never seems to have been popular in any other colony.[22]

The halberd, a weapon mentioned in the records of almost every colony, was a polearm bearing an axehead balanced by a beak or fluke and surmounted by a sharp point. The butt end of the shaft was usually shod with a cap of iron or brass, known as the ground iron, butt cap, or foot. Although it was sometimes used as a combat weapon, the halberd was more often carried by noncommissioned officers as a badge of rank or by governor's guards as a ceremonial arm during the 16th and 17th centuries.[23]

Records of the halberd in America during the period under consideration begin with the De Soto expedition, in which they were considered functional weapons, and continue throughout the rest of the period. The inventories of the forts of Florida in 1578 record halberds among the other arms. In 1595 and 1596, Don Juan de Oñate and Don Pedro Ponce de León each offered to supply 12 halberds if he were chosen to lead an expedition into New Mexico. Don Luís de Velasco, who went on the expedition after de Oñate had been chosen, took with him "a halberd, garnished with yellow velvet and purple tassels, and all studded with nails, which he bought for his sergeant to carry." Jacques Le Moyne's painting of the Indians in Florida worshipping a column, in 1564, clearly shows such a halberd with the concave blade typical of the middle of the 16th century (see frontispiece). It is held by a man who is obviously a subordinate officer of some type.[24]

Unlike the lance, the halberd is frequently mentioned in the records of

[93]

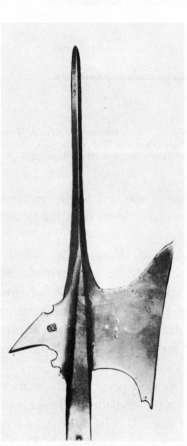

C. O. v. Kienbusch Collection
Plate 102. Halberd, c. 1530.

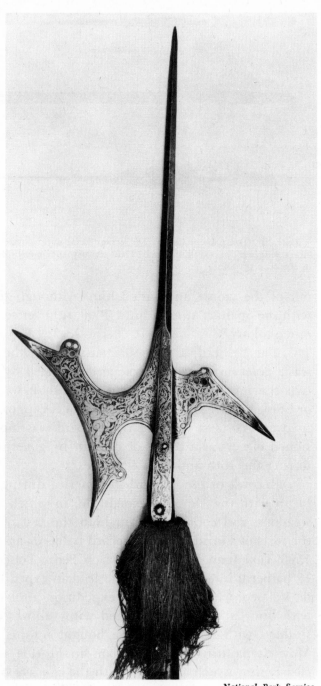

National Park Service
Plate 103. Etched halberd. German, c. 1560-1590.

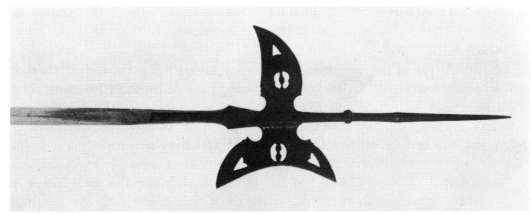

Pilgrim Hall, Plymouth
Plate 104. Seventeenth century halberd found in the cellar of the John Alden House.

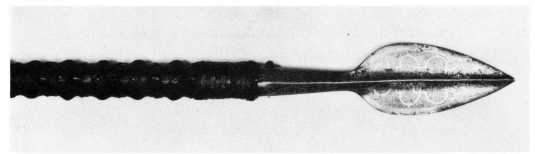

National Park Service
Plate 105. Etched officer's spear, German, mid 16th century.

the English and Dutch colonies during the 17th century. Strachey's *Martiall Lavves* of 1611 for Virginia required the sergeants to carry halberds for garrison duty but to abandon them for firearms in the field. There is a record of halberds actually being used in combat during the Pequot War in New England (1635-37). The settlers of Massachusetts Bay brought three halberds for their sergeants when they came to America. Later, the governor's guard of Massachusetts carried halberds, as did the governor's guard of New Netherlands and probably other colonies. "Pole axes" were listed in an account of the cost of King Philip's War for the United Colonies. Even as late as 1689, Governor Leisler in New York threatened to run one of the councilors through with a halberd, indicating that the weapon was still in use at the very end of the period.[25]

Another form of polearm mentioned occasionally by the early settlers was the partizan. This was normally an officer's weapon, about six or seven feet in length with a symmetrical head consisting of a point with one or more branches at the base. As used by the contemporary writers, however, it meant any type of officer's spear, and consequently one finds that the specimen illustrated by Jacques Le Moyne closely resembles the boar spears of contemporary Europe and is in reality closer to the true spear than to the normal partizan. It is an interesting specimen with a decorated head and two tassels. In 1628 the settlers outfitting for the expedition to found the Massachusetts Bay Colony purchased "2 partizans, for capten & lieftenant."[26]

A fourth type of polearm used in Colonial America was the bill or "brown bill" as it was frequently called because of the browned finish of its blade. The bill as a weapon evolved from the agricultural implement of the same name. It had a hook-shaped blade with a cutting edge on the concave side and various spikes and projections on the back. The bill was long a favorite weapon in England, and one would expect to find it mentioned frequently in early colonial records. Actually, however, bills appear only once, but then in such quantity as to warrant considerable attention. After the massacre of 1622, the Virginia Company petitioned the King for arms from the Tower of London. Among the arms asked for and received were 1,000 brown bills. Bermuda requested and was given 50 of the bills, but the remaining 950 reached Jamestown safely early in 1623. Remnants of six of these bills were recovered at Jamestown.[27]

The most popular form of polearm in Colonial America, however, was the pike. For the sake of convenience and since the difference lies only in the length of the shaft, both the full pike and the half-pike are here considered in the same

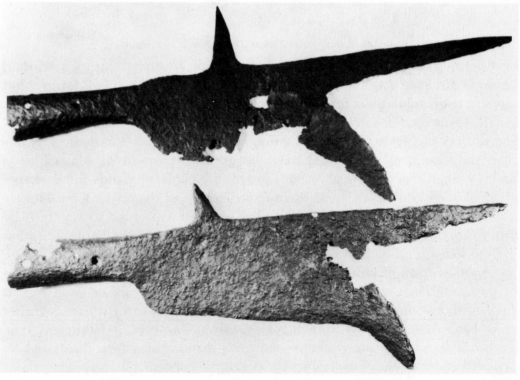

Plate 106. Bills excavated at Jamestown.

National Park Service

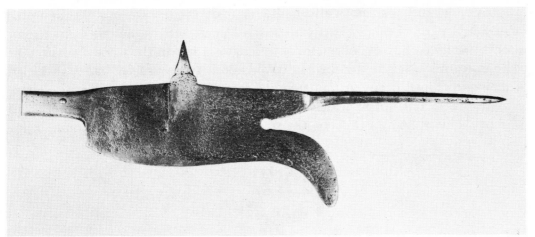

Plate 107. English bill, late 16th century.

Plate 108. Pikeman with his pike braced against his foot ready to receive a charge. Note that the French or Flemish armor shown differs from the English in the attachment of the tassets and the type of helmet used. From De Gheyn.

[97]

category. The full pike normally had a shaft of 14-16 feet, and the half-pike ranged in length normally between six and eight feet, although Connecticut records specify half-pikes "of ten foote in length at lest in the wood." As in most other polearms, ash was the favorite wood. Both types usually had leaf-shaped or diamond-shaped heads. Attenuated awl-shaped heads, rectangular in section, were also used, but not so widely. Long metal straps or langets were added to prevent the head being cut off by the stroke of a sword. It was also common for

Folger Shakespeare Library
Plate 109. Pikeman with his pike held short so that the head and long metal straps are visible. From De Gheyn.

the ground-irons of these weapons to be somewhat pointed to facilitate the bracing of the butts in the ground for added strength in meeting a cavalry charge.[28]

The records of almost every colony provide references to pikes in quantity. Large numbers of full pikes and half-pikes were reported by Alvaro Flores after his inspection of Spanish forts in 1578. At Jamestown in 1609, Captain John Smith reported there were more pikes and swords than men, and National Park Service archeological explorations have thus far recovered the ground-iron from one pike at that site. As early as 1603, on a visit to the shores of Massachusetts, Martin Pring described the appearance of a Mastiff with a half-pike in its mouth.

[98]

Somewhat later, the settlers of Massachusetts Bay brought with them 60 pikes and 20 half-pikes—almost as many pikes as muskets. In 1646, Plymouth required each town to provide one half-pike for every four men. Both New Haven and Connecticut maintained a large number of pikes throughout the period, using them not only to arm infantry, but also equipping the dragoons of New Haven, Fairfield, and New London with half-pikes. In New Netherland, the Dutch seemed to prefer the half-pike, for that weapon is mentioned frequently from 1633 to 1673, while the full pike is almost never listed.[29]

The history of the use of the pike varied greatly from colony to colony. Since pikemen formed the bulk of the infantry forces in Europe during the 16th century and into the opening year of the 17th century, it was natural that almost all colonies included a large number of these weapons among their public arms when the first settlements were made. Thereafter, patterns of use differ. Most colonies found them ineffectual against Indians and so abandoned them. In Virginia, for instance, George Thorpe wrote to Sir Edwin Sandys in 1621 stating that they had ceased using pikes against Indians "some time ago" but that now that there was the threat of a war with the Spanish who would fight in a civilized manner, it might be well to have some pikes on hand once more. In Massachusetts Bay, the General Court ruled in 1675 that:

> "Whereas it is found by experience that troopers & pikemen are of little use in the present warr wth the Indians . . . all pikemen are hereby required . . . to furnish themselves wth fire armes . . ."

One notable exception was Connecticut, which passed an exactly opposite resolution, and continued to use pikes right up to the end of the period. By way of comparison, it should be noted that the pike was abolished in England about 1700 and in France by a royal ordinance of 1703.[30]

In conclusion, the history of edged weapons in America for 1526-1688 may be summarized briefly. The development of the sword in America paralleled that in Europe. The different conditions in America caused no innovations in design. Before the end of the period, however, the tomahawk or hatchet began to supplant the sword for some privates. The dagger as an eminently practical weapon remained popular, but the trend was toward an all-purpose knife and away from the specialized types popular at the beginning of the period. Among the pole-arms, the lance was popular only among the Spaniards. The halberd and partizan as emblems of rank rather than functional weapons continued in use throughout the period. The pike, with a few notable exceptions such as Connecticut was dropped as a weapon by Virginia more than 80 years before it was abandoned in Europe, and as much as 25 years ahead of Europe by Massachusetts and the majority of other colonies.

NOTES—CHAPTER THREE

1. "List of the munitions of war required for 150 men, to be sent to the South River of New Netherlands," O'Callaghan, *Documents*, I, 645. "Proposed Freedoms and Exemptions for New Netherlands 1640," *ibid.*, 123. Proceedings of a General Court, November 25, 1639, Hoadly, *New Haven Records*, 25, 26. Minutes of a General Meeting, March 13, 1638, John R. Bartlett, editor, *Records of the Colony of Rhode Island and Providence Plantation in New England*, 10 vols., Providence, 1856-1865, I, 54. Minutes of the General Court, October 10, 1643, Shurtleff and Pulsifer, *Plymouth Records*, II, 65. Captain John Underhill, *Newes From America, A. D. 1638*, David H. Underhill, editor, n. p. 1902, 17. Shurtleff, *Massachusetts Records*, I, 25, 26. Minutes of the Grand Committee for the Ordering of the Militia, August 11, 1673, Hoadly, *Connecticut Records*, II, 207, 208, "An Act for Settling the Militia," *Laws Enacted by Governor Andros and his Council, ibid.*, III, 430. Strachey, *Lawes*, 32. Edward Waterhouse, "A Declaration of the State of the Colony and . . . a Relation of the Barbarous Massacre . . .," Kingsbury, *Records*, III, 578. "Acts, Orders and Resolutions of the General Assembly of Virginia," July 1, 1644, *Virginia Magazine of History and Biography*, XXIII, (July 1915), 231. Beauchamp Plantagenet, *A Description of the Province of New Albion*, in Force, *Tracts*, II, No. 7, 32. Edward Williams, *Virginia, More Especially the South Part Thereof, Richly and Truly Valued*, London, 1650, in Force, *Tracts*, III, No. 11, 10. "An Act Providing for the Supply of Arms and Ammunition," 1673, William G. Henning, *Statutes at Large, Being a Collection of All the Laws of Virginia*, 13 vols., various places and dates, II, 304. Simmonds, *Proceedings*, 197. "Meeting of a Committee for Smythes Hundred," May 18, 1618, Kingsbury, *Records*, III, 96.

2. "Inventory of the Personal Property of the Widow Bronck at Emaus," O'Callaghan, *Documents*, XIV, 43.

3. Sir Guy Francis Laking, *A Record of European Armour and Arms Through Seven Centuries*, 5 vols., London, 1920-1922, IV, 260-329. Alfred Hutton, *The Sword and the Centuries*, London, 1901, 45-172. Albert F. Calvert, *Spanish Arms and Armour*, London, 1907, 72-142. Bashford Dean, *Handbook of Arms and Armor*, New York, 1915, 54-59, 67-69, 73-78. Edgerton Castle, *Schools and Masters of Fence*, London, 1892, *passim*.

4. *Ibid.* Stone, *Glossary*, 524-526, 591-596. Mann, *Arms and Armour*, III, 637, 640, *et passim*. Castle, *Schools*, 318-333.

5. Laking, *Armour and Arms*, V, 59-79. Mann, *Arms and Armour*, III, 535. Castle, *Schools*, 331-335.

6. Laking, *Armour and Arms*, V, 96-102. J. D. Aylward, *The Small-Sword in England*, London, 1945, 11, 12. Castle, *Schools*, 335, 336.

7. Laking, *Armour and Arms*, V, 96-102. Aylward, *Small-Sword*, 30-46. Bashford Dean, *Catalogue of European Court Swords and Hunting Swords*, New York, 1929, *passim*. Castle, *Schools*, 335, 337.

8. *Ibid.*

9. *Ibid.* Aylward, *Small-Sword*, 46-79.

10. "Manifest made by Captain Don Luís de Velasco of the goods, arms, and horses which he is taking to serve his Majesty in the expedition to New Mexico, of which Don Juan de Oñate goes as Governor and Captain General," May 19, 1597, Hackett, *Historical Documents*, I, 428-433.

11. Louis B. Mason, *The Life and Times of Major John Mason, 1600-1672*. New York, 1935, 306.

12. Harold L. Peterson, "The American Cutlass," *Bulletin* of the Society of American Sword Collectors, III, No. 2 (October 1949), 8-11.

13. Joseph R. Mayer, "Fragments of a Seventeenth Century Sword," *Bulletin* of the Society of American Sword Collectors, I, No. 4 (July 1947), 3. John Esquemeling, *Bucaniers of America*, London, 1684. The same illustrations appear in the first edition of this work, published in Amsterdam in 1678 under the title, *De Americaensche Zee-Roovers*. Dwight Franklin, "Weapons of the Buccaneers and Pirates," *A Miscellaney of Arms and Armor*, New York, 1928, 11-17.

14. Simmonds, *Proceedings*, 181. Winthrop, *History*, II, 232.

15. Laking, *Armour and Arms*, V, 92-95. Castle, *Schools*, 338-341.

16. *Ibid.* Cecil C. P. Lawson, *A History of the Uniform of the British Army*, 3 vols., London, 1940— I, II, *passim*. Castle, Schools, 338-341.

17. John Hayward, *Swords and Daggers*, London, 1951, 2.

18. "Journal of the Council &c," November 23, 1675, Hoadly, *Connecticut Records*, II, 385.

19. "Manifest made by Captain Don Luís de Velasco of the goods, arms, and horses which he is taking to serve his Majesty in the expedition to New Mexico of which Don Juan de Oñate goes as Governor and Captain General," May 19, 1597, Hackett, *Historical Documents*, I, 428-433. Minutes of a Committee for Smythes Hundred, May 18, 1618, Kingsbury, Records, III, 96.

20. Laking, *Armour and Arms*, III, 1-81, V, 59-107. Bashford Dean, *Catalogue of European Daggers*, New York, 1929, *passim*. Hutton, *Sword*, 70-79, 109-122. Castle, *Schools*, 343-345.

21. Martin Ellehauge, *The Spear Traced Through its post-Roman Development*, Copenhagen, 1948, 44-48. Laking, *Armour and Arms*, III, 81-87, IV, 330, 331. Stone, *Glossary*, 407, 408. Mann, *Arms and Armour*, III, 632.

22. Elvas, *Narrative*, 139, 158, 159, 198, 199. De vaca, *Narrative*, 114. Castañeda, *Coronado*, 305, 325.

23. Mann, *Arms and Armour*, III, 630. Stone, *Glossary*, 275, 276. Laking, *Armour and Arms*, III, 120-123, IV, 348-350.

24. Elvas, *Narrative*, 160, 191, 215. Petition to the viceroy, Don Luís de Velasco, September 21, 1595, Hackett, *Historical Documents*, I, 228, 229. Statement of what Don Juan de Oñate and Don Pedro Ponce de León offer for the exploration, pacification and settlement of New Mexico, *ibid.*, 280-283. "Manifest made by Captain Don Luís de Velasco of the goods, arms, and horses which he is taking to serve his Majesty in the expedition to New Mexico, of which Don Juan de Oñate goes as Governor and Captain General," May 19, 1597, *ibid.*, 528-533. The Visitation made by Alvaro Flores of the Forts of Florida, 1578, Connor, *Records of Florida*, II, 117-203.

25. Strachey, *Lavves*, 32. Shurtleff, *Massachusetts Records*, I, 25, 26. Edward Johnson, *The Wonder-working Providence of Sions Saviour*, in Massachusetts Historical Society *Collections*, Boston, Series 2, IV, 48. Winthrop, *History*, II, 263, 268. "Defence of Henry van Dyck, Fiscal in New Netherlands," O'Callaghan, *Documents*, I, 510. "Abstract of Colonel Bayard's Journal," *ibid.*, III, 603. John Tuder to Captain Nicholson, August, 1689, *ibid.*, 618. Shurtleff and Pulsifer, *Plymouth Records*, XI, 105.

26. Shurtleff, *Massachusetts Records*, I, 25, 26. Stone, *Glossary*, 483, 484. Mann, *Arms and Armour*, III, 635. Ellehauge, *Spear*, 48-51, 57, 58. Laking, *Armour and Arms*, III, 109, 110, IV, 342-348.

27. Treasurer and Council for Virginia to Governor and Council in Virginia, August 1, 1622, Kingsbury, *Records*, III, 667. Warrant to the Lord Treasurer, September 1622, *ibid.*, 676. Minutes of a Court held for Virginia, August 14, 1622, *ibid.*, II, 99, 100; April 2, 1623, *ibid.*, 342. Stone, *Glossary*, 113, 114, 116. Mann, *Arms and Armour*, III, 621 Martin Ellehauge, *Certain Phases in the Origin and Development of the Glaive*, Copenhagen, 1945, *passim*. Laking, *Armour and Arms*, III, 110-115.

28. Minutes of the General Court, September 8, 1642, Hoadly, *Connecticut Records*, I, 74. Ellehauge, *Spear*, 52-54. Stone, *Glossary*, 501. Margerand, *Armement*, 13, 14. Grose, *Military Antiquities*, I, 132, 133n. Laking, *Armour and Arms*, IV, 352.

29. The Visitation made by Alvaro Flores of the Forts of Florida, 1578, Connor, *Records of Florida*, II, 117-203. Simmonds *Proceedings*, 158, 169, 170, 197. Martin Pring, *Voyage from Bristoll*, in Harry S. Burrage, editor, *Early English and French Voyages Chiefly from Hakluyt, 1534-1608*, New York, 1906, 348, 351. Shurtleff, *Massachusetts Records*, I, 25, 26. Shurtleff and Pulsifer, *Plymouth Records*, XI, 105. Minutes of a General Meeting, March 13, 1638, Bartlett, *Records of Rhode Island*, I, 54. Minutes of a General Court, August 6, 1640, *ibid.*, 104. Minutes of a General Court, September 8, 1642, Hoadly, *Connecticut Records*, I, 74. "Military Affairs," *Code of Laws*, 1650, *ibid.*, I, 543, 544. "Answers to Queries," 1679, *ibid.*, III, 295. "An Act for Settling the Militia," *Laws Enacted by Governor Andros and His Council, ibid.*, 430. Minutes of a Grand Committee for the Ordering of the Militia, August 11, 1673, *ibid.*, II, 207, 207. Deposition of John Johnson, O'Callaghan, *Documents*, I, 79. Deposition of Jacobus Elkins, *ibid.*, 80. "Extracts from the Papers of Director Kieft, *ibid.*, 415. "Nathan Gould's Account of the Capture of New York," 1673, *ibid.*, III, 201.

30. George Thorpe to Sir Edwin Sandys, May 15, 1621, Kingsbury, *Records*, III, 447. Minutes of the second session of the General Court, October 13, 1675, Shurtleff, *Massachusetts Records*, V, 47. "Answers to Queries," 1679, Hoadly, *Connecticut Records*, III, 295. Grose, *Military Antiquities*, I, 133. Margerand, *Armement*, 14.

Chapter Four

Armor

T HE HUNDRED YEAR PERIOD that began shortly before 1450 and ended just before the middle of the 16th century witnessed the climactic era in the history of defensive armor. Technically, the full suits of the period were often marvels of mechanical genius and craftsmanship; and they were effective and practical defenses against the weapons then generally in use. As such they were widely in demand. Some armor was considered an absolute necessity for every fighting man. Firearms, which were to cause such a change in the attitude of the soldier towards his armor as well as in the armor itself, were not yet the important factor they became after 1550.

This was the period in which the first settlements in America were made and the first large-scale explorations of the country undertaken. The men who made up these colonies and expeditions shared the universal respect for armor, and they came to America fully armed. Here they could not transport their armor in wagons or on pack animals and don it only on those occasions when danger threatened. There were few facilities for transporting such equipment on the long marches, and since danger was almost always imminent, it was necessary to wear the armor most of the time.

The hardships which the constant wearing of armor occasioned the early explorers can hardly be appreciated by the modern American. First, there was the discomfort of heat. No method for adequately ventilating a piece of armor was ever developed, and the Spanish suffered terribly from this defect as they made their way through the steamy heat of the Gulf states or across the treeless plains of the West. There was the discomfort of the extra weight which tired the men and sometimes caused their death as in the instance of eleven of De Soto's men who drowned in the Mississippi when their canoe was upset by Indians. There was the discomfort of chafing which occasioned the "galled shoulder"

Plate 110. Spanish infantryman, late 15th-early 16th centuries. This and the following four figures are probably typical of the infantry who accompanied De Soto. They wear brigandines, mail shirts and reinforcing pieces of plate. The head defense is a chapel de fer with a bevor.

Real Armeria, Madrid
Plate 111. Spanish infantryman, rear view showing alternate form of the same armor as the previous figure. The sword has been removed to show the frog construction better.

Plate 113. Spanish crossbowman, rear view. The archer's salade here is shallower and more typical. Note the quiver and crannequin carried on the belt.

Plate 112. Spanish crossbowman with a windlass crossbow. Note the deep archer's salade, almost a barbute.

C. O. v. Kienbusch Collection
Plate 114. German salade, late 15th century.

lamented by De Vaca's men. Finally, there was just the simple inconvenience which caused Champlain even at a later date and with lighter armor to complain:

> "We went through dense woods, and over swamps and marshes, with the water always up to our knees, *greatly encumbered* by a pike-man's corselet, with which each one was armed."[1]

Fortunately, there is enough evidence available to allow the student to determine fairly accurately the appearance of the armor which so sorely tried the patience of the early explorers and colonists while it protected their hides from Indian arrows. The documents often are fairly specific, but best of all, there are several drawings and a remarkable number of surviving specimens.

The Spanish, who made the long treks with De Vaca, Coronado, and De Soto and who founded the first permanent settlements in Florida, were the most heavily armored group ever to come to America. The infantry wore chain mail shirts probably with reinforcing pieces of plate in the form of cuishes to protect the thighs, knee-cops, and possibly brassards for the arms. Some carried targets, and all wore helmets. The Gentleman of Elvas, a native of Portugal, in describing the soldiers who left Spain with De Soto, noted that the Portuguese had good armor, but that "the Castilians had for the most part very bad and rusty shirts of mail, and all had headpieces and steel caps." The cavalry were more heavily armed, some very probably in full suits of plate armor. Even the horses were protected.[2]

[106]

C. O. v. Kienbusch Collection
Plate 115. German salade, late 15th century.

The chain mail, which played such an important part in the equipment of the Spaniards, was a form of armor that had been popular in Europe for many centuries. The exact origins of this defense are lost in antiquity. Probably it was developed in the Near East. It was known in Europe at least as early as the 3rd century, A. D., and remnants of mail attributed to the 4th and 5th centuries have been excavated in several places.[3]

The methods of making chain mail varied little from country to country or from century to century. In the 16th and 17th centuries, it was the usual practice to wind a wire tightly around an iron rod and then cut it off in rings. The ends of each ring were then customarily flattened and punched for a rivet. Garments were constructed from these rings by linking them together and then riveting the individual rings. Occasionally European mail is found in which the ends of alternating rows of the rings were welded instead of riveted, but the latter was more common. Normally each ring was linked with four others. An ordinary shirt of mail would weigh from 14 to 30 pounds depending upon the size of the rings and the over-all size of the garment.[4]

The defensive quality of the mail varied according to the quality of the metal used and the size of the rings. Some garments are known in which the links are so large that only a relatively heavy weapon such as the sword or broad arrow would be prevented from passing through the interstices. Other pieces are known which could not be penetrated by the sharpest dagger point. The majority of the chain mail brought from Europe by the Spanish was probably

[107]

C. O. v. Kienbusch Collection
Plate 116. Italian barbute, early 15th century.

of moderately good quality. The splinters from the reed arrows of the Indians, which split upon contact, could pierce it, but such splinters would normally be very thin and sharp. Also, the Gentleman of Elvas paints a picture of De Soto's men making flour in which they ground the corn with a mortar and pestle and "some of them did sift the flower through their shirts of maile." If the shirts were of any use as sieves, the apertures must have been relatively small.[5]

The size of the openings in chain mail could be decreased by two methods. The diameters of the rings could be made smaller, or a heavier wire could be used, thus making the diameter of the center opening smaller even though the overall diameter of the ring remained the same. Very closely woven mail made by the second method is known as double mail. It was frequently used to protect especially exposed or important parts of a garment while the rest was composed of regular mail in order to provide maximum protection at necessary points without greatly increasing the weight.[6]

In later Spanish expeditions into the Southwest, the mail shirt was also apparently standard equipment. The situation is not absolutely clear because of the difficulty of translating the Spanish word *"cotas."* The word was almost always used to denote a coat of mail, but occasionally it may have been used for armor in general. In most instances connected with the New Mexico expedition, however, the records refer to *cotas* and *escarzelas* separately. Thus, in 1596,

[108]

Don Pedro Ponce de León offered to supply 6 *cotas* and 6 *escarzelas* if he were chosen leader of an expedition into New Mexico. Don Juan de Oñate, who was finally chosen leader, also offered *cotas* and *escarzelas*. In 1602 *Maestre de Campo* Vincente de Zaldivar y Mendoza listed 100 *cotas* and 100 *escarzelas* among the armor which he intended to take on his expedition to New Mexico. The word *"escarzelas"* refers to a defense for the thigh and is normally translated as

Author's Collection and Joe Kindig, Jr. Collection

Plate 117. Italian archer's salades, late 15th century and early 16th century, indicating the evolution of the type.

Museum of New Mexico

Plate 118. Archer's salade, 1490-1510, excavated near Santa Fe where it had apparently been used by one of Oñate's men a century later.

Museum of New Mexico

Plate 119. Archer's salade, 1490-1510, excavated near Santa Fe where it had apparently been used by one of Oñate's men a century later.

[109]

Real Armeria, Madrid
Plate 120. Spanish chapel de fer, late 15th century.

Real Armeria, Madrid
Plate 121. Spanish chapel de fer, late 15th century.

"tassets." Tassets, however, are usually considered as integral parts of a cuirass and it would be strange to find them always listed separately. Thus it would seem that another form of thigh defense, the cuishe, is indicated by the word.[7]

If these premises are accepted, it would appear that most of the armored men on these later Spanish expeditions wore mail shirts or hauberks with reinforcing plates (cuishes) for the thigh and possibly the knee. The beginning of the 17th century seems late for this form of armor, but it may have been dictated by local conditions. Chain mail was cooler and less tiring to wear, and these factors may well have caused it to remain popular for long expeditions in hot climates against enemies whose weapons were not comparable to those which forced changes in Europe.

It should not be forgotten, however, that since the words *"cotas"* and *"escarzelas"* are in some degree ambiguous there is always the possibility of other translation. Of these other versions, the most logical is that *cotas* referred to full plate corselets, complete with tassets, and that the separate use of *escarzelas* indicated that cuishes to the knee were also worn.

The helmets which the Spanish infantry wore in conjunction with their mail shirts were of a variety of designs. Probably all of the forms then in use in southern Europe were represented among the "headpieces and steel caps" recorded by the Gentleman of Elvas. Among those types which were probably most prevalent were the later versions of the salade with its variant, the barbute; and the chapel de fer in all its forms. All of these were essentially close-fitting helmets and, in a general sense, open helmets as contrasted with the really closed helmets such as the armet.

[110]

As indicated above, there were two distinct forms of the salade. One type, usually associated with northern Europe, fitted the head closely in the front and both sides but extended back in a broad sweeping tail, which reached extreme lengths in some German examples. Some specimens left the face open. Others were equipped with a hinged visor. In still another variation there was no opening for the face, vision being provided for by a single narrow slot or ocularium.[8]

The other major form of the salade is known today as the barbute and is commonly associated with Italy and the south of Europe. In the barbute, the long tail was omitted, and a much closer fit for the head and neck was afforded. In some barbutes, the face was left open. Others were equipped with nasal guards, and still others had only a T-shaped opening for vision and breathing. In these forms, the barbute bore a pronounced resemblance to the ancient Greek casque. Both types of salade achieved their greatest popularity during the 15th century. The design carried over into the early years of the 16th century,

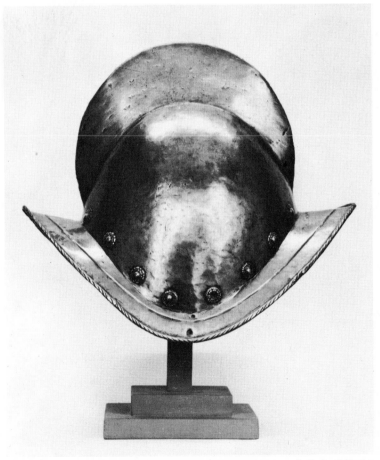

Author's Collection

Plate 122. German morion. The original dark finish is now missing.

however, particularly as modified in the open-faced varieties for archers and callivermen known as archer's salades, and it is quite likely that many of the early Spanish troops were equipped with some form of this helmet. Indeed, one rudimentary archer's salade was recently excavated at the site of Onate's capital, San Gabriel, New Mexico, and is now preserved in the Museum of New Mexico.[9]

The second major type of open helmet was the chapel de fer, or literally translated, iron hat. This simple but well-designed headpiece was made in a variety of shapes, but in all its modifications it possessed a well-defined bowl or crown and a brim. In its most common form it had a bowl in the shape of an elongated hemisphere and a broad brim turned down at the sides. The chapel de fer developed during the 13th century and achieved its greatest popularity during the 14th and 15th centuries. It was still in use in its pure form during the early 16th century, however, and it survived in the form of the pikeman's helmet until late in the 17th century. Still later, the helmets worn by both British

Author's Collection
Plate 123. Italian morion with original blued finish.

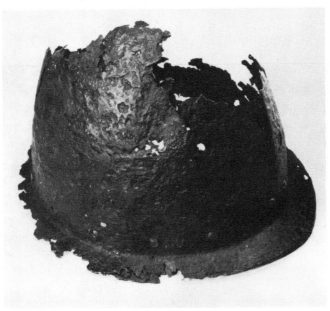

Plate 124. Cabasset excavated on an early 17th
century site at Yorktown, Virginia.

and American troops during World War I and by the British today are actually a
modern version of the chapel de fer.[10]

With both the salade and the chapel de fer it was often the practice to wear
a defense for the lower part of the face and the throat. These defenses, known
variously as bevors, mentonnieres or buffs, were entirely separate from the
helmet. They were attached usually by a strap or straps around the neck. Those
worn with full plate armor rather than mail were often bolted to the breastplate.[11]

Two other types of open helmet which derived their inspiration largely
from the chapel de fer began to develop during the early 16th century. These
were the morion and the cabasset. The morion was essentially a chapel de fer
with a comb added to the bowl and the brim elongated and turned up in peaks
before and behind. The word "morion" is a general Spanish term, meaning
simply "helmet" or headpiece." The specific type which is denoted by the term
today was frequently referred to in early records as a "comb morion" to distinguish it from the "Spanish morion" as the cabasset was often called. The
cabasset was simply a chapel de fer with a high keeled bowl surmounted by a
small apical peak normally pointing to the rear. The brim was reduced to a
minimum and was normally horizontal rather than turned down. The word
cabasset is relatively modern and has been derived from the Spanish word
"cabeza," meaning head. Both the morion and the cabasset reached their full development about the middle of the 16th century.[12]

[113]

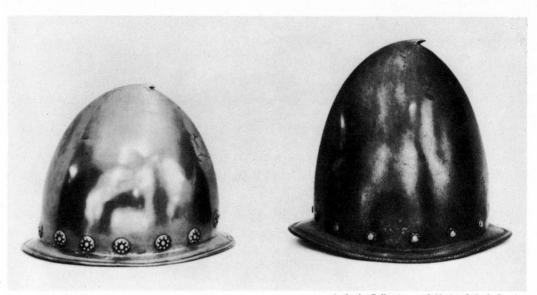

Plate 125. Cabassets, the one at left is of bright steel ornamented with large brass rivet bosses; the one on the right is of blued steel with lesser brass rivet bosses.

Some time during the second half of the 16th century a form combining features of both the morion and cabasset was developed. Usually it had the keeled bowl and apical peak of the cabasset and the crescentic, peaked brim of the morion. In modern parlance this hybrid form is denoted morion-cabasset. Another and still later form of the cabasset is found with a comb on the front half of the bowl. Both morions and cabassets are also found with scaled straps to protect the ears.[13]

The morion and cabasset achieved widespread and lasting popularity as infantry helmets. They continued in use as long as armor was generally worn, and the morion is still worn by such ceremonial guards as the Vatican's Swiss Guard today. Broadly speaking, the better morions and cabassets were forged from one billet of steel. Poorer—and usually later—specimens were forged in two pieces and fastened together along the crest of the bowl.

One final form of close-fitting open helmet, the burgonet, also began to make its appearance during the opening years of the 16th century. Its salient features were a comb and an umbril or brim over the eyes only. Often hinged ear pieces were added to protect the ears and cheeks. On early burgonets, the face was left open, but could be protected by the addition of a buffe. Later, nasals or barred cages, which could be let down over the face, were attached to the umbril. This became standard practice in the 17th century. In that century, the burgonet was sometimes elaborated upon until it ceased to be a light open helmet and was in fact a closed helmet. Typical of this form of development

[114]

was the so-called "death's head" burgonet used by sappers and miners which completely enclosed the head and neck and often weighed as much as 20 pounds.[14]

The burgonet was popular with both infantry and cavalry, particularly light horse. As such it is probable that many of the Spanish wore them, particularly those in the South West at the end of the 16th century. The documents are generally not specific on this point, usually using the general term *morion* or occasionally *celada*, but in many instances they refer to *moriones con sus sobrevistas* or *celadas con sus osbrevistas*. This would seem to indicate a helmet with a separate visor or bevor, and in that period, the burgonet with buffe or bevor would be the most likely candidate to fit the description. In one instance, however, in a list of armor supplied by Oñate himself for his expedition into New Mexico in 1597, there is a specific statement that one suit of armor included a "Burgundian helmet" as the burgonet was often called at that time.[15]

Among the Spanish explorers and settlers were a sizeable body of troops known as targeteers. These infantrymen were armed with a sword, and in addition to their other armor they carried a shield known as a target or buckler. Usually such targets were round or oval, but other shapes were also used. The so-called Codex Rios, although useless as far as other forms of armor are concerned, definitely shows small kite-shaped or triangular shields being used by Cortez' men in Mexico. Since the Narvaez and De Soto expeditions were only a few years later than Cortez, and since they all outfitted at the same place, it is logical to assume that some of the targeteers with these later expeditions also

National Park Service

Plate 126. Heavy siege helmet of the cabasset form excavated near Jamestown. Note the testing dent on the side and the two-piece construction.

[115]

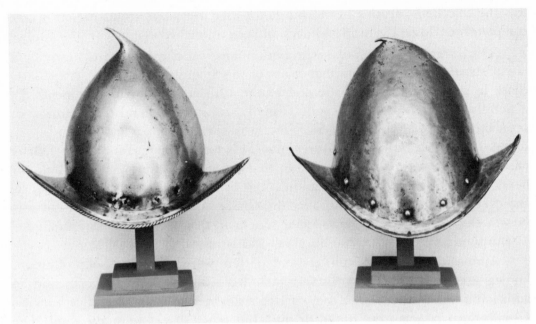

Author's Collection

Plate 127. Morion-cabassets, Italian (left) and German (right).

carried kite-shaped or triangular shields. In modern times an attempt has been made to distinguish between the terms target and buckler, applying the former to those shields with loops through which the forearm is passed and the latter to those with a handle designed to be held in the left hand. Apparently, however, no such distinction was made by the men who used them. The word "target" was most often employed in contemporary records, and will consequently be used in this work.[16]

Targets were made either of iron or of wood covered with leather. Probably there were more leather than iron targets in the early expeditions, although it is impossible to obtain any comparative figures. The Gentleman of Elvas mentions making targets after the disastrous fire at Chicaça and again on a later occasion of raw ox hides captured from the Indians. Since it is highly doubtful that the Indians had any oxen, it is probable that he referred to buffalo or elk hide. In 1596, Don Pedro Ponce de León offered to provide 6 leather shields for an expedition into New Mexico if he were chosen leader. Don Juan de Oñate, who got the appointment, offered 6 leather shields plus 4 round steel shields.[17]

In addition to the shirts of mail with reinforcing pieces worn by the infantry, there were also some full and some half suits of plate armor among the early Spanish explorers and colonists. The Gentleman of Elvas indicates their presence on the De Soto expedition by contrasting the effects of an arrow when it struck "an armor" and when it struck mail. Several complete corselets were listed in

[116]

the projected inventory of the Oñate expedition into New Mexico, and, during the battle between a Spanish Frigate and a French ship in San Mateo harbor [St. Johns River] in 1580, one Captain Gil was described as:

> "cased from head to foot in armor which was arquebus proof, and he died of an arquebus shot which struck him through the visor in the temple, for in any other manner it was impossible to kill him."[18]

As with all other forms of equipment, the armor brought to America by the Spanish was of a great variety of types, depending upon the taste and affluence of the individual wearers. Those who could afford it probably brought the latest forms. Others less well off financially brought older suits. Probably the majority of armor-wearing Spaniards with the de Ayllon colony and the Narvaez expedition of the 1520's wore suits of the transitional period between the Gothic and Maximilian schools. Perhaps some true Gothic suits were even present. With the De Soto and Coronado expeditions of the late 1530's and early 1540's, some of the so-called smooth Maximilian suits probably made their appearance. The typically channelled and fluted armor which is automatically called to mind when the term "Maximilian" is mentioned was never very popular in Spain, and probably little or none of it ever reached America.

Since almost all plate armor worn in America came from Europe, the

National Park Service
Plate 128. Burgonet, German, mid 16th century.

Author's Collection
Plate 129. Burgonet, probably English, late 16th-early 17th centuries.

[117]

Plate 130. Burgonet with barred visor, German, early 17th century.

Plate 131. Lobstertail burgonet, English or German, early 17th century.

evolution in this country roughly followed the trends on the Continent, the parallels becoming closer as colonies and expeditions became more frequent.

In a full suit of plate armor of the so-called transitional and Maximilian periods, the head was usually encased in a closed helmet. Such helmets consisted of a number of individual plates. First was the bowl or crown which protected the top and back of the head. This was normally forged from one piece of metal. Usually there was a low ridge or crest running along the center. Second was the bevor or mentonniere which defended the cheeks and chin. Sometimes the bevor was made of one plate, hinged at one side of the crown and hooking at the opposite side. In other, and usually later instances, it was made of two pieces, each hinged at the side of the crown and hooking together in the center of the chin.

The third important element was the visor, which covered the face. At the beginning of the period this also was usually of one piece pierced with horizontal slits or occularia for vision and smaller apertures for breathing. It was pivoted at the sides so that it could be raised and lowered. Sometimes the visor was held shut by gravity, but more often there were spring catches which held it more securely. By the end of the first quarter of the 16th century, however, a visor of two separate plates was common, and soon became standard. In these instances the upper plate containing the occularia is today denoted as the visor, while the lower piece with the breathing apertures is known as the

[118]

ventail or mezail. Both plates pivoted on the same rivet, and the visor fitted inside the ventail and fastened to it with a spring catch.

In addition to these standard parts of a helmet, there were sometimes additional plates. In the earlier helmets, the neck portion of the bowl and bevor were usually furnished with a hollow rim, often decorated with a rope or cable design. This rim fitted over a corresponding solid rim on the upper edge of the gorget or neck defense and thus permitted the helmet to be rotated while it was fastened to the gorget. Other helmets had a series of small plates or lames riveted to the bowl and bevor in place of the hollow rim. In these instances the helmet was designed to sit loosely over the gorget and not attached directly to it. This series of plates, known as a colletin, became more and more popular as the century progressed.

The gorget of the transitional and Maximilian Periods was primarily a neck defense, but it often spread over the chest and extended down the back as well. Normally it was constructed of several overlapping lames, riveted at the sides of the neck and working freely upon each other. As a rule, each plate overlapped the lower edge of the one above. In those instances where the helmet fastened directly to the gorget, these sliding plates were the only provision for raising and lowering the head.

The breast and back plates usually fitted up over the lower edges of the

Author's Collection
Plate 132. Sapper's and miner's siege burgonet,
late 16th—early 17th centuries.

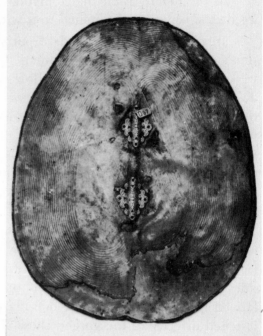

Real Armeria, Madrid

Plate 133. Spanish leather shields (adarga) of the 16th century.

gorget. These plates were normally of one major piece each, reaching to the waist. At the waist one or more articulated lames known as taces were added to permit the body to be bent at that juncture. Other lames, known as gussets, were attached to the arm holes for the freer movement of the arms. In shape the breast plate was generally smooth and globose, although occasionally a slight central ridge, forerunner of the later tapul, is found.

Attached to the taces at the lower edge of the breast plate were another series of lames known as tassets, which acted as defenses for the upper thigh. Unlike the taces, the tassets were divided in front to allow for the lateral movement of the legs. The back plate also had a series of lames attached to its lower border and corresponding to the taces in front. These have been denoted the garde rein or culet. Usually a skirt of mail or at least a mail brayette was worn under these defenses.

The shoulders were protected by pauldrons of lames, overlapping from the bottom up. These lames were carried well around over the back and breast, covering the gussets. Occasionally, for freer movement of the right arm, the lames were not carried around far enough to cover the gussets completely. In such instances a round plate, known as a roundel, was fastened to the breast plate to protect the joint. Frequently, one of the upper two lames was forged

[120]

with a large raised flange or pike guard as a protection for the neck region from a thrust or cut from the side.

The arms and hands were protected by a series of cleverly articulated plates. The defense for the upper arm, known as the rerebrace, attached to the pauldron with a rotating ring or "cannon." It was usually a complete cylinder, sometimes made of one plate, sometimes of several lames overlapping downwards. The elbow was protected by the elbow cop or coudiere, a small cup over the elbow which flared out into a large butterfly-shaped covering for the inside of the joint. The forearm was encased in the vambrace, which was usually made of two pieces hinged in a line on the outside of the arm and fastening with studs on the inner surface. Vambraces hinged on the inner surface, however, were by no means unusual. The gauntlets were characteristized by relatively short cuffs, usually square across the top or only slightly pointed. Some gauntlets had complete individual articulated fingers; others were of the mitten pattern. It should be noted that as a rule only the outside or back of the hand was protected by metal. The inside was covered by a stout leather glove.

Like the arms, the legs and feet were also defended by a skilfully arranged series of plates. The thigh was protected by the cuishe, which was composed sometimes of two or three lames. Normally it protected only the front and outside of the thigh and was held to the leg by straps. The knee cop or genouilliere was a shallow cup with one or two lames above and below and a large wing on

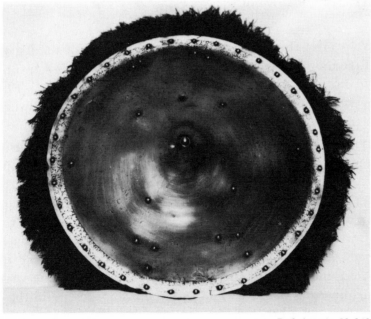

Real Armeria, Madrid
Plate 134. Spanish metal shield of the 16th century.

Plate 135. Late 16th century steel target. There is a large group of these shields in the Tower Armouries, and they are thus believed to be of English origin or at least made for English use.

the outside to protect the back of the knee. The calves of the leg were covered by greaves. Like the vambrace, the greave usually consisted of two plates hinged in a line on one side and fastening together on the other. The feet were protected by sabbatons of lames overlapping downward over the instep and upward over the toes.

As the century progressed, notable changes took place in the design of armor. The comb on the helmet became higher, and during the third quarter of the century the colletin completely succeeded the turning joint at the bottom edge. The burgonet form of helmet with buffe or barred visor became more and more popular after 1550. The breast plate developed a definite median ridge or tapul which came to a sharp point in about the middle of the chest by 1550. As the century waned, the point dropped lower and lower until in the full peasecod type it overhung the taces. The taces and tassets began to flare widely to cover the bombasted breeches of the period. In some instances, late in the century, the tassets were continued all the way to the knee in a series of a dozen or so lames, overlapping upward. There they joined the knee cop and thus eliminated the cuishe. When worn, the sabbatons gradually lost their square toes and evolved round ones.

Another change in armor can be found in the decorating techniques. Early armor usually depended upon the beauty of outline and the shape of the individual plates with some fluting and large embossings. By 1550, however, the trend toward surface enrichment was well advanced, with bands of etching and gilding and embossing until sometimes the entire surface of a suit was covered. This was more true of parade armor, but to a lesser degree it also affected field armor.

It should be noted also in the discussion of the treatment of the metal surfaces that black or russeted armor increased in popularity. Black, blued, and russeted suits had been used for many years for decorative effects and as a practical measure. All three treatments made the metal more resistant to rust and therefore easier to maintain. Sometimes these colors were produced by artificially induced corrosion in a manner generally similar to modern bluing and browning. In other instances, particularly for black armor, a pigment was applied. The field armor of the late 16th and early 17th centuries was almost universally blackened or russeted, and consequently the great majority of armor used in America during that period was either black or brown.

Finally, there was a distinct tendency away from the full suit. After 1550, the three-quarter suit to the knee and the half suit to the tassets became increas-

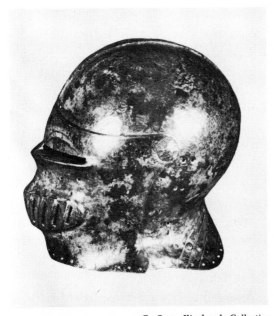

C. O. v. Kienbusch Collection

Plate 136. Closed helmet, c. 1500, painted in several colors.

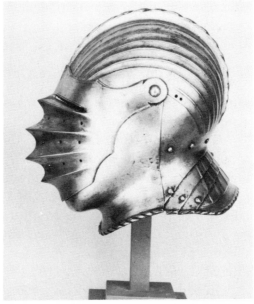

Author's Collection

Plate 137. Closed helmet, German, of the Maximilian form, c. 1525.

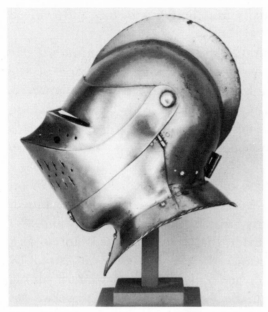

Author's Collection

Plate 138. Closed helmet, French, third quarter of the 16th century.

Bluford W. Muir Collection

Plate 139. Closed helmet with falling buffe, English or Flemish, last quarter of the 16th century.

ingly popular, and the older cap-à-pied armor gradually disappeared, although a few suits continued to be made into the beginning of the next century.

There is such a widespread and mistaken tradition about the weight and clumsiness of armor among the general public that a few actual figures are in order as a counter measure. Most everyone, no matter how infrequently he attends the movies, has been exposed at one time or another to the sight of an armored man being hoisted onto his horse by an imaginative derrick-like device. He is also thoroughly acquainted with the theory that once a man in armor was knocked from his feet he could not rise again but was completely at the mercy of his adversary.

There is no truth in either of these conceptions. A full suit of field armor would weigh on the average about 60 pounds; a half-suit, about 35 pounds or somewhat more if it were bullet-proof. This weight was distributed all over the body, and the men were accustomed to it through long use. There are many tales of exceptional men vaulting into or over their saddles while wearing full suits of armor. The average man was expected to mount by himself. As for the idea of a man in armor being helpless when prostrate, even a man of today, unused to wearing armor, can rise without difficulty.[19]

In addition to their metal armor, the Spanish also wore a species of padded cloth armor. Although padded garments had long been worn as protective devices, particularly by the poorer classes in Europe, these *escaupiles,* as they

[124]

were called, were patterned more directly after those worn by the Aztecs whom the Spanish had encountered in Mexico. These garments were normally made of canvas and stuffed with cotton. They had the advantage of being light and easy to wear, and in addition they were effective against the arrows of the Indians who had, indeed, devised them for that very purpose. One instance of their effectiveness is given in an account of the De Soto expedition:

> ". . . and Rodrigo Ranjel returned to the Governor [De Soto] and had him draw out more than twenty arrows which he bore fastened in his armour, which was a loose coat quilted with coarse cotton."[20]

Since this cotton armor was so practical and also so inexpensive, it rapidly gained in popularity among the Spaniards, especially those in Florida. It was issued to soldiers at Santa Elena in 1573, and in 1577 and 1578 there were repeated requests for them from Spain and instructions that every soldier was to have one issued both for Santa Elena and St. Augustine. In the inspection of the forts of Florida made by Alvaro Flores in 1578, *escaupiles* were the only kind of armor listed in the official stores with the exception of one buckler. Since this form of armor was known so early and since it was so popular in Florida, it would seem logical that the Spanish elsewhere would be well provided with it. The standard inventories for expeditions into the South West, however, fail to mention it.[21]

Finally, before leaving the Spanish, it should be noted that the horses also wore armor. Horses were extremely valuable to the early explorers. They provided rapid transportation, gave decided advantage in battle, and above all, terrified the Indians. For this reason the Spanish protected them carefully. In one instance, when his horses were without armor, De Soto ordered his infantry to form around the horses and protect them with their bodies. Armor, however, was the logical device, and it was widely used.[22]

In Europe, steel armor which covered all but the horse's legs was frequently used for tournament and parade, but leather was generally used for field service. In America, the same situation seems to have held true. The Gentleman of Elvas mentions making horse armor of raw "ox" hide after the fire at Chicaça, and when Don Luís de Velasco went to New Mexico in 1597 he took with him:

> ". . . three sets of horse armor of buckskin, lined with undressed leather, for the flanks, foreheads, breasts, necks,—all, without anything lacking."

If steel armor was used at all, it probably consisted of a chanfron for the forehead and perhaps a crinnet of overlapping plates for the back of the neck, these pieces serving as reinforcements for the leather.[23]

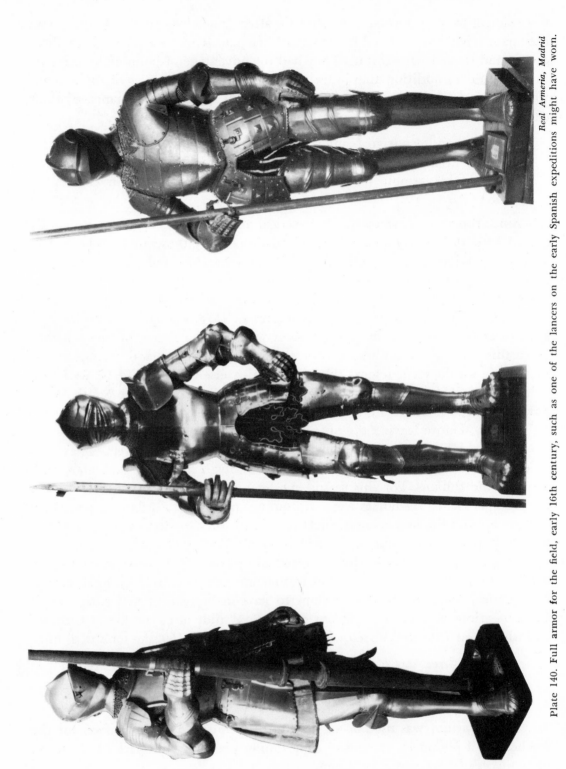

Real Armeria, Madrid

Plate 140. Full armor for the field, early 16th century, such as one of the lancers on the early Spanish expeditions might have worn.

Real Armeria, Madrid
Plate 141. Full armor for the field, second half
of the 16th century.

Real Armeria, Madrid
Plate 142. Half suit of armor, late 16th century.
This suit could fit the description of armor on the
Oñate expedition: *"Cotas con escarzelas y moriones
con sus sobrevistas"*. The gauntlets do not belong
with this suit, and it is doubtful if two-handed
swords were ever used in this country.

[127]

Aside from the Spanish, the other major attempts at colonization in the 16th century were the ill-fated French settlement in Florida and Sir Walter Raleigh's unsuccessful colony on Roanoke Island. Little is known about the types of armor worn in the Roanoke colony. The anonymous military adviser to Raleigh recommended considerable armor be taken on the expedition. His list included:

> "100 swordes and lyght moddena targetes; . . . Then 100, Armed men with millan corsseletes lyght; Then 50, Armed men with lyght corsseletes & short weapons."

The Modena targets and Milan corselets reflected the preference of the Englishman of the period for Italian arms and armor. The fact that he called for light corselets would probably indicate half suits to the tassets, some possibly with arm defenses, some without. Whether Raleigh accepted any of this advice is unknown, but it does reflect the general attitude of contemporary military men toward the requisites for a colony.[24]

Fortunately, there is more specific information available concerning the French colony in Florida. Jacques Le Moyne de Morgues, who was present, has

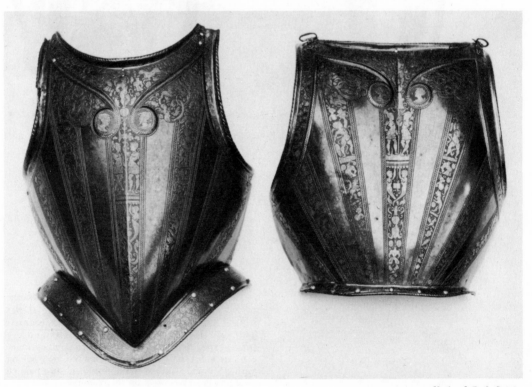

National Park Service

Plate 143. Italian, etched, blued and gilded breast and back plates, second half of the 16th century.

National Park Service

Plate 144. Italian morions etched with French designs (left) and Spanish designs (right).

National Park Service

Plate 145. Italian cabasset with etched, blued and gilt decorations.

left two pictures portraying the colonists in armor. One of these paintings is known only through an engraving made from it by Theodore De Bry in 1595, but the original of the other survives in full color.

Le Moyne's pictures of the Florida colony are particularly valuable because they depict two different situations, a ceremonial occasion and a battle. In the ceremonial painting, the original of which has survived, de Laudonnière, the leader of the expedition, is shown in a breastplate with a pronounced tapul, although it is not yet peasecod in form. It is blued or blackened and decorated

Horseman   *Arquebussier*   *Sergeant*   *Captain Velasco*   *Lancer, dismounted*

Oñate Expedition, 1597-1598

Company of Military Collectors & Historians
Plate 146. Men of the Oñate expedition illustrating the forms of arms and armor referred to in the manifests and inventories. Drawing by H. Charles McBarron, Jr.

with etched and gilded bands. The backplate does not show. De Laudonnière wears a civilian hat, but the men behind him wear decorated morions. Some of these helmets have banded decorations while on others the entire surface is etched. All have roped borders on comb and brim, and all have scaled straps under the chin.

In the battle picture, the officer wears the same breastplate or one similar to it. On his arm he carries a circular steel target, and on his head is a cabasset decorated to match the breastplate. The soldiers are also wearing cabassets,

Metropolitan Museum of Art

Plate 147. Late 16th century Italian half suit of armor. This was undoubtedly the type of armor Raleigh's advisor referred to as "millan corseletes—lyght."

but these are undecorated except for the brass rosettes around the rivet heads. All the cabassets have scaled chin straps and all are incorrectly drawn with the apical peak forward. In place of the finery in the pageant picture, the men are wearing padded clothing as a further protection against arrows or blows from war clubs.

Shortly after the beginning of the 17th century European colonies began to multiply rapidly. As the population increased, so did the amount of armor that was imported, for armor was still considered a necessity. One suit of armor for every two men was accepted as a moderate estimate, and almost every able-bodied man had at least a helmet or a target.[25]

The armor that was used in America during the 1600's was much the same as that worn in the second half of the preceding century. The target was used everywhere, and the morion and cabasset continued to be very popular. Shirts of mail were still in use, and so were quilted and padded garments. In the English colonies, the latter were frequently called jacks or jack-coats, and they derived

Deffaite des Yroquois au Lac Champlain.

A (1) Le fort des Yroquois.
B Les ennemis.
C Les Canots des ennemis faits d'ef-
   corce de chefne, qui peuuent tenir

chacun 10. 15. & 18. hommes.
D. E. Deux chefs tués, & vn bleffé
   d'vn coup d'arquebufe par le fieur
   de Champlain.

F (2) Le fieur de Champlain.
G (3) Deux Arquebufiers du fieur de
   Champlain.
H (4) Montaignets, Ochaftaiguins &

Algoumequins.
I Canots de nos fauuages aliés faits
   d'efcorce de bouleau.
K (5) Les bois.

(1) Cette lettre manque dans le dessin. — (2) La lettre manque; mais il est facile de reconnaître Champlain posté seul entre les combattants. — (3) Cette lettre manque dans le dessin; mais on reconnaît aisément les deux arquebusiers sur la lisière du bois. — (4) La lettre H a été mise par inadvertance sur les canots des alliés, où il y a déjà la lettre I. — (5) Cette lettre, qui manque aussi, est facile à suppléer.

P. 344

Folger Shakespeare Library

Plate. 148. Champlain's drawing of his fight with the Iroquois.

Virginia Historical Society

Plate 149. Arm defense excavated at Jamestown, consisting of vambrace, elbow cop, and a portion of the rerebrace.

more from European antecedents than from the Aztec prototypes of the *escaupiles.*

The biggest changes are to be found in the field of plate armor. The full suit had all but vanished. In its place were half-suits to the tassets and three-quarter suits to the knee. Champlain wore a half-suit, which he described as a "light armor" in his famous battle with the Iroquois near the lake that now bears his name. Fortunately, he made a sketch of the event, and although the details are not clear, it is possible to make out the fact that it consisted of a back plate, a breastplate, flaring tassets, and a burgonet with an open face for the helmet. Apparently there were no arm defenses, which was not unusual. The three-quarter suits, however, normally did possess arm defenses and gauntlets, and the tassets were extended to the knee-cop in a series of lames overlapping upward. This form of tasset has been designated in modern parlance the lobstertail tasset. An arm defense for such a suit was excavated at Jamestown during the Civil War by Confederate soldiers throwing up breastworks.[26]

Probably the most popular form of plate armor, however, was the so-called pikeman's suit. This normally consisted of a backplate, a breastplate, wide tassets, sometimes a gorget, and an open helmet. The breastplate was high waisted and had a moderate median ridge. It was relatively square across the bottom, where it flared out in a narrow flange. To this flange the tassets were hooked. These plates

Plate 150. Three elements of a suit of pikeman's armor used by an early Massachusetts colonist.

usually were made each from one piece of metal although they were embossed to resemble a series of overlapping lames.

The helmet was most often of a type derived from the chapel de fer, and known colloquially as a pikeman's pot. It had a wide brim turned down at the sides and a low comb. Almost always it was made from two pieces of metal joined together down the center of the helmet from front to back. Sometimes, however, a variety of the cabasset was used, and in these instances it was often of the type with a half comb in front and scaled chin straps. These, too, were almost always made from two pieces of metal and joined down the center.

Several fragments of pikeman's armor used in this country have survived the ravages of time. In the Massachusetts Historical Society collections are a helmet of the broad brimmed variety, a back plate and a right tasset which

[134]

Plate 151. English pikeman's armor bearing the cypher of James I (1603-1625).

Plate 152. Swedish pikeman's helmet excavated in Pennsylvania.

belonged to an early settler. Recently a tasset was found behind the fireplace of the John Howland House in Plymouth, and it is now preserved in Pilgrim Hall there. Another helmet of the chapel de fer type was found on the skull of an Indian in a burial in Lancaster County, Pennsylvania. The general shape and the area from which this last specimen came definitely identify it as coming from one of the Swedish settlements.

Another special form of armor was worn by mounted troops, and was known as Cuirassier armor. In the first years of the 17th century, this frequently referred to three-quarter suits, but gradually it came to denote a lighter harness, consisting of a breastplate, backplate and helmet. Sometimes an elbow gauntlet was also included. The breastplate closely resembled those worn by pikemen, except that there was no provision for attaching tassets and it was normally somewhat heavier. The helmet, however, was almost always of the burgonet type. Usually it possessed a long defense for the back of the neck made of four lames overlapping upwards, and this feature won for it the name of "lobster-tail burgonet." As in most burgonets there was an umbril over the eyes, but there was no comb. The face was guarded either by a single nasal bar which would be raised or lowered at will and fixed in position by a thumb screw, or by a series of three bars which attached to a pivoted umbril. Movable ear pieces fastened to the crown by straps protected the sides of the face.

An excellent example of a somewhat better than usual suit of this armor, including an elbow gauntlet, is preserved in the Massachusetts Historical Society. It was worn by Fitz-John Winthrop, grandson of the first John Winthrop and a famous military leader in Connecticut. It dates from the middle of the 17th century.

In addition to the plate armor and the padded jacks, another form of defensive clothing was also popular. This was the buff coat, so-called because it was made of a thick and heavy leather known as buff leather. Originally the name

Kungliga Livrustkammaren, Stockholm
Plate 153a. Swedish pikeman's armor.

Kungliga Livrustkammaren, Stockholm
Plate 153b. Swedish pikeman's helmet.

had applied to the thick leather from buffalo hides, but later cow and ox hides
were more generally used. In Virginia elk skins were recommended as excellent
for the purpose. Such coats were normally close fitting to the waist where they
flared widely in skirts reaching halfway to the knee. Some were made with
sleeves, but many were not. The thickness of the leather from which these coats
were constructed made them a good defense against sword cuts and arrows,
and as such they became increasingly popular. At first they were worn under
metal corselets. but later it frequently became the practice, especially for musketeers, to be armed simply with a helmet and buff coat. An excellent example
of a buff coat which belonged to Governor John Leverett of Massachusetts and
dates from the middle of the 17th century is preserved in the Massachusetts Historical Society.[27]

The pattern of armor use in America in the 17th century may be traced
through a brief survey of some of the more important references to it in the
various colonies. The settlers who arrived at Jamestown in 1607 were well
equipped with armor. There were both leather and steel targets for the targe-
tiers, and there were jacks, helmets, and plate armor in ample quantity: In fact,
when John Smith left the colony in 1609, he reported that there were more
helmets and cuirasses than there were men.[28]

The appearance of the Virginia settler when he sallied forth completely
armed is excellently described in the *Martial Lawes* of 1611:

Hee [the Governor] shall not suffer in his Garrison any Souldier to
enter into Guard, or to bee drawne out into the field without being

[138]

Plate 154. Three-quarter armor made for the mounted retainers of the Earl of Pembroke, early 17th century. This would be typical of the three-quarter suits worn in the English colonies.

armed according to the Marshals order, which is, that every shot [musketeer] shall either be furnished with a quilted coate of Canuas, a headpeece, and a sword, or else with a light Armor, and Bases quilted, with which hee shall be furnished: and every Targiteer with his Bases to the small of his legge, and his headpeece, sword and pistoll or Scuppet provided for that end. And likewise every Officer armed as before, with a firelocke, or Snaphause, headpeece, and a Target, onely the Serieant in Garrison shall vse his Halbert, and in field his Snaphaunse and Target.

The Gouernor shall have a Principall care, that he vse his Garrison to the dayly wearing of these Armors, least in the field, the souldier do finde them the more uncouth strange and troublesome.[29]

The word "base" used in the quotation referred to a defense for the lower body and thighs. Traditionally it designated a padded skirt, but by 1611 it is possible that it was also used to describe padded or quilted breeches.[30]

In 1622, Jamestown suffered severely from an Indian attack. Many lives and much material were lost, and the Virginia Company petitioned the King for a grant of arms and armor to help them recover from the loss. The petition was granted, and the shipment of arms donated from the Royal arsenals reached Virginia in 1623. Along with the offensive weapons in the lot were 2,000 open helmets (skulls of iron), 400 shirts and coats of mail, 40 plate cuirasses, and 100 brigandines. These last were a type of armor that had not been used actively in Europe for 100 years. They consisted of a series of small metal plates riveted or sewed to a canvas backing and covered with another layer of canvas, or, in better specimens, leather, silk or velvet.

In many instances the rivet heads were allowed to pass through the outer cloth also and were formed into ornamental designs. In early specimens the metal plates were fairly large, but in later types they were seldom larger than one by two inches. The garments constructed in this manner were most frequently sleeveless vests, but occasional specimens with sleeves and even legs are known.[31]

In 1625, the now-famous military census of Virginia was conducted. It was incomplete because some areas failed to file reports, and because of peculiar overlapping and unspecific groupings it is not as helpful on the subject of armor as it might have been. Nevertheless it does contain some useful information. There were 342 "complete armors" listed along with 260 "coats of mail and head pieces," 20 quilted and buff coats," and 26 "jackets, jack coats and corselets." More informative are those individual returns that are still available. Such statements range all the way from individuals with only a helmet and a padded coat to men like Sir Francis Wyatt who provided for his servants also

Plate 155. Armor of Fitz-John Winthrop. The helmet originally had ear pieces, and there is a reinforcing plate for the breastplate which is not shown in the photograph.

and thus listed "4 armors, 1 Jack Coat, 2 Coats of mail, 1 steel coat, 1 corselet, 2 good head pieces" at his plantation, and "6 armors" at his Jamestown residence.[32]

Armor continued popular in Virginia until the middle of the century. In 1644 the men who were to march in an expedition against the Indian chief Opecancanough were ordered each to wear "some defensive coat of armor and head piece." In 1648 Beauchamp Plantagenet advised a group of "undertakers and subscribers" in England who had agreed to bring 3000 men to the colony that each man should have "halfe an old slight Armour, that is, two to one Armour;" and in 1650 Edward Williams advised all prospective planters to bring with them one suit of light armor.[33]

After 1650 interest in armor rapidly waned. There were no more serious troubles with the Indians, and armor was of little use against European adversaries. Curaissiers' armor was the last to go, and as late as 1687 men of sufficient means in Middlesex County were required to supply their own horse and armor when called out for military duty. Such regulations, however, were exceptional.[34]

In New England the pattern was generally similar; but there were some notable differences. The settlers at Plymouth in 1620 were not so well equipped as those who first landed at Jamestown. Nevertheless they managed to provide a corselet, probably of the pikeman variety, for every man on their early exploring expeditions. When settlers of the Massachusetts Bay Colony left London they brought plate armor only for the 60 pikemen in the public stores, the presumption being that the 90 musketeers would wear buff or quilted coats although none are listed. Privately owned armor undoubtedly augmented the number in public possession, but there were no records of the number and types of such items.[35]

Twenty of the corselets that the Massachusetts Bay settlers brought with them were purchased on March 6, 1628 from Thomas Stevens of London, and the purchase agreement is most informative:

> Agreement with Thomas Steevens, in Buttolph Lane for 20 armes, viz, corselet, breast, back, culet, gorgett, tases, & head piece, all varnished and black. 17s each except 4 with closed helmets, these 24s each.[36]

In this agreement it should be noted that the word "tases" referred to both the taces and tassets, the distinction between the two being purely modern. This document has significance for Virginia as well as Massachusetts. Thomas Stevens also sold armor to the Virginia colonists, and since the two prices quoted are about the same as the Virginia agreement ("23 armors at 17s a piece, 2 armors, better than ordinary for Mr. Middleton & son 25s ea.") it may be inferred that they were generally similar.[37]

The first major Indian war to engulf the New England Colonies was the Pequot War of 1635-1637. In that conflict there was a noted break with the practice of wearing armor. The Connecticut troops under Captains Mason and Underhill, who stormed the Pequot stronghold in 1637, were all "completely armed, with Corselets" according to the latter, but especially among the Massachusetts troops there began to appear more and more "unarmed" men as the settlers began to grow contemptuous of their adversaries. By the beginning of King Philip's War in 1675, probably the majority of men were without armor.[38]

The colonies of New Haven and Connecticut which had fought together during the Pequot War united in 1643, and their records provide a few useful sidelights on armor in New England. Most important of these was the fact that the possession of armor was a subject of legislation, and the colony government was particularly interested in it. Thus, in 1645, the General Court ordered every family to provide "a canvas coat quilted with cotton wool as a defense against arrows." In addition to the armor owned by individuals, the separate settlements were also required to maintain public armor. The older settlements on the Connecticut River had begun this practice as early as 1637 for the Pequot War when Hartford was ordered to produce 21 corselets, Windsor, 12, Wethersfield 10, and Agawam 7. In 1650 cotton coats were allowed as well as metal, and the figures were revised sharply downward as follows: Windsor 9, Hartford 12, Wethersfield 8, Seakook 3, Farmington 3, Fairfield 6, Stratford 6, Southampton 3, and Pequett 3.[39]

In general, it may be stated that in New England the practice of wearing armor was abandoned earlier than in Virginia. As was seen above, armor was considered necessary in Virginia up until the middle of the century and was

Massachusetts Historical Society
Plate 156. Governor Leverett's buff coat.

still required in some places as late as 1687. In New England, on the other hand, men were fighting Indians without it as early as 1637 and shortly thereafter armor began to disappear entirely until it was almost completely a thing of the past by 1675.

The Dutch and Swedish records which are relatively informative on the subject of firearms and equipment are not at all helpful about the armor used. Undoubtedly the same general types of armor were used in these colonies as in the others, but the available documents give no details. Armor is mentioned frequently in the records of New Netherlands, but always the term *malj rocken*

Company of Military Collectors & Historians

Plate 157. Jamestown settlers of 1611-1615 based on Strachey's *Martial Laws.*
The word bases is here interpreted as the quilted skirts shown. Drawing by
H. Charles McBarron, Jr.

Plate 158. Fragment of brigandine, c. 1530, found in an Indian site near Panama City, Florida.

(coats of mail) is used, and this obviously is a general euphemistic term meaning body armor of any sort.[40]

A particular important phase of the study of armor in America is, of course, concerned with its effectiveness against Indian arrows. In such a study, it must be remembered that all Indians were not alike. Some groups possessed much stronger weapons and greater skill in using them than other groups. This fact is most important because it is the only really variable factor that must be considered in the analysis. The quality of plate armor, mail and quilted garments in one colony was roughly similar to that in the others and so does not have to be evaluated.

The Spanish, who were the first settlers to come in contact with the Indian warriors, had a hearty respect for them. It should be said in their behalf that the Indians they met were hardy warriors who possessed strong weapons and considerable skill in using them. Nevertheless, many of the Spanish accounts of the effect of Indian arrows must be discounted as somewhat exaggerated, especially when contrasted with the calmer account of the Gentleman of Elvas, who encountered the same Indians.

Typical of the accounts which seem to be slightly exaggerated are two found in De Vaca's narrative:

Some of our men were wounded in this conflict, for whom the good armor they wore did not avail. There were those this day who swore that they had seen two red oaks, each the thickness of the lower part of the leg, pierced through from side to side by arrows. . . . I myself

Plate 159. Brigandine, showing outer view of the front and inner view of the back.

saw an arrow that had entered the butt of an elm to the depth of a span.[41]

Also,

> We found their corpses traversed from side to side with arrows; and for all some had on good armor, it did not give adequate protection or security against the nice and powerful archery of which I have spoken.[42]

According to the Gentleman of Elvas who fought the same Indians about 10 years later, however, the arrows were not nearly so effective, although he was impressed by the marksmanship. Describing the effect of arrows upon armor, Elvas wrote:

> For the most part when they light upon an armor, they breake in the place where they are bound together. Those of cane do split and pierce a coate of maile, and are more hurtful than the other.[43]

Further west, the Indians who were encountered by the Spaniards under Coronado and the English under Sir Francis Drake were apparently poor warriors. Almost anything served as protection against their bows, which were described as:

[146]

"more fit for children then for men, sending the arrowes neither farre off nor with any great force . . ."[44]

The English in Virginia met Indians similar to those encountered by De Vaca and De Soto a century earlier. Like their Spanish predecessors, the English also maintained a hearty respect for their adversaries, especially after a demonstration of their armor designed to impress the Indians backfired. George Percy, a witness, recorded the scene:

"One of our Gentlemen having a Target which hee trusted in, thinking it would beare out a slight shot, hee set it up against a tree, willing one of the Savages to shoot; who tooke from his backe an Arrow of an elle long, drew it strongly in his Bowe, shoots the Target a foote thorow, or better: which was strange, being that a Pistoll could not pierce it. Wee seeing the force of his Bowe, afterwards set him up a steele Target, he shot again, and burst his arrow all to pieces. He presently pulled out another Arrow, and bit it in his teeth, and seemed to be in a great anger."[45]

The fallacy in the colonists' thinking which caused their surprise when the arrow pierced the pistol-proof leather target lay in failing to realize the different actions of the two projectiles. The round pistol ball would strike the target a heavy but dull blow and could be expected to bounce off. An arrow, on the other hand, although its velocity was much lower, would deliver a sharp, slicing blow which would be more effective against such materials.

In New England also the Indians were hardy, but as a rule they preferred to shoot from a distance with a high trajectory rather than point blank. This action, plus a relatively low velocity of the arrows, permitted the colonists to dodge them when they were seen in advance. Normally when the arrows struck plate armor they bounced off, but if the Indians were close enough they could dent the metal. In such an instance during the Pequot War one Captain Turner:

"received a shot upon the breast of his corselet, as if it had been pushed with a pike, and if hee had not had it on, hee had lost his life."[46]

In the expedition of Connecticut men led by Mason and Underhill against the Pequots in 1637, there occurred some fighting at close quarters. Captain Underhill referred to it only briefly in his narrative but still gave some indication of the effectiveness of the armor the men wore.

Captain *Mason* and my selfe entring into the Wigwams, hee was shott, and received many Arrows against his head-peece, God preserved him from any wounds; my selfe received a shotte in the left hippe, through a sufficient Buffe coate, that if I had not been supplied with such a garment, the Arrow would have pierced through me; another I received betweene necke and shoulders, hanging in the linnen [lining] of my Head-peece, others of our souldiers were shot some through the shoulders, some in the face, some in the head, some in the legs.[47]

Musketeer   *Colonel*   *Sergeant*   *Pikeman*   *Ensign*

The North Regiment, Massachusetts Bay Colony, 1636

Company of Military Collectors & Historians
Plate 160. Drawing by H. Charles McBarron, Jr.

It should be noted that all the areas listed by Underhill in which the men were wounded were places that probably were not protected by armor. The only exception to this is his reference to the head, but in that instance he may well have been referring to the occipital region which was not protected by some types of helmet.

When these accounts and numerous other references to the effect of arrows upon armor are correlated, certain conclusions can be reached. Plate armor was effective against the arrows of all Indians. In all the records examined there is no definite instance in which an arrow pierced plate. The success of mail as a defense varied. If the wilder Spanish tales are discounted somewhat and Elva's account taken as slightly conservative, it would seem that the arrows of the hardy warriors in the South could pierce it if the range were short, but that normally the arrows splintered and delivered painful but not necessarily dangerous wounds. In the Far West and South West, mail was highly effective against the weaker weapons encountered in those areas. No specific comments on the effectiveness of mail in the English colonies have been found, but the Indians there were no hardier than those encountered by De Vaca and De Soto. Consequently it is safe to assume that it was at least as efficient.

Leather and cloth armor were tried everywhere, and they were universally efficient. Arrows were stopped or at least sufficiently slowed by the quilted armor and the buff coats to make them excellent secondary defenses, with vital areas covered by plate. Their lightness was a great recommendation, and frequently this was given more consideration than absolute safety. This circumstance combined with the fact that they were inexpensive to produce and to maintain were the main reasons for their widespread popularity.

It was this simple factor of effectiveness that caused armor to remain in active use in America as long as or even longer than it was really used in most of western Europe. As long as the colonist had a sure defense against the weapons of his adversaries, he was inclined to use it. When the Indians began to acquire a substantial number of firearms, and when the settler began to find himself pitted more and more against other Europeans with their more effective weapons, he abandoned his armor just as his former countrymen abroad were doing for the same reason. Except for special instances it was no longer sufficiently effective to be worth the effort and expense of acquiring and wearing it.

1. Samuel de Champlain, *The Second Voyage to New France in the year 1610*, W. L. Grant, editor, *Voyages of Samuel de Champlain, 1604-1618*, New York, 1907, 180. Elvas, *Narrative*, 256, 257. De Vaca, *Narrative*, 28.

2. Elvas, *Narrative*, 139, 199, 200, 209, 256. De Vaca, *Narrative*, 28, 31, 32, 36. Casteñada, *Coronado*, 321-333.

3. J. Starkie Gardner, *Foreign Armour in England*, London, 1898, 17-22; *Armour in England*, London, 1897, 9-12. Charles H. Ashdown, *British and Foreign Arms and Armour*, London, 1909, 84-88. Stone, *Glossary*, 424-430.

4. Ashdown, *Arms and Armour*, 84-88. Stone, *Glossary*, 424-430. Bashford Dean, *Helmets and Body Armor in Modern Warfare*, New Haven, 1920, 49.

5. Stone, *Glossary*, 424-430. Elvas, *Narrative*, 148, 156. Elvas, *Virginia Richly Valued*, 29.

6. Stone, *Glossary*, 424-430. Ashdown, *Arms and Armour*, 84-88. Gardner, *Foreign Armour*, 17-22.

7. "Statement of what Don Juan de Oñate and Don Pedro Ponce de León offer for the exploration, pacification, and settlement of New Mexico," Hackett, *Historical Documents*, I, 280-283. "Manifest made by Captain Don Luís de Velasco of the goods, arms, and horses which he is taking to serve his Majesty in the expedition to New Mexico, of which Don Juan de Oñate goes as Governor and Captain general," May 19, 1597, *ibid.*, 428-433. The Council on the Indies to the president of the Casa de Contractación, June 12, 1602, *ibid.*, 403.

8. Mann, *Arms and Armour*, III, 620, 638. Stone, *Glossary*, 93, 94, 536, 537. Ashdown, *Arms and Armour*, 217-221. Gardner, *Armour in England*, 57-59.

9. *Ibid.*

10. Stone, *Glossary*, 173, 174. Mann, *Arms and Armour*, III, 624, 643. Ashdown, *Arms and Armour*, 258-260.

11. Mann, *Arms and Armour*, III, 621, 623. Stone, *Glossary*, 152, 153. Ashdown, *Arms and Armour*, 219-221. Gardner, *Armour in England*, 58; *Foreign Armour*, 52, 53.

12. Laking, *Armour and Arms*, IV, 193-217. Stone, *Glossary*, 158, 159, 455, 457. Mann, *Arms and Armour*, III, 623, 634.

13. Stone, *Glossary*, 455, 457.

14. Laking, *Armour and Arms*, IV, 125-193. Mann, *Arms and Armour*, III, 623. Stone, *Glossary*, 156, 157, 204.

15. *Ibid.* "Statement of what Don Juan de Oñate and Don Pedro Ponce de León offer for the exploration, pacification, and settlement of New Mexico," 1596, Hackett, *Historical Documents*, I, 280 283. "Manifest made by Captain Don Luís de Velasco of the goods, arms, and horses which he is taking to serve his Majesty in the expedition to New Mexico, of which Don Juan de Oñate goes as governor and captain general," May 19, 1597, *ibid.*, 428-433. The Council of the Indies to the president of the Casa de Contractación, June 12, 1602, *ibid.*, 403. The King to the president of the Casa de Contractación, June 23, 1602, *ibid.*, 409.

16. Mann, *Arms and Armour*, III, 623, 641. Stone, *Glossary*, 151, 152, 605. *Il Manoscritto Messicano 3738 Dette Il Codice Rios*, Rome, 1900, 87-94.

17. *Ibid.*, Elvas, *Narrative*, 199, 200, 209. "Statement of what Don Juan de Oñate and Don Pedro Ponce de León offer for the exploration, pacification, and settlement of New Mexico," 1596, Hackett, *Historical Documents*, I, 228, 229. "The Visitation made by Alvaro Flores of the Forts of Florida," 1578, Connor, *Records of Florida*, II, 137. Castañeda, *Coronado*, 333. Hammond and Rey, *O ate*, I, 226.

18. "A Most Truthful Relation of What Happened in Florida in the Month of July of this Year MDLXXX," Connor, *Records of Florida*, II, 322. Elvas, *Narrative*, 148. "Statement of what Don Juan de Oñate and Don Pedro Ponce de León offer for the exploration, pacification, and settlement of New Mexico," Hackett, *Historical Documents*, I, 280-283. Hammond and Rey, *Oñate*, I, 226-286.

19. Dean, *Helmets and Body Armor*, 45-50.

20. Oviedo, *Narrative*, 125. Testimony of Baltasar Lopez, "Investigations made in Madrid by Licentiate Gamboa on Matters Concerning Florida," February 4, 1573, Connor, *Records of Florida*, I, 97.

21. *Ibid.* Pedro Menéndez Márques to the King, October 2, 1577, *ibid.*, 275. "Investigation of the Return from Florida of Esteban de las Alas," *ibid.*, 307. "Instructions Given to the Treasurer, Martín Quiros, and to Iñigo Rúiz de Castresana," October 12, 1577, *ibid.*, II, 13. Petition of Pedro Menéndez Márques, June 15 (?), 1578 (?), *ibid.*, 77. "The Visitation Made by Alvaro Flores of the Forts of Florida," 1578, *ibid.*, 117-203.

22. Elvas, *Narrative*, 209.

23. Laking, *Armour and Arms*, III, 147-208. Elvas, *Narrative*, 209. "Manifest made by Captain Don Luís de Velasco of the goods, arms, and horses which he is taking to serve his Majesty in the expedition to New Mexico, of which Don Juan de Oñate goes as governor and captain general," May 19, 1597, Hackett, *Historical Documents*, I, 428-433.

24. *For Mr. Rauleys Viage*, ms. *Loc cit.*

25. Edward Waterhouse, "A Declaration of the State of the Colony and . . . a Relation of the Barbarous Massacre...," Kingsbury, *Records*, III, 578, "Meeting of a Committee for Smythe's Hundred," May 18, 1618, *ibid.*, 96. Beauchamp Plantagenet, *"A Description of the Province of New Albion*, 32.

26. Champlain, *The Voyage to the Great River St. Lawrence from the Year 1608 to that of 1612*, Grant, *Voyages of Champlain*, 164.

27. Plantagenet, *New Albion*, 31. Stone, *Glossary*, 152. Mann, *Arms and Armour*, III, 623. Grose, *Military Antiquities*, I, 101-111. Underhill, *Nevves*, 38, 39.

28. George Percy, *Observations*, Lyon Gardiner Tyler, editor, *Narratives of Early Virginia*, 1606-1625, New York, 1907, 13, 17, 58, 168, 172, 173. Smith, *True Relation*, 53, 58. Simmonds, *Proceedings*, 168, 181, 197. Percy, *Trewe Relacyon*, 259-282.

29. "Instructions of the Marshall for better inhabling of the Colonell or Gouernor, to the executing of his or their charges in this present Colony the 22. of June. 1611.", Strachey, *Lavves*, 32.

30. Mann, *Arms and Armour*, III, 620. Stone, *Glossary*, 102.

31. Warrant to the Lord Treasurer, September 1622, Kingsbury, *Records*, III, 676. "Minutes of a Court held for Virginia," April 2, 1623, *ibid.*, II, 342. Stone, *Glossary*, 149, 150. Mann, *Arms and Armour*, III, 623.

32. "Military Census of Virginia," *Virginia Magazine of History and Biography*, VII, 364-367 (April 1900). Brown, *First Republic*, 610-627.

33. "Acts, Orders and Resolutions of the General Assembly of Virginia," July 1, 1644, *Virginia Magazine of History and Biography*, XXIII, 231 (July 1915). Plantagenet, *New Albion*, 32. Williams, *Virginia*, 10.

34. "Military Census of Middlesex County," November 23, 1687, *Virginia Magazine of History and Biography*, VIII, 189 (October 1900).

35. The Leader of the Pilgrims to the Adventurers, August 3, 1620, Arber, *Story*, 338. Bradford, *History*, 98, 103. Bradford and Winslow, *Relation*, 411, 415. See also Peterson, "Military Equipment," 198, 199. Shurtleff, *Massachusetts Records*, I, 25, 26.

36. Shurtleff, *Massachusetts Records*, I, 31.

37. "An order to Mr. Ferrar," Kingsbury, *Records*, III, 262.

38. Underhill, *Nevves*, 7, 17, 38, 39. Winthrop, *History*, I, 231, 233, 235, 236.

39. Hoadly, *New Haven Records*, 214. Hoadly, *Connecticut Records*, I, 9, 14, 15, 17, 543, 544.

40. "Extracts from the Papers of Director Kieft," O'Callaghan, *Documents*, I, 415. "Report of the Board of Accounts on New Netherland," 1644, *ibid.*, 151, *et passim*.

41. De Vaca, *Narrative*, 31, 32.

42. *Ibid.*, 36.

43. Elvas, *Virginia*, 22.

44. *The World Encompassed by Sir Francis Drake*, 1579, Burrage, *Early English and French Voyages*, 170.

45. Percy, *Observations*, 17.

46. Underhill, *Nevves*, 7, 40, 41. Winthrop, *History*, I, 231, 233, 236. Bradford and Winslow, *Relation*, 411-415. Bradford, *History*, 98-110. Underhill, *Nevves*, 38, 39.

BOOK II

The French Wars
and the Revolution

1689-1783

Introduction

IN THE HISTORY of arms and armor, the period from 1689-1783 was in many ways the antithesis of the preceding period. Arms in America had developed rapidly under the pressure of the new environment until they had far surpassed those in general use in Europe. After 1689, aside from the development of the rifle, the rate of progress in America declined while European arms improved. Towards the end of the period, in fact, Americans began to abandon their own distinctive military tactics and the weapons connected with them and once more patterned their military modes after European models.

This transformation, like the one before it, was the result of a change in environment. The colonists faced different enemies under different conditions.

Militarily, the period from 1689-1783 was characterized by a series of wars between England and France for control of the Continent and by the American Revolution, which was closely connected with the previous struggles. King William's War, 1689-1697, began the long conflict. It was followed by Queen Anne's War, 1702-1713; King George's War, 1740-1748; and the French and Indian War, 1755-1763. By the treaty ending the French and Indian War, France was deprived of all her colonies in America, and Great Britain reigned supreme. From these conflicts, however, stemmed many of the conditions which produced the Revolutionary War of 1775-1783 and ended the colonial period of American history.

In the French wars the bulk of the important fighting was done by European troops. The Indian allies on both sides contributed little except through their terrorizing activities and their harassment of the frontier which made it necessary to maintain garrisons all along the line and thus kept many men out of the active campaigns. American troops in general lacked discipline and training in European tactics, and aside from a few brilliant exceptions they were considered unreliable by the English commanders. A small group, however, did render valuable service as scouts and rangers.

As the French wars continued, an attempt was made to raise the caliber of American troops and thus remove some of the load from the British regulars. Colonial governors were encouraged to raise and train special regiments. This was done within the existing militia laws, and there were wide deviations in the way the individual governors interpreted and executed their authority. In some colonies there was little or no improvement over the old militia, but in others, such as Virginia and New Jersey, there developed relatively well disciplined and well equipped American regiments, the first such ever raised in this country.

From the very beginning military leaders in the English colonies had studied English drill manuals. They patterned the American militia system with its muster days after the English militia. Insofar as possible they used the English drill. But the nature of the country and the character of the enemy had prevented them from putting much of it into practice.

By the 18th century, however, conditions had begun to change. The Eastern Seaboard was becoming civilized. Cleared land had begun to replace the forests in many sections. The Indians were no longer a constant menace. In general, conditions there were beginning to approximate those in Europe. Also, the enemy was no longer a savage hiding in a dense forest, but another white man who fought in an open field or behind fortifications. Thus, most of the reasons for the tactics and armament of the earlier period had been removed. In their place were an entirely new set of conditions which called for a return to European tactics.

At the same time, however, there was still a frontier in America, and there the evolution of arms and tactics continued as it had in the early years. Along the Western borders of the colonies, conditions were much the same as they had originally been on the coast. The forests were still thick, and the Indians were still a continuing threat. It was on this frontier that the rifle was developed. The same conditions which had caused the first settlers to seek the lightest, most accurate and fastest shooting guns that they could purchase in Europe continued in the 18th century to foster the evolution of these European types into a purely American gun that met the requirements even better.

Although the rifle was an effective weapon for the purposes for which it was designed, it had little effect on the overall arms picture. It was almost unknown to military men during the French wars, and the Revolutionary War was fought under conditions which relegated the rifle to a minor supporting role. During that war, which was largely confined to the cleared lands of the East Coast, both armies relied heavily on the standard European linear tactics. In such warfare, the rifle, which lacked the bayonet and which required more time for loading than the musket, was useful only under special conditions.

Thus at the end of the period Americans were once more fighting like Europeans. The rifle was restricted to special troops which acted as light infantry, and the musket and bayonet of European pattern was retained as the standard weapon. The return to linear tactics also had another effect on the development of arms. The pole arm, which had all but disappeared a century before, came back into vogue as American Revolutionary troops were equipped with spontoons, trench spears, pikes and lances.

Chapter Five

Firearms

HE HISTORY of firearms in America from 1689 to 1783 follows a
pattern entirely different from that of the preceding period. The
first 162 years had seen rapid developments and radical changes.
Three entirely different systems of ignition had followed one another
in quick succession, and there had been many variations and improvements in
each. In design these firearms had advanced from heavy, clumsy and ill-balanced
contraptions to comparatively light, well-balanced, and relatively efficient
weapons. As each of these advances was made, its effect was quickly felt in
America where the dependence of the colonist upon his arms caused him to
demand the very best that Europe produced and to adopt them as standard arms
before they were so recognized abroad.

The last of these major developments had taken place well before 1689,
and the next big stride, the invention of the percussion system of ignition, did
not occur until well after 1783. Thus the period under consideration was one
of refinement and systematization. Older forms were improved upon, resulting
in finer guns. Even the rifle and the breech-loader which are often considered
the outstanding achievements of this period were but further developments of
already known principles.

The other major contribution of the period, the standardization of arms, was
also not absolutely new. Some small groups had already begun to try to equalize
calibers and to use similar guns before 1689. It was during this period, however,
that the heterogeneity of arms in most national armies was gradually done away
with and definite models for firearms were developed which can be described
and dated. By the end of the period, all the guns of a well-equipped organization were as nearly alike as hand-craftmanship could make them.

The principal firearm of the period was the flintlock musket. This smoothbore weapon of large caliber answered perfectly the requirements called for by the military tactics of the day. The basic formation for an enagement was the line of battle. This consisted of two or sometimes three lines of men drawn up shoulder to shoulder, one line close behind the other. About six feet behind these lines was another line of "file closers" or reserves to take the place of casualties. From this formation soldiers advanced to the attack, marching to within sure range of the enemy, delivering a volley, and then charging to decide the issue hand to hand. Likewise, it was in this formation that soldiers received an attacking force in the open fields. They waited until the enemy was within range, fired a volley, loaded, and if possible fired one or two more vollies before the enemy closed with them.[1]

Volley-firing from a line of battle was a very formal practice. All loading

Author's Collection
Plate 161. British musket by I. Hawkin of the period of William III-Queen Anne, used in this country.

and firing was done by command, or, as a modern soldier would say, "by the numbers." There was little or no aiming as it is understood today. The volley was delivered directly ahead or to the right or left oblique as commanded. The theory was to lay down a pattern or field of fire, and consequently rapidity of fire was prized much more highly than accuracy.[2]

Thus the musket, which could be loaded rapidly, was considered a fine weapon, even though its accuracy left something to be desired. Some idea of the speed of loading and firing expected of the soldier armed with the musket can be obtained from the following entry in a military treatise of 1768:

> "No recruit to be dismissed from the drill, till he is so expert with
> his firelock, as to load and fire fifteen times in three minutes and three
> quarters."[3]

This would mean a sustained fire of one shot every fifteen seconds, a rate which would assure at least two volleys at an approaching enemy in any average charge.

Thus, if, as was often the case, a charge involved only one regiment on each side, and if each regiment consisted of 500 men, it would mean that the attacking force would have to suffer the effects of 1,000 bullets in two volleys in the 20 or 25 seconds it would take them to negotiate a charge of less than 100 yards. The second volley would be received, if delivered properly, at a range of no more than 30 yards.

[160]

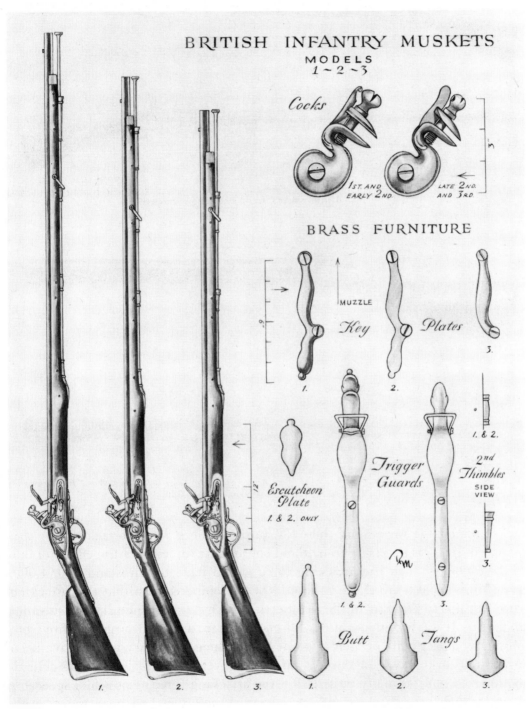

Plate 162. Drawing by Robert L. Miller.

Company of Military Collectors & Historians

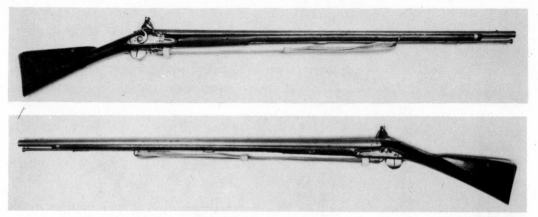

Plate 163. British officer's fusil. The sling is modern.

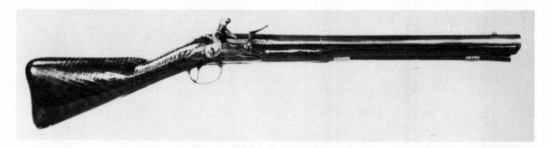

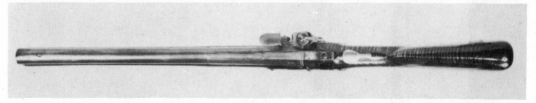

Plate 164. Cavalry musketoon, c. 1690-1700.

If the charge were more than 100 yards, if there were obstacles to be surmounted, if it was necessary to halt and consolidate forces after the effects of one of these volleys, then the attacking force would have to withstand 500, 1,000, or possibly 1,500 more shots. It should be remembered also that this attacking force was not spread out in the manner in which modern infantrymen advance under fire. It was a compact and solid mass of men, a perfect target for fire from another compact body of men at point blank range. Accuracy would have been superfluous in this type of warfare. Speed was everything. Speed for the defending force to pour as many bullets into the attacking force as possible; speed for the attacking force to close with its adversary before it had been too severely decimated to have sufficient strength to carry the position.

There were some instances, however, in which an accurate weapon was to be desired, and here the musket was weak. Troops detached to act as flankers on a march through hostile territory, pickets, rangers, and other similar small groups where the action was apt to involve only a few men or perhaps single individuals felt the need of accurate weapons. It was to these troops and in these instances that the rifle later proved a valuable arm.

These men wanted accuracy, and they practiced marksmanship even with the musket. There are many orders and references to such target practice, and in one instance the procedure is well described. Frederick Mackenzie, an officer of the Royal Welch Fusiliers, then stationed in Boston, left the following account of British target practice in January 1775:

> 15th Jany. The Regiments are frequently practiced at firing with ball at marks. Six rounds p^r man at each time is usually allotted for this practice. As our Regiment is quartered on a Wharf which projects into part of the harbour, and there is a very considerable range without any obstruction, we have fixed figures of men as large as life, made of thin boards, on small stages, which are anchored at a proper distance from the end of the Wharf, at which the men fire. Objects afloat, which move up and down with the tide, are frequently pointed out for them to fire at, and Premiums are sometimes given for the best Shots, by which means some of our men have become excellent marksmen.[4]

The limitations of the musket with which these men fired have been well described by one of the most famous marksmen and authorities on shooting of the time. Major George Hanger, who was also well versed with both the German and American rifle, reported that:

> A soldier's musket, if not exceedingly ill-bored (as many of them are), will strike the figure of a man at eighty yards; it may even at 100; but a soldier must be very unfortunate indeed who shall be wounded by a common musket at 150 yards, provided his antagonist aims at him; and as to firing at a man at 200 yards with a common musket, you may just as well fire at the moon and have the same hopes of hitting your object. I do maintain and will prove, whenever called on, that no man was ever killed at 200 yards, by a common soldier's musket, by the person who aimed at him.[5]

These were the general characteristics of the musket and the reasons for its ascendancy as the principle military firearm of the period. Muskets from many nations were used in America in addition to those made here. Great Britain, France, Holland, the various states of Germany, and Spain were all represented.

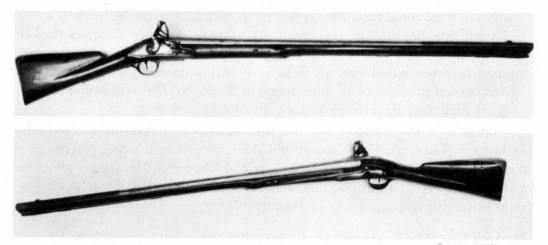

Colonial Williamsburg

Plate 165. British musketoon of the type described in the warrant of 1756, although this specimen is somewhat earlier.

The models differed, but the overall principles and characteristics were the same.

The nation whose muskets wielded the dominant influence in America until the very end of the period was Great Britain. Almost all arms purchased by individuals and by Colonies prior to the Revolution came from there. During the wars with France from at least as early as the reign of Queen Anne (1702-1714), England sent arms to equip colonial troops, and most of these arms remained in America. The British musket was thus the one with which Americans were familiar, and when war broke out between the colonies and Britain in 1775 and the committees of safety of the various colonies began contracting for arms with local gunsmiths, it was the British musket which they chose as their pattern.[6]

When William III ascended the British throne in 1689, there was no standard British musket. Rather, he inherited a great mass of heterogeneous firearms, most of them matchlocks, from his predecessors. William quickly began to make the flintlock the standard weapon for his armies and to eliminate the matchlock. Unfortunately, he was shortly embroiled in a Continental War with repercussions in America, and thus could not proceed to make the conversion as systematic as might have been desired. The need for arms was such that he proceeded to convert what matchlocks he could, to contract with private English gunsmiths, and to purchase many muskets from his allies abroad, especially Holland. By these means he managed in a broad sense to make all his muskets of the same general type and of fairly uniform caliber.[7]

An average example of one of the British manufactured flintlocks of King William's reign would have a roughly made flint lock possibly with a dog catch, of about the same size and shape as the older matchlocks and thus interchangeable with them. It would be attached by three screws and might bear upon the lock plate in front of the cock the initials "WR" (William Rex) and a crown. There would be no bridle for either the tumbler or the frizzen. The barrel would be 46 inches long and about .75 caliber. It would be octagonal for about 18 inches at the breech. There would be a small fore-sight, but no rear sight. The mounts would be iron except for the brass butt plate. There would probably be no screw plate and no rear ramrod thimble. The stock would be black, and the barrel and iron mounts would also be blackened or russeted.[8]

King William was succeeded in 1702 by Queen Anne, and it was during her reign that the famous "Brown Bess" musket was adopted. There is some question, however, as to whether it actually got into production during her life-time. This almost legendary arm was selected by John Churchill, Duke of Marlborough, and introduced into the Army under his auspices. The "Brown Bess" was a fine gun, and a great improvement over its predecessors. With only a few modifications it served the British army for well over 100 years. It had a good flint lock attached by two screws with bridles for both the tumbler and frizzen. On the lock plate it bore the cypher of the Queen and the broad arrow denoting government ownership. Sometimes it bore the name of the maker instead. The barrel was 46 inches long, round for its entire length, and of about .75 caliber. It was fastened to the stock by four pins in addition to the tang screw, and there was an ornamental raised band at the breech. An artificial oxidation or acid pickling process colored the barrel brown and thus gave rise to its nickname "Brown Bess." The stock was walnut, and the mounts were brass throughout,

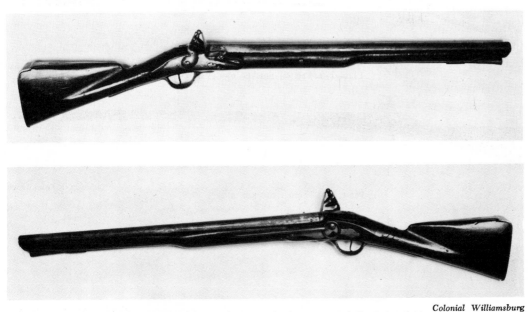

Colonial Williamsburg

Plate 166. British musketoon of the type described in 1764.

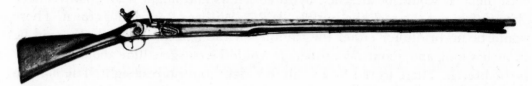

Plate 167. French musket, model 1717. Muskets of this model conforming exactly to specifications are almost impossible to find. This one has a straighter butt than usual and lacks the barrel band and fore-end cap.

Plate 168. French musket, model 1728. Note that this specimen lacks the band retaining springs.

Plate 169. French musket, model 1746, surcharged "U.S." during the Revolution.

Plate 170. French musket model 1763.

Plate 171. French musket model 1777.

Plate 172. French musket model 1777. (Dragoons)

although some early examples were mounted in iron. The ramrod was wooden, and there was a lug for the attachment of a bayonet on top of the barrel.[9]

It was with this arm that Queen Anne set out to replace the motley array of firearms that William III had gathered. The number of these earlier arms with Queen Anne's cyphers on them that are found in America may indicate that it was these arms which she sent to the colonies for their use as she replaced them with the new model at home.

The changes that occurred in the British musket during the remainder of the period were mainly concerned with the length of the barrel, the shape of the brass mountings and the introduction of the iron ramrod. The first change in barrel length occurred late in the reign of George II, probably just before 1760. At that time the length was reduced to 42 inches. It continued that length until sometime in the late 1770's when a final reduction cut it to 39 inches.[10]

During this period there were several changes in the mountings. The length of the tang of the butt plate was reduced about the same time as the introduction of the 42 inch barrel. The key or side plate, which was cast with a convex surface and a long tail in the first model was made flat in the 42 inch model, but retained the tail. The first guns of the 39 inch model used the same key plate as the 42 inch, but soon changed to a convex plate without a tail. Both of the first two models had four ramrod thimbles with the upper one usually trumpet shaped. The third model reduced the number to three and made the first two thimbles trumpet shaped. The heavy mouldings of the trigger guard of the first two models were done away with, and the guard was much lightened in the third model.

The introduction of the iron ramrod was a slow and gradual process. It began about 1724 and continued sporadically over a long period. As late as 1757 some regiments still were only partly equipped with them. These new iron ramrods were usually made with flat "button" heads and without a worm for removing cartridges.[11]

There were also two significant changes in the cock. In the first model and early years of the second model, a tenon on the top jaw of the flint vise slid in a mortise in the tang of the cock. In later years on the second model, a slot was cut in the back of the jaw so that it fitted around the tang, which had been modified somewhat to make this possible. Finally, whereas the head of the flint screw on the first two models was slotted only, the head of the screw of the third model was both slotted and pierced.

It should also be noted that while it was not related to any particular model, the general shape of the lock plate followed the same evolutionary changes found in contemporary locks on other guns. That is, the earliest specimens had lockplates that curved sharply downward at the rear while in other specimens

Plate 173. French musketoon, model 1776.

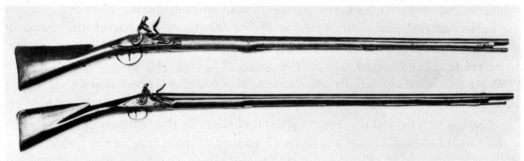

Plate 174. Semimilitary guns. Top: New England, c. 1690-1710, iron mounted with fruit wood stock. Bottom: New England, c. 1770, brass mounted with curly maple stock. Note the bayonet stud underneath the barrel.

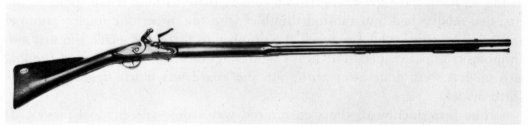

Plate 175. American Revolutionary musket by Deacon Barrett of Concord, Mass.

the lock gradually straightened across the bottom. Also the surface varied between convex and flat according to contemporary preference.

Finally, of course, the locks were marked differently. Each sovereign used his own cypher, although all three Georges used the same one. Some locks, particularly those made before 1760, are dated and bear the names of the individual contractors who made the arm. Others simply bear the words "Tower" or "Dublin Castle" depending upon the arsenal from which they were issued. Exactly when the practice of marking arms with "Tower" or "Dublin Castle" instead of makers' names began is not known. Some of the later examples of the first model are so marked, and towards the end of the period of the second model, it seems to have become universal.

In addition to the standard infantry musket, there was also a lighter officer's model known colloquially by the older term of fusil or fuzee. Throughout the entire period it generally followed the design of the regular musket but was lighter, better made, and often embellished with decorations. The brass mounts were usually cast or engraved with ornamental designs, and there was often a silver wire inlay on the wrist of the stock. The normal practice in most British regiments at the beginning of the period was for the officers to carry espontoons and the sergeants to carry halberds. As the period progressed, however, officers in some regiments began to carry fusils, and during the Seven Years War and later, in the Revolution, the officers, including sergeants, changed to fusils almost exclusively for field use in America.[12]

There are also plain muskets with government locks and broad arrows indicating government ownership which are otherwise exactly similar to these officers' fusils. According to tradition, these are artillery and light infantry muskets. It is known that the artillery had long been issued muskets lighter than the usual infantry model. When the concept of light infantry was developed, whether by General Wolfe as some claim or by some more obscure military

U. S. National Museum

Plate 176. Committee of Safety musket by H. Watkeys of New York.

Warren Hay Collection

Plate 177. Committee of Safety musket by Lewis Prahl of Pennsylvania. The cock is an early replacement. The original was undoubtedly flat with a bevelled edge.

Author's Collection

Plate 178. Committee of Safety musket bearing the Maryland proof mark.

[169]

genius, about the middle of the 18th century, these troops were armed with the light artillery musket. No one has as yet been able to produce definite documentary evidence that these are indeed the artillery or light infantry muskets, but the assumption seems justified since no other light muskets of the period are known.[13]

One other form of the smoothbore long arm carried by British troops was the musketoon or carbine. Both terms were used synonymously during at least the first half of the 18th century, the later differentiation based upon the presence or absence of rifling had not yet developed. Several different forms of these

Plate 179. Maryland proof mark.

musketoons are known. Some are found made from regular infantry muskets with eight or ten inches cut off the barrel. Most of the earliest specimens seem to have been made in this manner. A warrant dated April 17, 1756, calls for carbines 4 feet 3 inches long with a ring and bar for attachment to a swivel, and in 1764 the standard carbine had a 28½ inch barrel of about .66 caliber and an overall length of about 44 inches. In all instances the general design and decoration followed that of the contemporary infantry musket.[14]

After the English models the French were probably the next most widely used muskets in America during the years from 1689 to 1783. From the outset,

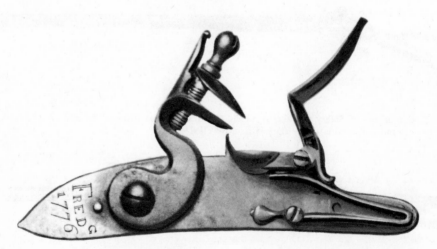

Robert L. Miller Collection
Plate 180. Lock from a Fredericksburg Manufactory musket.

Arthur A. O'Neill Collection

Plate 181. Rappahannock Forge musket.

Arthur A. O'Neill Collection

Plate 182. Lock from Rappahannock Forge musket.

the period was characterized by wars involving England and France. For most of the period the colonies fought with England against France and knew the French musket only as an enemy weapon. But with the coming of the Revolution and the beginning of the shift in alignment which brought France into the struggle on the side of the colonists, French arms began to become more and more common weapons to Americans. By the end of that struggle the colonists had begun to prefer the French pattern to the Brown Bess, and soon set out to make it the basis for American muskets for the next fifty years. Many of the early French arms are still found in America, mostly in New England and New York, and the evidence is that these arms were used here for many years after they had been discarded in France. A specific instance of this is the fact that a lock from a French musket model 1717 was found on the battlefield of Guilford Courthouse where it had apparently been dropped by an American soldier in 1781.[15]

Unlike the British musket which underwent only a few easily recognizable changes, the French musket of the period passed through 15 different models. The differences in these models were often slight and hard to detect, and the

[171]

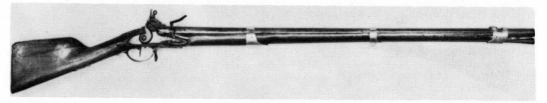

Plate 183. Banded German musket.

Richard K. Sprague Collection

Plate 184. Pin-fastened German musket.

Robert James Collection

Plate 185. Prussian musket.

West Point Museum

picture is further complicated by the fact that many guns were produced that differed slightly from the specifications.

The first really regulation French musket was the so-called model of 1717. Prior to that time muskets had varied widely. Both matchlock and flintlock were used until 1699, when the matchlock was formally abandoned. Then, although the King supplied the new flintlocks to his troops, they varied widely according to the ideas of the different makers. Also, the individual troop commanders were responsible for replacements, and there was no effective check on the selection of arms that they made as long as they were flintlocks. A regulation of January 4, 1717 contained the specifications for a new infantry musket, and the Royal Manufactories at St. Etienne, Maubeuge, and Nozon near Charleville were shortly placed under the control of inspectors of the Royal Artillery Corps, thus setting the stage for the first standard French musket. The model 1717 and its successors through the model 1777 are cataloged briefly below: [16]

Musket, Model 1717

Round barrel 46 inches long with a flat face on top running to within 5 inches of the muzzle. Bayonet stud on top of barrel, which is fastened to the stock by 4 pins. There is also one band around the barrel and

[172]

stock at about the normal position of a middle band. All mountings are iron. Sling swivels are round and are fastened on the left side of the piece, one on the barrel band and the other on a ring bolt set in the stock just to the rear of the screw plate. The butt plate is prolonged up the comb of the stock and fastened by a pin. There are 3 ramrod thimbles. The lock plate is flat. The pan is iron, chamfered, and with a fence. There is a vertical bridle from the frizzen screw to the frizzen spring screw. The goose neck cock is flat, and the jaw screw is slotted only. The ramrod is wood. Total length: 62½ inches. Caliber: .69.

Musket, Model 1728

Similar to the preceding with the following differences: The barrel is held to the stock by 3 bands, of which the upper band has two rings and a funnel for the ramrod. All bands are held in place by springs set to the rear of the bands. The vertical bridle between frizzen screw and frizzen spring screw is abandoned and instead there is a bridle in the normal fashion from pan to frizzen screw. The wooden ramrod has a slightly bulbous metal band at the tip.

Musket, Model 1746

The barrel has 8 long flat faces. The first band is very short, and the middle and lower bands are held in place only by friction. The bridle has been removed from the lock, and the iron ramrod has a button head.

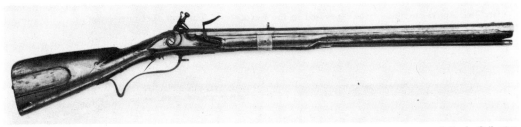

Author's Collection

Plate 186. German pattern rifle dated 1725 used in Pennsylvania.

Bucks County Historical Society

Plate 187. Rifle made in Pennsylvania and carried by Edward Marshall on his "Indian Walk" of 1737.

Total length reduced to 62 inches. Otherwise similar to the preceding model.

Musket, Model 1754

Same as the preceding except that the bridle is returned to the pan, the upper band is lengthened again, and the sling swivels are moved underneath the gun.

Musket, Model 1763

Barrel 44½ inches long with two short flat faces, one on either side at the breech. Mountings similar to the preceding except that the upper

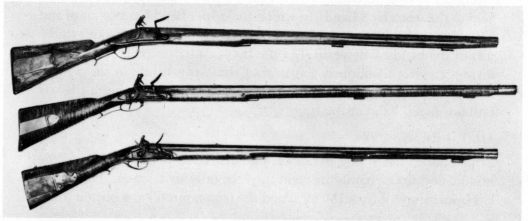

Joe Kindig, Jr. Collection

Plate 188. American rifles of the type used in the Revolution. The top specimen is mounted in iron.

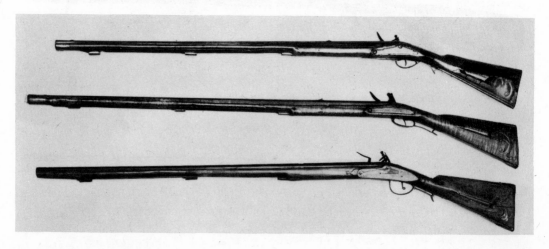

Joe Kindig, Jr. Collection

Plate 189. Reverse side of the rifles in the previous illustration. Note that the rifles have been reversed in order from top to bottom.

Joe Kindig, Jr. Collection

Plate 190. Detail of the lock of the iron-mounted rifle showing construction details. Even on this very crude specimen there is some relief carving.

band carries both a brass front sight and a ramrod retaining spring and the tang of the butt plate has been shortened. The sling swivels are oval instead of round. The cock is reinforced, and the head of the jaw screw is pierced. The iron ramrod has a trumpet head. Total length: 60 inches. Otherwise it resembles the preceding model.

Musket, Model 1766

Similar to the preceding except the construction is lighter, the ramrod retaining spring is attached to the underside of the barrel, the swivels are flat, and the ramrod has a button head.

Musket, Model 1768

The trigger guard is a separate piece passing beneath the trigger bow and holding the trigger. The swivels are oval once more, and the total length is reduced to 59 inches. Otherwise it resembles the preceding model.

Musket, Model 1770

Exactly the same as the model 1768 except that the lockplate is convex, the bands are stronger, and the ramrod retaining spring is moved to the lower band.

Musket, Model 1771

The only changes from the model 1770 consist of the removal of the bayonet stud to the underside of the band, the strengthening of the barrel, and the increase in total length to 60 inches. In some specimens the comb of the stock is quite small.

[175]

Musket, Model 1773

Exactly similar to the preceding except the ramrod retaining spring is once more attached to the underside of the barrel.

Musket, Model 1774

The tail of the frizzen is cut square. The ramrod retaining spring is returned to the lower band, and the ramrod itself has a pear-shaped head. Otherwise no changes from the model 1773.

Musket, Model 1777 (Infantry)

The barrel has five short flat faces at breech and a tenon at the muzzle to receive the retaining screw of the front band. The front band carries the ramrod retaining spring and a brass front sight. The middle band is held by a screw which enters the stock. The lower band is held by a spring. The changes on the lock consist primarily of the addition of a brass pan without fence but set at an angle, a convex reinforced cock, and the return of the curled tail on the frizzen. Total length: 60 inches.

Musket, Model 1777 (Artillery)

Resembles the infantry musket except that the barrel is reduced to slightly over 36 inches in length, and the furniture except the swivels is brass. The total length is $51\frac{1}{2}$ inches.

Musket, Model 1777 (Dragoons)

Resembles the infantry musket except that the barrel is reduced to $42\frac{1}{2}$ inches. All furniture is brass except the middle band which has two rings over the barrel and is iron. Total length: $57\frac{1}{2}$ inches.

Musket, Model 1777 (Navy)

Similar to the infantry musket except the length, which is the same as the dragoon. All furniture, including swivels, is brass.

Just as with the British, there were also light muskets for French officers. The spontoon which had previously been regulation for commissioned foot officers was abandoned in 1754, and the regulation officers' fusils begin with the model of that year. In each instance they resembled the contemporary infantry musket but were lighter and better made, and the furniture was often decorated with engraving.[17]

Although the infantry musket had been standardized in 1717, the carbine or musketoon was left to the discretion of the various corps until 1763. The only consideration given was that they should all be of the same caliber. In 1763,

Company of Military Collectors & Historians
Plate 191. Revolutionary rifleman in typical
dress and equipment. Drawing by H. Charles
McBarron, Jr. Courtesy the Company of Military Collectors & Historians.

however, a standard model was adopted. A second followed in 1766, and a third
in 1777. These arms may be described briefly as follows: [18]

Musketoon, Model 1763

Round barrel 31 inches long. Full stock prolonged to the very muzzle.
The lock resembles the infantry musket. All furniture is brass except
the swivels and swivel bar, which are iron. Both the front and middle bands are double, the middle band supporting a sling swivel, and
the rear band supporting the forward end of the swivel bar. The rear
end of the swivel bar is held by the rear lock plate screw. A second
swivel is fastened to the underside of the butt. Thus, having both reg-

[177]

Plate 192. German jaeger rifle of the type used in the Revolution.

ular sling swivels and a swivel bar the musketoon could be carried either on a regular sling or on a shoulder belt and snap. The iron ramrod has a button head. Total length: 45 inches.

Musketoon, Model 1766

The stock is shortened, stopping 14 inches from the muzzle. There is one band, of iron, to which the swivel band is attached. The iron front sight is attached to the barrel.

Musketoon, Model 1777 (Heavy Cavalry)

Similar to the model 1766, but longer. The barrel is $33\frac{1}{3}$ inches long, and the overall length is 46 inches. The bands and swivel bar are brass. The stock has a cheek piece, and the iron ramrod has a pear-shaped head.

The British and French muskets and musketoons thus far described made up the bulk of such arms found in America during the period under consideration. There were also, however, some American made firearms and, particularly during the Revolution, some arms from other European countries.

From the earliest periods American gunsmiths had made and repaired military firearms. There were certain general characteristics that marked their production, but individual tastes and abilities as well as a lack of specific regulations prevented any approach to uniformity. Militia laws usually required every man to own a firearm. It had to be a flintlock but there was normally no other restriction. A few colonies did set minimum lengths for musket and carbine barrels. Massachusetts and Connecticut, for instance, required musket barrels to be at least 42 inches long and carbine barrels at least 30 inches long, but no maximum was set. Thus all manner of variation was possible.[19]

The bulk of these American made firearms of the early 18th century resembled their British contemporaries. The barrels were almost always pin fastened. Escutcheon plates similar to those on the Brown Bess are often found, and in general the hardware resembled that on British pieces, although it was frequently iron instead of brass. Sometimes, of course, actual pieces from British or French muskets were used to produce these arms. The thrifty colonist would not think of throwing away anything so valuable as a gun part, and consequently these parts were used over and over again in many different combinations until they finally wore out.

The stocks also normally followed British design although there were two distinctive local variations. Particularly noticeable is the fat belly and massive comb of the muskets and other long arms made in the Hudson Valley where the Dutch influence carried over in stocks as well as in hardware. In New England generally, the slender so-called "Queen Anne" stock with the bottom line of the butt slightly concave, was highly popular. There were some fat bellied stocks in New England, too, but normally they were flatter and lacked the heavy comb of the Hudson Valley products. Naturally these stocks were made of American woods, usually either black walnut or maple. It is possible for an expert in such matters to distinguish American walnut from European varieties even after it has suffered the rigors of two or more centuries, but a curly maple stock is a relatively sure sign of American workmanship recognizable even to the layman.

The average colonist could not afford to own a selection of guns, and so he normally chose one which would serve him well in hunting and also pass inspection on muster days. Thus the distinction between military and sporting arms is almost lost. Some examples of each, of course, are quite obvious, but a great many fall in between and are known to collectors generally as "semi-military." These arms are usually sturdy pieces. Their caliber varies normally between .70 and .75. They do not have sling swivels, and since a man was allowed his choice between a sword and a bayonet, they usually do not have bayonet studs.

With the coming of the American Revolution and the consequent dire need

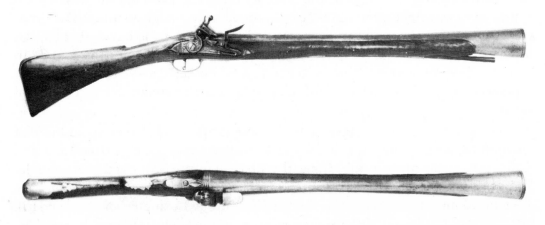

Author's Collection, National Rifle Association
Plate 193. American blunderbuss stocked in curly maple, c. 1720-1730.

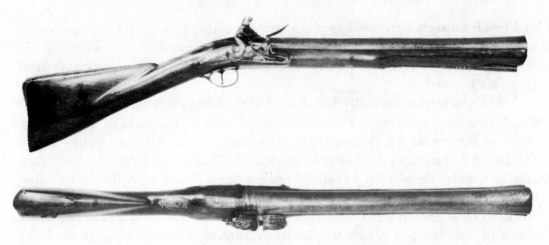

Plate 194. English blunderbuss by Oakes of London, dated 1718. Despite its very slight flare, this gun scattered shot in a wider pattern than the widely flared American gun illustrated above.

for arms, however, there was a decided change in the entire situation. Every means to obtain arms was exploited including confiscation, contract production by American smiths, purchase abroad, and the purchase of all available arms already in the country. In addition many soldiers brought their own weapons with them and theoretically received a special compensation for doing so.

Those firearms made by individual gunsmiths under contract to local committees and councils of safety have so caught the attention and fired the imagination of collectors that considerable confusion has developed over what may and what may not legitimately be called a Committee of Safety musket. The term is frequently used to denote any American musket made and used during the Revolution, but this is obviously inaccurate usage. Many arms were made in America and used during the war with no connection whatsoever with a committee of safety. Again, the phrase cannot be used to designate all muskets purchased and issued by committees or councils of safety, for these included foreign arms as well as nondescript guns picked up wherever they could be found. In its pure sense, the phrase "Committee of Safety musket" can refer only to those muskets made under a specific contract for a particular committee or council of safety.

Once these premises are accepted, it immediately becomes apparent that the number of guns that can be accurately called Committee of Safety muskets is sharply curtailed. For one thing, the first committee contracts were not let until the late spring and early summer of 1775. Therefore there could have been no Committee of Safety muskets at Concord or Lexington or Bunker Hill. Also, as new state constitutions were written and new governments established, the functions of the committees and councils of safety devolved upon other

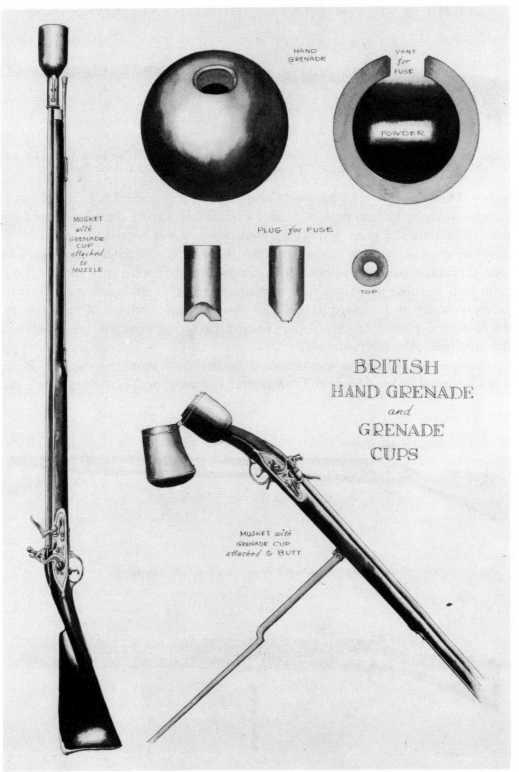

HAND
GRENADE

VENT
for
FUSE

POWDER

MUSKET
with
GRENADE
CUP
attached
to
MUZZLE

PLUG *for* FUSE

TOP

BRITISH
HAND GRENADE
and
GRENADE
CUPS

MUSKET *with*
GRENADE CUP
attached to BUTT

Company of Military Collectors & Historians
Plate 195. Drawing by Herbert A. Sherlock.

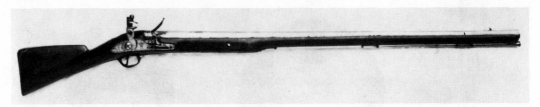

U. S. National Museum

Plate 196. British wall piece believed to have been used on a gunboat in the naval battles on Lake Champlain. The caliber is 15/16 of an inch, and the overall length is 72¾ inches.

bodies. Thus the period of the true Committee of Safety musket lasted only two or three years on the average, and since the output during that time was never great the number of guns falling into that category was remarkably small.

The most important fact about these Committee of Safety muskets, however, is that the contracts under which they were made were very specific. From them it is possible to obtain not only descriptions of the guns manufactured for each colony in that short period, but also, through a survey of all these contracts, a good picture of the type of firearm preferred generally in America at the outbreak of the Revolution.

Before reviewing the specifications of the individual colonies in detail, it is of interest to note that the Continental Congress in Philadelphia took con-

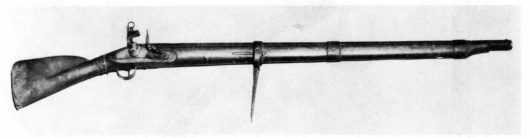

Joe Kindig, Jr. Collection

Plate 197. American iron-mounted swivel gun from the Chesapeake Bay area.

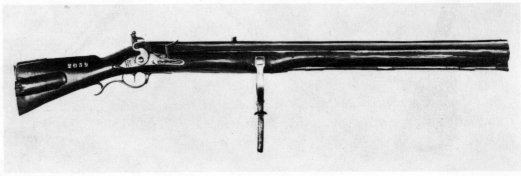

West Point Museum

Plate 198. Rappahannock Forge wall rifle.

siderable interest in the local programs and frequently offered advice to individual colonial governments. In July 1775, two resolutions were passed indicating the type of musket in favor with that national body. Then, on November 4, the following detailed resolution was passed:

> *Resolved* That it be recommended to the several Assemblies or conventions of the colonies respectively, to set and keep their gunsmiths at work, to manufacture good fire locks, with bayonets; each firelock to be made with a good bridle lock, 3/4 of an inch bore, and of good substance at the breech, the barrel to be 3 feet 8 inches in length, the bayonet to be 18 inches in the blade, with a steel ramrod, the upper loop thereof to be trumpet mouthed: that the price to be given be fixed by the Assembly or convention, or committee of safety of each colony. . . .[20]

Massachusetts set up its specifications the day before Congress passed its detailed resolution; yet the musket called for is of the same design preferred by Congress:

> . . . *Resolved*, That for every effective and substantial Fire-Arm which shall be manufactured in this Colony with a barrel of three feet and nine inches in length that will carry an ounce ball, a good bayonet with a blade not less than eighteen inches in length, a steel ramrod with a spring to retain the same, two loops for gun strings, and the maker's name stamped or engraved on the lock . . . and resemble in construction, and, as nearly as may be, equal in goodness with the King's new arms there shall be allowed . . . the sum of three Pounds.[21]

The maker of the gun was required to prove it at his own risk with 4½ inches of powder, a ball, and wads on each. Some of the guns were then to be stamped MB (Massachusetts Bay) on the barrel near the lock.[22]

Connecticut set its standards as early as April 1775, when the following bill was passed by the General Assembly:

> *Resolved*, That the three thousand stands of arms to be procured for the use of this Colony be of the following dimensions, to wit: the length of the barrel three feet ten inches, the diameter of the bore from inside to inside three-quarters of an inch, the length of the blade of the bayonet fourteen inches, the length of the socket four inches and one quarter; that the barrels be of a suitable thickness, with iron ramrods, a good substantial lock, and a good stock well mounted with brass and marked with the name or initial letters of the maker's name.[23]

All such arms manufactured in the colony by May 1, 1775 were to be purchased "at a reasonable price." In March 1776, the committee purchased some imported barrels and locks that fitted the specifications and passed them out to local gunsmiths for stocking and mounting. After May 1776 Connecticut also began the practice of impressing needed guns from their owners. These impressed arms were then stamped with the initials of their former owners with the promise that payment would be made in due time.[24]

Rhode Island apparently set up no specifications for its arms. For the most part it relied on the unusually ample supply of public arms which had been built up in the magazines of its various towns throughout the entire colonial period. Beginning in 1776, these guns were supplemented by purchases from individual citizens and dealers and later by imports from foreign countries. One distinguishing characteristic, however, is found in the fact that all arms purchased were ordered to be stamped with the Rhode Island coat of arms and the letters CR.[25]

New Hampshire, like Rhode Island, let no specific contract for arms. Instead the colony periodically appropriated money and sent out agents to purchase whatever they could find in the line of serviceable firearms. One of the

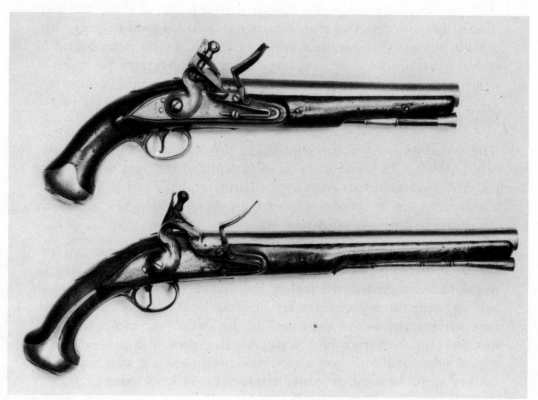

Author's Collection

Plate 199. British military pistols, late type above. early model below.

favorite hunting grounds for these agents was the Salem-Marblehead area of Massachusetts. Eventually conditions became so bad that when Washington wrote the colony in 1777 to ask about the possibility of purchasing some muskets for the use of Continental troops, the Committee of Safety was forced to reply:

"Fire arms cannot be procured from us that can be depended upon."
They added they were also practically without undependable ones.[26]

In New York, the Committee of Safety supplied contracting gunsmiths with a "Brown Bess" and an English lock as patterns and required them to follow them both in design and quality.[27]

Pennsylvania required that its muskets have barrels 3 feet 8 inches long "well fortify'd, the bore of sufficient size to carry 17 Balls to the Pound." The bayonets were to have blades 16 inches long. Contractors were issued a pattern, apparently a "Brown Bess," to guide them in the construction of the desired gun. Since Pennsylvania gunsmiths were so well known, the colony was faced with a particular problem. Buyers from other states were purchasing most of their products. To put an end to this situation, the Pennsylvania Council of Safety passed a law forbidding anyone to take a firearm out of the colony without a specific license. In March of 1776 the council established a provincial gunlock factory since the main deterrent to the swift production of muskets was a shortage of locks.[28]

Complete data on the arms purchases of New Jersey are not available, and nothing at all has been found on those of Delaware. From such records as are obtainable, however, it appears that New Jersey relied more on scattered purchases than on systematic contracts. The nearby Pennsylvania gunsmiths were a special temptation until that state forbade the exportation of firearms.[29]

Maryland defined its standards on August 30, 1775, when it required:
. . . good subsantial proved Musquets, 3½ Feet in the Barrell, and of three Quarters of an Inch in the Bore, with good double Bridle Locks, black walnut or Maple Stocks and plain strong brass mountings, Bayonets with Steel Blades 17 Inches long, steel Ramrods, double Screws, priming Wires, and Brushes fitted thereto, with a pair of brass Molds for every Eighty Musquets to cast 12 Bullets on one Side, and on the other side, to cast Shot of such Size, as the Musket will chamber three of them, for such a Sum not exceeding Ten Dollars and two Thirds of a Dollar in Bills of Credit. . . .[30]

Another statement a short time later indicated that the barrels were pin fastened. Some barrels were later especially ordered with full inch bores. The Council appointed Thomas Ewing as an inspector in Baltimore, and there he proved all submitted muskets with an ounce of powder and two balls. He

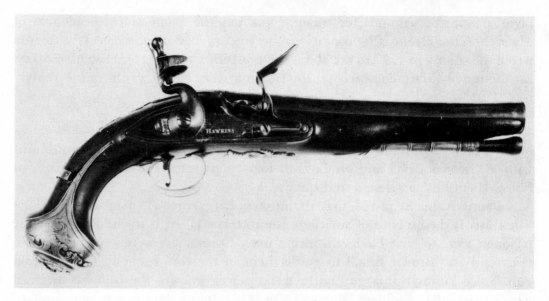

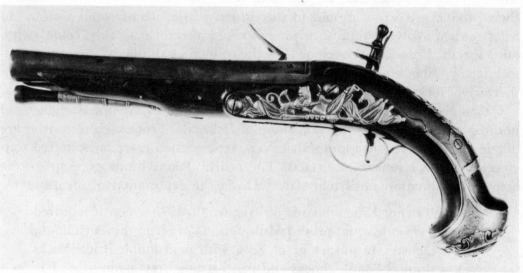

Plate 200. One of a pair of silver-mounted pistols by Hawkins of London which are believed to have belonged to George Washington.

[186]

had a proof stamp made at that time. The initials or device that this stamp bore are not definitely known, although two muskets found in Maryland and conforming to that Colony's specifications bear a proof mark somewhat resembling a *fleur de lys* [see cut].

Ewing was a rigid inspector, once rejecting as many as 19 out of 32 muskets presented to him; but the Council was forced to abandon its standards at least to the extent of accepting iron as well as brass mountings and single-bridled as well as double-bridled locks. Which bridle was omitted is not clear, but it was probably the arm from the pan to the frizzen since that was the second of the two bridles to come into general use. Like Connecticut, Maryland was also forced to import suitable barrels and locks in March 1776 and hire local gunsmiths to stock and mount them. In another move to correct the shortage of locks, the Council established a state gun lock factory at Frederick in 1776.[31]

Virginia pursued a path somewhat different from those of the other colonies and established a state manufactory in the very beginning. Under the leadership principally of Fielding Lewis and Charles Dick, the Fredericksburg Manufactory proceeded in the fall of 1775 to repair arms already in the colony and in the late spring of 1776 it began also to manufacture arms, generally following the British pattern but somewhat lighter and often mounted in iron instead of brass. Two complete muskets made in the Fredericksburg Manufactory have survived along with one lock on a repaired musket. The barrel lengths in the two complete specimens measure 39 inches and 37 inches respectively. The Manufactory continued in operation until 1783, but lack of funds and labor after 1780 seriously hampered its work and relegated it primarily to the position of a repair shop.[32]

At the same time Virginia contracted with individual gunsmiths and such private establishments as James Hunter's Rappahannock Forge at Falmouth, across the river from the Fredericksburg Manufactory. A typical contract called for 200 stands of arms:

> . . . to consist each of a Good Musket three feet eight Inches in the Barrel, three quarters of an Inch bore Steel rammers, the upper thimble trumpet mouthed the lower thimble with a spring to retain the ramrod, bridle Lock, brass mounting, a Bayonet eighteen inches blade with a Scabbard, one pair bullet moulds, to mould sixteen Bullets, to every forty guns; a priming wire & brush to each musket.[33]

In the southern colonies of North Carolina, South Carolina and Georgia an entirely different situation prevailed. The war came more slowly to this area, with only two engagements before 1777. Consequently there was more time in which to procure arms. Also, the West Indies and Bermuda were close at hand and easy to reach. The ports of these islands were soon swarming with war profiteers who possessed large stocks of good and bad European arms. It was natural, therefore, that these colonies should turn to that source for the bulk of their supplies. Even so, some few arms were purchased locally, and in regard to these, the Georgia Council of Safety on January 2, 1776, passed a resolution to the effect that all such guns should conform as nearly as possible to the specifications set forth by the Continental Congress.[34]

An analysis of all of the above specifications leads to some interesting conclusions. There is a remarkable similarity in the requirements for all these muskets. All specify iron or steel ramrods and bridle locks. Calibers are all about .75. Barrel lengths are remarkably even, most of them 44 to 46 inches with only Maryland and possibly New York and Pennsylvania as short as 42 inches. In every instance barrels are to be pin fastened. In fine, all resembled the British "Brown Bess." Also, contrary to the popular myth that Committee of Safety muskets were not marked because of the fear British reprisals, many were marked, some colonies even requiring it.

With all these specifications available, it would seem reasonable that a student could expect to examine a given specimen and determine immediately whether it was or was not a Committee of Safety musket. This, unfortunately,

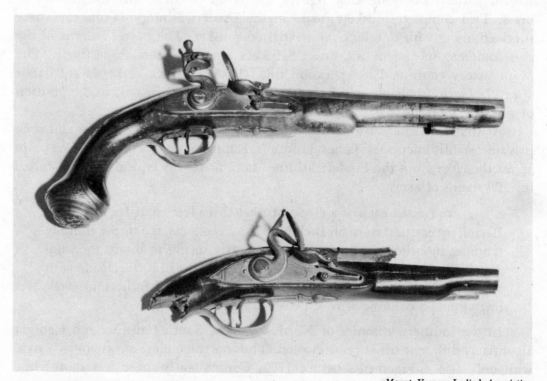

Mount Vernon Ladies' Association

Plate 201. Pair of British brass barrelled pistols by Wooley which are believed to have been owned by George Washington.

[188]

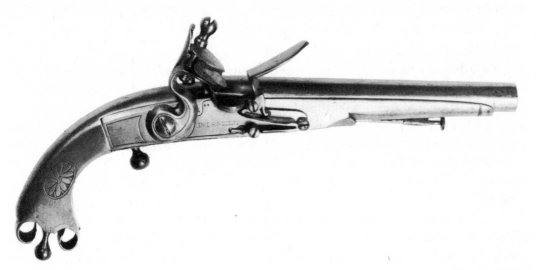

Herbert A. Sherlock Collection
Plate 202. Scottish enlisted man's pistol by Bissell marked "RHR" on the barrel.

is not the case. There are very few muskets in existence today which meet all the qualifications established by any colony.

There are two possible explanations for this situation; either practically no Committee of Safety muskets have survived, or individual contractors deviated from the specifications. In regard to the first possibility, it is true that such muskets would be expected to have an unusually low rate of survival. They were made and issued during the early years of the war; they saw severe service; and there was no steady supply of replacements. Also, since they were worn out and since they were not of the newer and more popular French pattern and caliber, many of those that remained in government arsenals at the end of the war were weeded out when the "third class" arms were sold or broken up for spare parts. Thus the possibility of almost total destruction is good.

On the other hand, the possibility that individual contractors deviated somewhat from specifications is also good. This possibility is enhanced by the fact that there are muskets in existence today which bear the names of men who had Committee contracts and which, while conforming in general to the Committee pattern, differ in one or two details. The most frequently found variance is in the barrel length, but in some few instances it is the caliber that differs from the specified size. Naturally, the marks on some of these specimens are suspect. On others, however, the marks are apparently genuine, and the piece is obviously American. With these latter pieces, then, the important question is posed: Are these guns Committee of Safety muskets or does the fact that they differ in some degree from the contract specifications disqualify them? In this connection it is known that Maryland was forced to accept iron as well

[189]

as brass mountings and single-bridled as well as double-bridled locks, and it seems probable that other colonies made similar exceptions as long as the pieces complied with the general specifications.

In addition to the arms produced in America, many more firearms were imported from Europe both by individual colonies and by Congress. Benjamin Franklin, who had been a colonial representative in England, left orders for arms with French, Dutch and even English dealers before returning to America at the outbreak of hostilities. Pliarne Penet et cie, a French firm, sent one of their members to Philadelphia in 1775 and contracted with the Secret Committee of Congress for firearms. In the spring of 1776 Congress sent Silas Deane, a merchant and former member of Congress from Connecticut, to France to obtain arms and military equipment as well as to induce the French government to lend money and perhaps to enter the war as an ally. In addition to these contacts, emissaries from various colonies traveled in Europe, purchasing arms in France, Holland, and Prussia; while European concerns sent arms to ports in the West Indies and Bermuda where they made contact with colonial agents.[35]

Of all the arms imported from foreign countries, by far the most came from France. The largest number of French arms and the best ones were obtained by Deane from the French government. France had been severely beaten in the series of wars with England for control of the American Continent, and the French government was therefore predisposed to help the colonies in their struggle with Great Britain in any way it could. One way was to supply arms. To sell arms directly to the colonies could be construed by England as an overt act of war, and so a dummy corporation was set up under the name of Roderique Hortalez et cie.

In charge of this corporation was an agent named Pierre Caron de Beaumarchais, who took his orders directly from the French foreign minister. It was with these men that Deane had his dealings, and through this subterfuge arms and equipment were released from the French arsenals and shipped to America. Because of English protests the ships were forced to clear for the French West Indies, and some actually went there and left their stores to be picked up by American ships. Others sailed directly to America. In all, 10 ships carried these stores to the colonists, the first arriving in April, 1777 and the last in November of that year. Only one was captured by the British. By early 1778 the French were openly at war with Great Britain, and the false trading company and private means of shipping were no longer necessary. Thereafter arms were sent directly from the Government, and also French officers like Lafayette sometimes brought arms with them for their own troops.[35]

Other arms purchased in France were not necessarily as good as the standard French army muskets. The profiteers bought their stocks just as cheaply

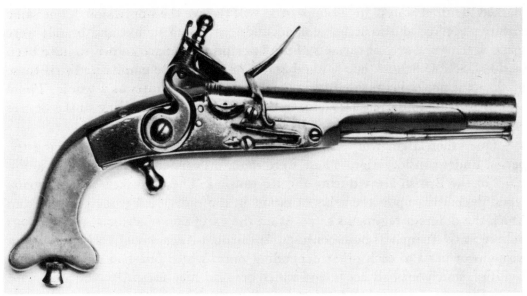

Author's Collection

Plate 203. Scottish enlisted man's pistol by Waters.

as they could, and consequently they had many obsolete and poorly made arms. Pliarne Penet et cie were among the worst offenders. An offshoot of this company operating under the name of James Gruel & Co. bought their guns in Liege in the Austrian Netherlands (modern Belgium); and the Belgian muskets of that period were just as bad as those of the 19th century.[37]

The muskets obtained by contract in Holland, although relatively few in number, were good arms. They were both shorter and lighter than either the English or French muskets, comparing almost to the officers' fusils of those countries. The .65 caliber barrel was round and attached to the stock by three brass bands, the first of which was double and very long (8 inches). It is the light construction and the long front band which form the most easily recognizable characteristics of these guns. Among those specimens still surviving, the name most often found on the lockplate is Thone, Amsterdam. The barrel usually bears the Amsterdam proof mark. Almost every known surviving specimen of a Dutch musket in America can be traced to Massachusetts, indicating the probability of a state contract. Since Franklin was a representative of the Colony of Massachusetts when he placed his contract in Holland, it is possible that these arms derive from that source.

All of these arms, domestic or imported, that belonged to the regular army were supposed to be so marked. The first order was issued January 30, 1777, and follow-up orders were sent out periodically during the next three or four months directing that all arms of any sort belonging to the United States should be marked "United States" in "such parts as will receive the impression." The same directive applied also to accoutrements and tools. Both stamps and brands were made bearing the several variants of the inscription that are known to have been used—"US," "U States," and United States." It should be emphasized that these marks were put only on those arms belonging to the country as a whole. Those arms belonging to individual states were marked or not according to the desires of the local authorities.[38]

One other large group of muskets was also present in America during the period under consideration. These were the arms carried by the German auxiliaries of the British army during the Revolution. These muskets were of many types, depending upon the arms situation in the individual principalities from which the different regiments came. With the exception of Prussia, the weapons picture in Germany was most confused. Individual rulers bought and sold entire weapons or parts to each other depending upon which one had manufacturing facilities, which one had needs, and which one had surpluses. Also, the arms with which they equipped the forces they rented the British were not necessarily their best but often represented the dregs of their arsenals.

Nevertheless there are certain characteristics that mark most German muskets (or Hessian muskets as they are popularly called). No matter whether the piece is pin-fastened or banded, the mountings are brass. The butt plate is thin so that it frequently cracks through at the angle of the tang, which is long, and extends far up the comb. The stock is heavy, having a particularly massive butt with a high comb. The lock also is large, particularly the frizzen, which is often square across the top. All have an elliptical brass front sight either on the barrel or front band. The bayonet stud is usually under the barrel.

One particular type of German musket that can readily be recognized is the Prussian model. It is slightly lighter than the others. The wrist of the stock is long, and the short comb is particularly angular and narrow. The barrel is fastened to the stock with 10 separate pins and a tang screw. Because of Frederick the Great's well-known opposition to sending German troops to America, few of these muskets reached this country. Nevertheless two are known, both traditionally captured at the Battle of Bennington. If this tradition is correct, and the fact that the only two known specimens are both attributed to this engagement seems to indicate that it may be, it is possible that the Brunswick grenadiers may have been equipped with this arm.[39]

In addition to the smooth bore musket which formed the principal weapon of the period, there were also some rifles. Most important of these was the American rifle or 'Kentucky" or "Pennsylvania" rifle as it is popularly called. Developed on the frontier, principally by the German gunsmiths who settled in Pennsylvania, it attracted world-wide attention during the American Revolution, and the development and perfection of this rifle was the only American contribution to military science during the entire period from 1689-1783. In all other respects, American military men retreated from their advanced position and followed the lead of Europe, sometimes, in fact, becoming even more conservative than the older countries.

There was no new principle involved in the American rifle. The theory of rifling was centuries old. The use of greased cloth patches around the ball to insure a tight fit in the rifling has often been advanced as an American innovation, but in reality it had long been used in Germany. What the Americans did do was to lengthen the barrel for greater accuracy, improve the balance, and develop a new and distinct style of construction and decoration. More important, however, the dependence of the frontiersman on his gun for food and protection and his daily use of it for these purposes led to a high degree of proficiency in its use by a relatively large segment of the population. In Germany, the ancestral home of the American rifle, shooting contests with the rifle had once been a very popular sport, but in the 18th century the custom almost ceased. Only a few foresters and wealthy individuals had either the opportunity or the inclination to become marksmen.[40]

There is little or no reliable information concerning the formative years of the American rifle. The German and Swiss gunsmiths who developed it did

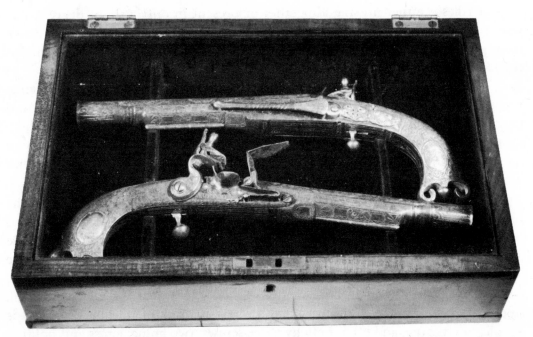

Lexington Historical Society

Plate 204. Scottish pistols carried by Major Pitcairn at the battle of Lexington.

not reach Pennsylvania in any numbers until after 1710. Undoubtedly their first products were exactly the same as those they had been accustomed to manufacture at home, although they probably used the native maple that later became almost the trademark of the American rifle. In all such developments change comes gradually, and it is probable that the first true American or "Kentucky" type did not emerge until almost the middle of the century, and even after that some smiths still made rifles that were predominantly German in character.

There is much popular misunderstanding today concerning the dating of the developments in Kentucky rifle design. It is a common mistake for the layman to assign a Revolutionary date to the much more numerous specimens of the late 1780's and 90's. Once a few of the scarce specimens that are truly Revolutionary have been studied, however, the difference becomes apparent.

Despite the differences that are to be expected wherever individual craftsmanship is involved, there are certain characteristics common to most of these early rifles. The lock is hand-forged, usually without a mark. The lock plate is attenuated at the rear to a long point. The lower line of the plate is often slightly concave. The cock is goosenecked and lacks the incised decorations of the later imported locks. The lines of its curves are also usually less angular. The pan is often filed with several facets rather than being rounded, and frequently there is no bridle for the frizzen.

The stock is relatively straight and heavy. The deep drop so characteristic of later rifles is either missing altogether or present in only a slight degree. The wrist appears slender when viewed from the side, but is actually quite thick from side to side as it joins the butt which is sometimes as much as 3 inches thick. The shoulder end of the butt lacks the sharp crescent so characteristic of later rifles and is relatively straight. There is almost always some raised carving. It may be slight, perhaps no more than a slight decoration around the lock and tang mortises, the beginning of the comb, or on the cheek piece, or sometimes a raised edge along the ramrod groove. Some examples, naturally, have more than this, but almost all have some. Other decoration is slight or non-existent. The multiple brass and silver inlays are of a later period.

There are two or three equally characteristic shapes for the mountings. The fore-end cap is normally short, usually only about an inch long, and it is attached by a screw which enters the bottom flat of the barrel. The trigger guard is wide and heavy. It is double; that is, there is a section behind the loop in which the trigger is housed. The strip of metal that crosses this space is almost straight, not sharply crescentic as in later models. Usually this guard is attached to the stock by a pin in front of the bow and a screw in back of it. The key plate is simple, fairly large, and often held by three screws, two going across and holding the lock, and the rear one simply entering the wood of the stock. The patch box cover is simple, usually of brass, hinged at the fore end, but sometimes it is a sliding cover of wood.

As has been emphasized before, when individual craftsmanship and initiative are involved, it is impossible to date a given piece accurately by the presence or absence of any one feature. The general appearance of the whole gun and the relationship of all the features to each other must be carefully weighed, in addition to the known facts about the maker if it is a signed piece, before a tentative date can be assigned to it.

Since the period of the greatest production and variation of the American rifle occurred after 1783 and also since the rifle was only secondarily a military weapon, it would be beyond the scope of this work to trace the development

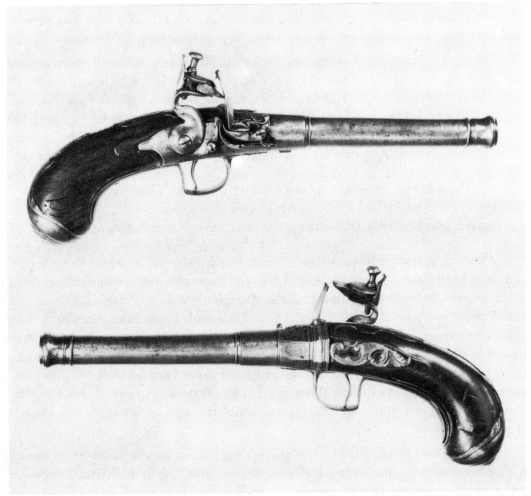

U. S. National Museum

Plate 205. Queen Anne screw-barrelled pocket pistols by Cornforth.

of the type any further. Rather, it is more to the point to trace its appearance and influence on the military scene.

The rifle was used only slightly in the French Wars. Insofar as those wars involved settlers on the frontiers of Pennsylvania and Maryland in raids and Indian depredations, these frontiersmen used their rifles in reply, and after the end of the last of the French Wars in 1763, they continued to use their rifles against the Indians until the end of the troubles caused by Pontiac's conspiracy when relative peace along the frontier allowed them to concentrate principally upon hunting. Rifles, however, were not used to any extent in the military campaigns conducted by the British. The anonymous author of a letter describing the Braddock expedition against the French at Pittsburg in 1755 said of the French fire that it was "like Poping shots, with little explosion, only a kind of Whiszing noise; (which is a proof the Enemy's Arms were rifle Barrels)." Actually, there is no evidence that the French had rifles, but the letter is an indication that the men on the expedition were acquainted with that weapon.[41]

When the American Revolution broke out, however, riflemen were among the first to spring to the colors. The Act of June 14, 1775 which was the birth of the United States army, authorized the raising of 10 companies of riflemen, six from Pennsylvania and two each from Virginia and Maryland "to join the army near Boston, to be employed there as light infantry. . . ." John Adams wrote his wife concerning this act and added of the ten companies of riflemen:

"These are an excellent species of light infantry. They use a peculiar kind of musket, called a rifle. It has circular or—grooves [sic] within the barrel, and carries a ball with great exactness to great distances."[42]

The first of these rifle companies under Daniel Morgan reached Washington at Cambridge, Massachusetts late in July, and soon the other companies joined them. Hugh Stevenson's company from what is now West Virginia, Cresnap's and Price's companies, both raised in and around Frederick, Maryland, and eight companies from Pennsylvania organized into a battalion under Col. William Thompson. Here these rifle companies, now 12 in number, put on demonstrations of skill with the rifle that spread their fame far and wide, as one company reputedly placed all their shots in a 7-inch target at 250 yards, and a marksman from Virginia put eight successive shots through a board 5 x 7 inches at 60 yards.[43]

The rifle had thus arrived upon the military scene as a force to be reckoned with. Many modern accounts have been written praising it highly as a weapon and making extreme claims for it as the most important single arm of the war. It is interesting, however, to examine the actual record and see just how well

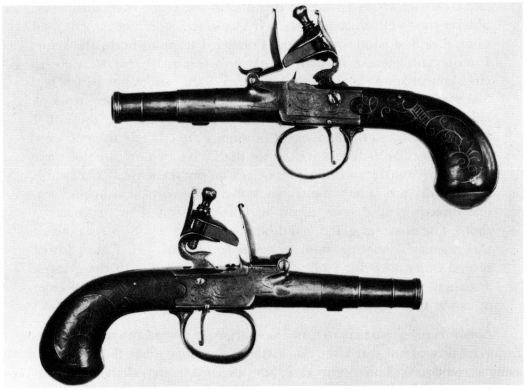

Plate 206. Screw-barrelled pocket pistols with box locks and silver wire inlay.

the rifle really did serve in that conflict and what contemporary soldiers thought of it.

First of all, the rifle's greatest asset was its accuracy even at long range. Many tales have been recounted about this quality, but perhaps the best comments are those of Major George Hanger, the trained British marksman, whose comments about the musket were quoted above. Recounting an experience, Major Hanger wrote:

Colonel, now General Tarleton, and myself, were standing a few yards out of a wood, observing the situation of a part of the enemy which we intended to attack. There was a rivulet in the enemy's front, and a mill on it, to which we stood directly with our horses' heads fronting, observing their motions. It was absolutely a plain field between us and the mill; not so much as a single bush on it. Our orderly-bugler stood behind us about three yards, but with his horse's side to our horses' tails. A rifleman passed over the milldam, evidently observing two officers, and laid himself down on his belly; for in such positions, they always lie, to take a good shot at a long distance. He took a deliberate

[197]

and cool shot at my friend, at me, and at the bugle-horn man. Now observe how well this fellow shot. It was in the month of August, and not a breath of wind was stirring. Colonel Tarleton's horse and mine, I am certain, were not anything like two feet apart; for we were in close consultation, how we should attack with our troops which laid 300 yards in the wood, and could not be perceived by the enemy. A rifle-ball passed between him and me; looking directly to the mill I evidently observed the flash of the powder. I directly said to my friend, "I think we had better move, or we shall have two or three of these gentlemen shortly amusing themselves at our expense." The words were hardly out of my mouth when the bugle-horn man behind me, and directly central, jumped off his horse and said, "Sir, my horse is shot." The horse staggered, fell down, and died. . . . Now speaking of this rifleman's shooting, nothing could be better. . . . I have passed several times over this ground and ever observed it with the greatest attention; and I can positively assert that the distance he fired from at us was full 400 yards.[44]

Major Hanger participated in the Burgoyne campaign, and consequently became a prisoner of war after the battle of Saratoga when that whole British army surrendered. This event gave him an even better chance to study the American rifle, as he reported:

I have many times asked the American backwoodsman what was the most their best marksmen could do; they have constantly told me that an expert rifleman, provided he can draw good and true sight . . . can hit the head of a man at 200 yards. I am certain that provided an American rifleman was to get a perfect aim at 300 yards at me standing still, he most undoubtedly would hit me, unless it was a very windy day. . . .[45]

So much for the rifle's advantages; its disadvantages were serious. It was not equipped with a bayonet, and it was slow to load. The lack of a bayonet left the rifleman helpless in the face of a charge and powerless to charge himself. The technique of loading was briefly this. A charge of powder was poured down the barrel. Then a greased patch was centered over the bore, a bullet placed on this and both rammed down together with the bullet being wrapped in the patch and thus ensuring a tight fit. It was impossible to use prepared ammunition such as that employed with the muskets, although a device was developed which helped with the patching of the bullet. This device consisted of a board with several holes bored through it. In each hole the user inserted a patched bullet so that when the time came he could place the hole over the bore and push the patched bullet right down the barrel. Still the charge had to be measured separately, and the patched bullet had to be seated accurately, instead of just being thrown in as was the case with the musket.

It will be remembered from the discussion of the musket how much emphasis was placed on rapidity of fire and consequently how adversely the slowness of the rifle would affect it as a military weapon can well be imagined. The emphasis on the use of the bayonet was not then mentioned, but it should be borne in mind that battles were frequently decided in hand-to-hand combat with the bayonet. Once the opposing troops closed with each other there was no time to reload. The American defeat at Bunker Hill was at least partially attributable to the lack of bayonets, and Samuel Webster, pleading for bayonets after the battle, declared "'tis barbarous to let men be obliged to oppose Bayonets with only gun Barrells. . . ." With this Gen. John Sullivan agreed and

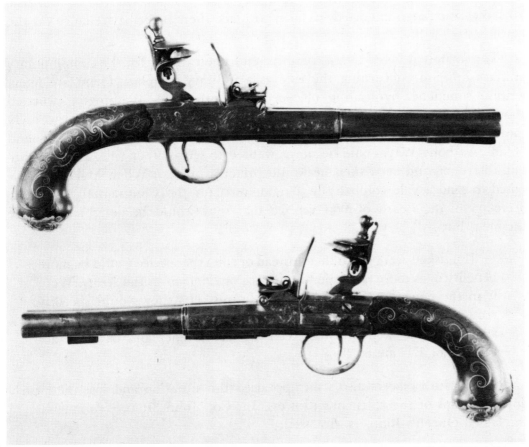

U. S. National Museum

Plate 207. Double-barrelled holster pistols with box locks and silver mounts by Parke of London which belonged to Gen. Daniel Roberdeau.

added his plea for more bayonets so that the same situation would not be repeated.[46]

The popular myth that the Revolution was fought between American troops who shot from behind trees and stone walls and British soldiers who were silly enough to stand in tight formations in the open is completely fallacious. With the exception of Kings Mountain, and of the retreat from Concord and Lexington no major battle of the war followed this pattern. Even at Concord the American forces charged down the hill toward the British at the Bridge, and at Lexington the Minute-men were drawn up in a line across the village green, quite in the open. American troops generally fought in the accepted European fashion as any tactical study of the battles of the Revolution quickly reveals. The Continental "Regulars" took pride in their firm ranks and their bayonet charges. At Stony Point the muskets were unloaded and American bayonets alone carried the day. Baron von Steuben, the celebrated drill master of the Continental Army, never taught "backwoods" warfare, and Washington in the climatic Yorktown campaign exhorted his men to place their principal reliance on the bayonet.[47]

Fortunately it is not necessary to depend upon theory for the contemporary military opinion concerning the rifle as a military weapon. There are many written comments by leading officers from both sides. Washington worried about the lack of bayonets and for that reason ordered Morgan's men to carry spears. He also felt there were far too many riflemen in the army. General "Mad" Anthony Wayne said he never wanted to see another rifle, at least without a bayonet, and even then he would prefer a musket. When Maryland proposed to send a rifle company to Philadelphia for the Continental Army, the Secretary of the Board of War replied that they would be delighted to have the men, but—

"If muskets were given then instead of rifles the service would be more benefitted, as there is a superabundance of riflemen in the Army. Were it in the power of Congress to supply musketts they would speedily reduce the number of rifles and replace them with the former, as they are more easily kept in order, can be fired oftener and have the advantage of Bayonetts."[48]

The British officers also soon appraised the situation and lost their early apprehensions of the rifleman's prowess. Lt. Col. John Simcoe, commander of the famed Queen's Rangers, declared:

"The riflemen, however dexterous in the use of their arm, were by no means the most formidable of the rebel troops; their not being

[200]

armed with bayonets, permitted their opponents to take liberties with them which otherwise would have been highly improper."[49]

The *Middlesex Journal* of December 31, 1776 quoted another British officer as remarking:

> ... about twilight is found the best season for hunting the rebels in the woods, at which time their rifles are of very little use; and they are not found so serviceable in a body as musketry, a rest being requisite at all times, and before they are able to make a second discharge, it frequently happens that they find themselves run through the body by the push of a bayonet, as a rifleman is not entitled to any quarter.[50]

Even Major Hanger, the great admirer of the rifle's accuracy, wrote:

> Riflemen as riflemen only, are a very feeble foe and not to be trusted alone any distance from camp; and at the outposts they must ever be supported by regulars, or they will constantly be beaten in, and compelled to retire.[51]

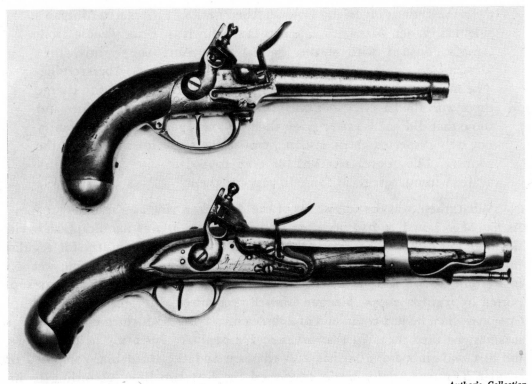

Author's Collection

Plate 208. French enlisted men's pistols. Model 1776 above, model 1763 below.

[201]

Plate 209. American made pistol of the Revolution with brass mounts and a maple stock found in Pennsylvania.

Again, Hanger:

. . . meeting a corps of rifle-men, namely *riflemen only*. I would treat them the same as my friend Colonel Abercrombie, . . . treated Morgan's riflemen. When Morgan's riflemen came down to Pennsylvania from Canada, flushed with success gained over Burgoyne's army, they marched to attack our light infantry, under Colonel Abercrombie. The moment they appeared before him he ordered his troops to charge them with the bayonet; not one man out of four, had time to fire, and those that did had no time given them to load again; the light infantry not only dispersed them instantly but drove them for miles over the country. They never attacked, or even looked at, our light infantry again, without a regular force to support them.[52]

What, then, was the usefulness of the American rifle as a military weapon? As has been noted, it had accuracy and range, but it was handicapped by its slowness and lack of a bayonet. Obviously it was useless as an arm for regular infantry, but its assets and the special skills of its users made it a fine weapon for certain troops, such as light infantry, scouts, snipers, and skirmishers supported by regular troops. Morgan himself recognized this, and at the battle of Cowpens when he had command of a force embodying both riflemen and regular infantry, he used them in that manner. He deployed his army in three lines, the first two embodying militia and riflemen and the third line composed of regular infantry. As the battle developed the first two lines, according to instructions, took as heavy a toll of the advancing British as they could and then retired behind the line of regulars which met the enemy with a volley and the bayonet.

Riflemen were also expert in coping with the Indian allies of the British in the North. They had long been used to dealing with the Indians on their own frontiers, and so took to this task naturally. Washington had this in mind when he sent Morgan's riflemen to join the army opposing Burgoyne on his march south from Canada. In announcing the action he wrote to General Horatio Gates:

> I am forwarding . . . Colonel Morgan's corps of riflemen, amounting to about 500. These are all chosen men, selected from the Army at large, well acquainted with the use of rifles, and with that mode of fighting which is necessary to make them a good counterpoise to the Indian . . .[53]

The rifle, then, was not, as some have claimed, "the gun that won the American Revolution," but supported by musketry and used in accordance with its special attributes, it was a very useful and deadly weapon.

In addition to the American rifles, there were also two types of rifles used in the British army, the British Ferguson and the German jaeger. The Ferguson will be discussed later with other breech-loading and repeating weapons, but since both the American and German rifles were descended from a common ancestor, the close relationship between the two invites a comparison here. Their advantages and disadvantages were similar, and the men who used them had much in common.

The German soldiers who carried the jaeger rifles were trained woodsmen and hunters, and they were expert marksmen. Shortly after the war began, George III realized the need for such men to act as light infantry and skirmishers in the forests of America. Consequently, beginning with the treaty of January 9, 1776 with Brunswick, companies of these men were frequently requested from the various German states who supplied troops. Thus these riflemen filled from the very beginning the role that was assigned to the American riflemen only after much trial and argument.[54]

The rifles that these men used differed from one another as greatly as did the American rifles of the period. Most of them were privately purchased or presentation pieces and thus were non-regulation. Yet, like the American rifles, there was a general uniformity of design which characterized them. They were short, usually about 44 or 46 inches in overall length. The locks were comparatively large and closely resembled those on the German muskets. The mountings, which were normally brass, included two ramrod thimbles, an exceptionally deep and long trigger guard, and a butt plate and screw plate similar to those on the muskets. Sometimes there was a brass fore-end cap on the stock, but often

[203]

there was none. Almost all had patch boxes in the butt with sliding wooden covers, but some hinged brass covers were also used. Attachments for a sling were provided by a brass swivel near the fore end and a button-like stud on the butt below the extension of the trigger guard. The barrel was pin-fastened, and the ramrods were of wood.

Much has been written about the effectiveness of the German rifle. Unfortunately much of it has been purely imaginary. One of the most popular of all these myths about these arms, is that the ball fit the bore so tightly that the soldier was forced to carry a mallet with him in order to drive it down the barrel. All of this was advanced to prove that the German rifle was a slow and laborious weapon to load and required special paraphernalia which was apt to be lost. Actually such was not the case. No mallet was needed. In fact, the same system of greased patches used in America was widely known and practiced in Germany, and the jaeger could load his rifle just as swiftly as the Pennsylvanian.[55]

The chief drawbacks of the German rifle were the same as those of its American counterpart. Although loading was not the long laborious process that some have pictured it, it was still slower than the musket, and it had no bayonet. Because of these factors, the jaegers carried swords and were used only as light infantry or as marksmen supported by musketry, just as their American counterparts finally came to be employed.

Conversely, the advantage of the German rifle was the same as that of the American. It was highly accurate and effective at long ranges. This was a source of contemporary amazement to some Americans, and even as late the siege of Yorktown one of the Continental soldiers posted opposite some jaegers wrote with apparent surprise:

> ". . . a few shot were fired at different times in the Day and about sunset from the Enemy's Redoubts—we had five or six men wounded; one mortally & two others by the same Ball. The Execution was much more than might have been expected from the Distance, the dispersed situation of our Men and the few shot fired."[56]

There were, in addition to the standard muskets and rifles, certain special purpose military firearms. These included the blunderbuss, the genade launcher, and the wall piece or rampart gun.

The blunderbuss, so often erroneously associated with the early 17th century in the popular mind, really came into its own in the 18th century. As was noted previously, there were a few blunderbusses in America prior to 1700, but they were rare. The blunderbuss was a weapon designed to do great execution against a tightly pressed group in a confined space. A contemporary work described them as "proper for the defence of a barrack, stair case, or door."

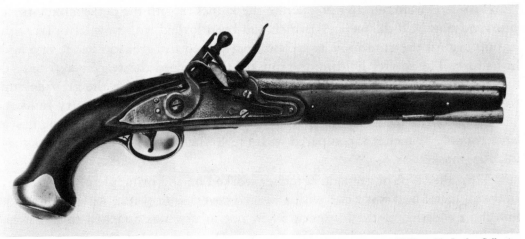

Plate 210.   Rappahannock Forge pistol.

It was also a fine arm for quelling a riot in a street or courtyard or for re-pelling boarders on ships. The greater urbanization that came with the 18th century as well as a coinciding increase in naval activities considerably enlarged the demand for this type of fire arm, and hundreds were produced to satisfy it.[57]

Washington at one time considered arming the American cavalry with blunderbusses and wrote the Board of War:

> It appears to me that Light Blunderbusses on account of the quantity
> of shot they will carry will be preferable to Carbines, for Dragoons, as
> the Carbines only carry a single ball especially in case of close action.[58]

The Board, however, demurred, and the carbine remained the standard cavalry weapon.[59]

Nevertheless, the Americans did make use of the blunderbuss as a naval weapon, and so did the British. These weapons are found with both iron and brass barrels. Usually for naval use the iron barrels were covered with black paint as a deterrent to the corrosive action of salt air and water. In all respects except for the shorter barrel, the large bore, and the flaring muzzle, these arms resembled the contemporary muskets, and consequently they can be dated by the same characteristics.

The grenade launcher as part of a standard musket seems to have been a specifically English development, and from there it spread to America. Two types of launchers were made. One consisted of a detachable launching cup that attached to the muzzle of a modified musket, and the other was a mortar-like arrangement built into the butt of a specially designed gun. Examples of both types exist in the Tower of London, the earliest bearing the cypher of James II, and later ones dated 1728, 1739, 1740, 1744, and 1747.[60]

[205]

Two men were required to operate the launcher with the detachable muzzle cup. One man held the musket (which had been loaded with powder only) with its butt against the ground. The second man placed the grenade in the cup and lit its fuse. The soldier holding the musket then pulled the trigger and prayed that the piece wouldn't misfire. Muskets intended for use with the grenade cup were made with shorter and stouter barrels than the normal infantry musket. One example in the museum of the Royal United Service Institution has a barrel of only 33 inches as compared with the 46 inch barrel of the contemporary infantry musket.[61]

The other type of grenade launcher worked on the principle of the mortar. In the all metal butt was a cup with a hinged cover. A steel rest, which folded up into the underside of the forestock when not in use, was attached to the stock between the trigger guard and the "swell." In order to fire this launcher, the musket was placed with the muzzle (presumably plugged) on the ground. The rest was pulled out to steady the piece, and the hinged cover of the cup was opened. The cup in this instance was fired like a mortar and was provided with a vent and pan with a sliding cover. Consequently the next step was to place a charge of powder in the cup; then open and prime the pan, seat the grenade and light its fuse; and then fire the charge in the cup. Probably two men were required to operate this launcher also.[62]

In 1694 Maryland ordered 10 "hand mortars" from Great Britain. It is not absolutely clear from the comments what type it was that Maryland received, but indications are that it was the type with the muzzle cup. It is a matter of record, however, that the Maryland authorities were not pleased with them when they were received. They admitted that they were "good of the Sort," but directed their agent in England to try to find some that could be discharged in such a way that the fire from the charge in the barrel would ignite the fuse of the grenade and thus enable one man to operate the apparatus without assistance and with less danger to himself and his gun if the piece misfired.[63]

The final form of special purpose weapon, the wall or rampart piece, almost enters the field of heavy ordnance. It has been included here, however, because it followed the general design of the contemporary musket, differing only in size and in the addition of a bar for a swivel. The idea of the rampart gun is almost as old as the conception of the fire arm. Known variously as an *arquebus á croc* or amusette, it was simply a huge musket—or later sometimes a rifle—designed to fire at greater ranges than the ordinary arm. It could not carry the power nor approach the range of even a small cannon, but its vastly lighter weight made it adaptable for use on small boats and in quickly erected forts where it was not practical to transport cannon.

The usual wall piece of the early 18th century and the Revolution was a smooth-bored flintlock. In France, some matchlocks were still used for the purpose at the very beginning of the century. It remained for America, however, to introduce the real innovation in the form of the rifled rampart gun.[64]

These rifled wall pieces were made early in the Revolution and quickly proved effective. On February 4, 1776, Fielding Lewis, Commissioner of the Fredericksburg Manufactory, wrote his brother-in-law, George Washington, that:

"... I propose making a Rifle next week to carry a quarter of a pound ball. If it answers my expectation, a few of them will keep off ships of war from our narrow Rivers, and be usefull in the beginning of an engagement by land..."[65]

It is not definitely known that Lewis achieved his goal and produced these rifles. No surviving specimens are known. There are, however, four surviving specimens made at the famed Rappahannock Forge, a private enterprise under

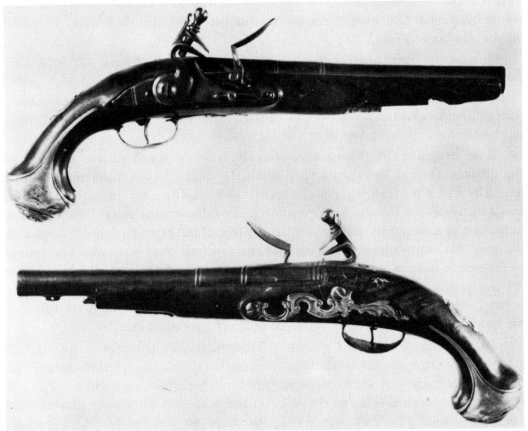

U. S. National Museum

Plate 211. European silver-mounted pistols with Rappahannock Forge locks which belonged to Gen. Charles Lee.

the direction of James Hunter and located directly across the river from Fredericksburg. These huge rifles all weigh in the neighborhood of 50 pounds and are roughly five feet long. They are full stocked, have sliding wooden patch boxes and wooden ramrods. The brass mountings are reminiscent of those on the lighter rifles of the period. Three of the surviving specimens have round barrels, the fourth is octagonal. The design of the exterior parts of the locks resemble those on the Fredericksburg muskets so closely that a common origin or at least a common pattern is suggested.[66]

General Charles Lee attested to the effectiveness of these weapons when he wrote Washington from Williamsburg on May 10, 1776, "I am likewise furnishing myself with four-ounced rifle-amusettes, which will carry an infernal distance; the two-ounced hit a half sheet of paper 500 yards distance."[67]

In addition to these various long arms, pistols were also an important weapon in the period under consideration. They were carried by officers of all branches of the service, by cavalry troopers and by sailors. And, as always, they were the personal weapon of the well-to-do private citizen with which he protected his person and his possessions against intruders and defended his honor on the duelling ground.

Just as the British musket wielded the dominant influence on American long arms up through the early years of the Revolution, so the British pistol held sway among the hand guns. The reasons for this situation were the same: the predominance of imports from Great Britain and the familiarity with British service arms through the frequent wars of the period.

The British military pistol apparently was not standardized as early as the musket. During the reigns of William III and Queen Anne these pistols normally had a barrel length of 14 inches and a caliber of approximately .66. In all instances the barrels were pin fastened to the walnut stock. The butt was bulbous and covered by a brass cap with projections extending up the sides of the grip. All mountings were brass, and the ramrods were wooden. The points of difference were minor, but generally included the length to which the butt cap projection extended up the grip, the presence or absence of a bridle on the frizzen, the design of the key plate, the presence or absence of square filing at the breech, and the presence or absence of an escutcheon plate.[68]

By the time of George I (1714-1727), however, British service pistols had achieved the same degree of uniformity as the muskets. The 12 inch .60 caliber barrels were round for their entire length, and there was an ornamental raised band at the breech similar to the ones on the muskets. There was neither rear nor front sight. The lock was similar to those on the muskets but smaller. Usually it simply bore the maker's name, although some carried the royal cypher. The extensions of the butt cap ran well up the sides of the grip. The

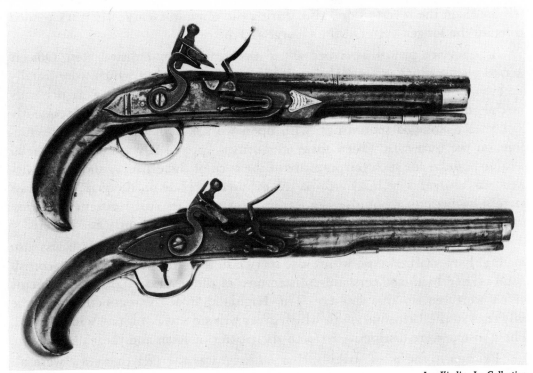

Plate 212. "Kentucky" pistols of the Revolution. Both are maple stocked, and the lower is signed J. Hills.

two ramrod thimbles resembled those on the musket, and the wooden ramrod was capped with brass. There were occasional differences in two items: most escutcheon plates resembled those on the musket, but some were oval; and some key plates were irregular although the majority were of the standard musket pattern, convex with a tail.

About 1760 the second really standard model of the holster pistol was adopted. In this model the barrel length was reduced to 9 inches, and the calibre was increased to .69. The lock resembled that on the 3rd model Brown Bess with the pierced and slotted jaw screw and the top jaw of the flint vise notched to fit around the tang of the cock. Markings were stamped instead of engraved. The extensions of the butt cap were reduced to vestigial lobes. The grip became thicker and shorter, and the escutcheon plate disappeared. The key plate was flat and without a tail, and the number of ramrod thimbles was reduced to one.

In addition to the service holster pistols for cavalry, there were also some government pistols made for navy use. These pistols differed from the holster pistols in that they sometimes had flat reinforced cocks and were equipped with belt hooks on the reverse side. Also, during the reign of George III, they tended to retain the longer barrel of the George II type.

The service pistols described above were carried by enlisted men. Officers carried pistols which generally resembled the issue arms, but which were usually better made and frequently shorter and lighter. Since these pistols were privately purchased and remained the personal property of the officers, they frequently bore nicely modeled mountings, with open work key plates and mask decorations on the butt caps. Often these mountings were of silver since that metal became popular for such purposes about the turn of the century, and frequently there was a silver wire inlay around the escutcheon plate on the grip. The brass barrel also became a popular innovation because of its rust resistant qualities, and officers' pistols of the period with such barrels are frequently encountered.[69]

In addition to the standard British pistols described above, there was also one highly specialized type which saw service in America. This was the Scottish pistol carried by the officers and enlisted men of the several Highland regiments which were sent to this country. The Highland infantry regiments were the only ones in the British army in which every private was equipped with a pistol. These pistols were distinctive in both their exterior form and their mechanism.

Externally the most striking characteristic was the fact that they were all metal, the stock being made of brass. They had no trigger guards, and the trigger itself was usually ball-shaped. The butt was often bilobate in what was known as a kidney or fish-tail shape or else it possessed two scroll-like extensions curving inward below the termination of the butt proper which gave rise to the descriptive "ramshorn" butt appellation. In the center of the butt was a finial which coud be unscrewed and used as a vent pick or oiler. The lock plate was normally cut square across the rear end, and there was usually no bridle from the pan to the frizzen. The ramrod was iron, and there was an iron belt hook on the left side of the stock.

Internally the lock mechanism was reminiscent of the earlier dog lock. The sear acted laterally. There was no half-cock position, and the cock was secured in the full position by the end of the sear which passed through the lock plate and protruded in front of it.

These service pistols were made usually in England, rather than Scotland. Many of those surviving today bear the mark of John Waters of London. Before 1758 these pistols were also often marked HR (Highland Regiment). After 1758 the markings RHR (Royal Highland Regiment) is more frequently found.

Officers' pistols resembled those of enlisted men except that they were usually better made and elaborately decorated. Usually the stocks of officers' pistols were iron instead of brass, and they were frequently inlaid with precious metals. A fine pair of such Scottish officers' pistols with chiseled iron stocks said

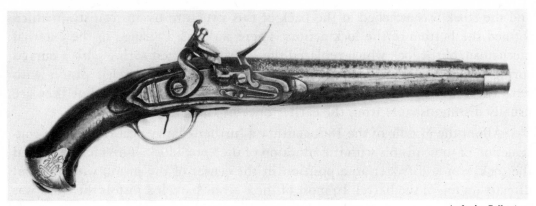

Plate 213. Prussian pistol. The jaw screw and upper jaw of the cock are inaccurate replacements. Virginia bought some Prussian pistols during the Revolution.

to have been used by Major Pitcairn of the Royal Marines at the battle of Lexington is now located in the Hancock-Adams house there.

In England where a network of roads made coach travel the common means of transportation, the holster pistol was largely replaced by smaller belt and pocket pistols for all but military purposes early in the 18th century. In America, however, the changes were not so rapid. Nevertheless, some of the smaller pistols were used here from the beginning, and when the Revolution began some American officers used them as the only weapon they had.

Some of these civilian pistols differed only from the military types in the matter of size. There was, however, one important variety quite distinct from the holster type—the screw-barreled pistol. The principal of this weapon, which allowed the barrel to be unscrewed and loaded at the breech, had been known and used in a limited way from the middle 1600's. It was not until the closing years of the 17th century and the early 1700's, however, that it became popular.

In their earliest form these pistols had barrels which screwed into a breech which extended approximately as far forward as the front end of the lock plate. The lock was of the conventional type. The stock, narrower in the grip and not so bulbous in the butt, extended as far forward as the fore-end of the breech. The butt cap lacked the side extensions of the military type but often had a single extension which carried a short distance up the back of the grip. The escutcheon plate, when there was one, and the key plate were of the standard type, often finely molded and decorated with open work design. The usual metals for these mountings were brass or silver, although a few with chiseled iron or steel mounts are known.[70]

With the reign of Queen Anne an important innovation occurred in the design of these arms. The breech and lock housing were forged in one piece, and the stock was attached at the back of this structure by an iron strap which formed the bottom of the lock action. There was also a change in the external mechanism of the lock which replaced the V-shaped frizzen spring with a curved spring fitted between the pan and the cock. Some screw-barreled pistols with separate locks of the conventional pattern continued to be made, but they are usually distinguishable from the earlier ones by their mounts.[71]

About the middle of the 18th century a further change occurred in the construction of these pistols with the adoption of the "box" lock. This change shifted the cock, pan and frizzen to a position in the center of the pistol, with the pan directly on top of the barrel. In most of these screw-barreled pistols the stock was round in cross section. Some, however, are found with flat sided grips and without butt caps, but most of these were made after 1783.[72]

Second to the British pistols in the influence they wielded on American arms were the French hand guns. Prior to the American Revolution the number of French pistols in America was small. There were, of course, a few in the French colonies, and some were carried by French soldiers in the colonial wars. Yet, since English pistol production in the early 18th century far outdistanced that of any other country in Europe, many of these even had British-made weapons. Just as with the musket, the era of French dominance in American pistols came with the Revolution. Then quantities of the French arms were imported and used, and after the conflict a French pistol was chosen as a model for future American hand guns.

Unlike the British hand guns, there was no standard French pistol model until 1763. Prior to that time the type of arm was left to the decision of the individual corps, the only qualification being that all calibers in the units should be the same. In 1763, an approved model was adopted and fabricated in the Royal manufactories, which previously had been concerned only with the infantry muskets.[73]

There were two versions of the model 1763 pistol, one for cavalry and one for navy use. The difference lay in the mountings which were iron for cavalry, brass for navy. Otherwise they were exactly the same. The .67 caliber barrel was 9 inches long and round throughout its entire length. It was attached to the stock by a tang screw and a long double band at the muzzle, which was held in position by a retaining spring on the obverse side. The walnut stock was long and relatively straight with a hardly noticeable swell at the butt. The butt cap fitted the butt closely and possessed a single short extension up the back of the grip. The key plate resembled those on the contemporary muskets. The ramrod was iron with a button head and decorative turnings just below it. The lock was similar to that on the 1763 infantry musket. It was marked with the name of the manufactory on the lock plate in front of the cock. The year of manufacture was engraved on the barrel tang, and the last two digits of the year of manufacture were stamped on the breech immediately behind the proof marks. As the years passed the lock of the pistol was modified more or less in keeping with the changes in the musket. The cock became convex as did the rear of the lock plate, and the pan changed from its original faceted design to a rounded shape. Even in the navy model, however, the pan remained iron.[74]

In 1776, the French adopted a second model which was first manufactured and marked in 1777. The new model differed considerably from its predecessor and indeed resembled no other contemporary pistol. The .67 caliber barrel was 7½ inches long. It was round and tapered gradually toward the muzzle. It was received in a breech casing of brass which fitted around it on both sides and underneath. This housing also held the lock and received the iron ramrod. The cock and frizzen were iron, but the pan was brass and cast as an integral part of the housing. The frizzen spring was inverted underneath the pan, running in a direction opposite from the conventional one. The butt dropped sharply and was covered by a brass butt cap somewhat similar to the one on the preceding model. A back strap of iron connected it with the barrel tang. There was no fore stock. Those pistols intended for naval use were equipped with a belt hook. The lock was marked with the name of the manufactory in an arc under the cock, and the barrel was marked in the same manner as the preceding model. It was this pistol that served as the model for the first pistols made under contract to the new United States government at the end of the Revolution.[75]

What few pistols were made in America during the early years of the 18th century generally followed the standard British forms. Most Americans of the social classes that were apt to own personal pistols preferred to purchase the products of British gunsmiths, and so it was not until the period of the Revolution that a sufficient number of pistols were made in America to permit a general description or classification. During the conflict there appear to have been two general types of pistol manufactured here. One was a close imitation of the British holster pistol of the period. The other was the so-called "Kentucky" pistol. The former differed from its prototype only in workmanship and materials, such as the wood used in the stocks and the very thin brass used in the mountings. The latter was a distinct American type.[76]

These American pistols differed markedly from other contemporary pistols in a number of respects. They were stocked most often with curly maple or a fruit wood, although some with walnut stocks are known. They usually had octagonal barrels or were at least octagonal at the breech. They had both front and rear sights in a period when few pistols had either; and they were frequently rifled.

There were also other distinguishing characteristics. The grips were sharply

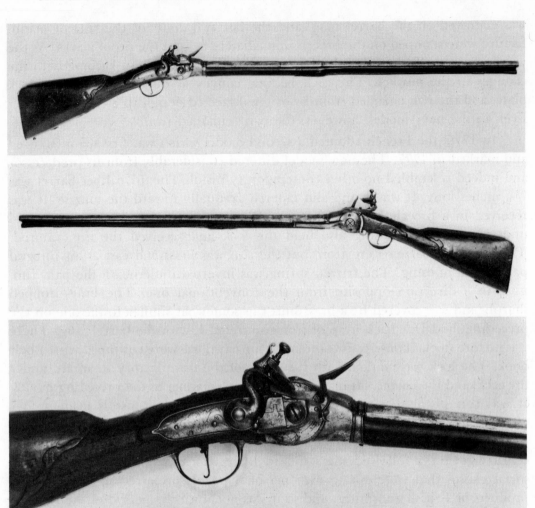

Plate 214. English "Cookson" rifle, late 17th century.

curved, ending in a slender butt with either a close-fitting butt cap or none at all. The mountings were usually brass and resembled those on contemporary American rifles. Frequently there was neither fore-end cap nor ramrod thimble. The barrels were pin-fastened, and the locks were hand-forged, differing only in size from those on the rifles.

Many theories have been advanced concerning whether the "Kentucky" pistol was a civilian or military arm. Probably it was a little of both. However, since almost all known specimens appear to have been made either during the Revolution or War of 1812, it would seem that they were originally made primarily as side arms for American officers in those conflicts.

With the coming of the American Revolution two other types of pistol were introduced to the American scene, the Dutch and the German. Just as the colonists purchased muskets from the Dutch so they also acquired pistols, although in much smaller quantities.

The German pistols used in this country were extremely few in number. The officers of the German troops brought their own personal weapons just as did their French and British counterparts, and they differed just as widely. There were only a few mounted units, and some of these relied principally on the carbine. And there were no German sailors. The service pistols that were used were acquired in the same way as the muskets and thus varied just as greatly. There were, however, certain general similarities. They were brass mounted, the barrels were round, pin-fastened, and of large caliber, often about .75. Cocks were frequently convex and reinforced. Ramrods were iron and occasionally attached to the barrel by a swivel. And almost always there was the typical elliptical brass front sight.

In addition to these standard muzzle-loading firearms of the period, there were also some breech-loaders and even some repeating arms. The desire for breech-loading and repeating weapons is almost as old as the history of firearms, and there were numerous attempts to achieve this goal, beginning at least as early as the opening years of the 16th century.

The first mention of a repeating weapon in America was made by Samuel Niles, who recorded that in September 1722 certain Indians

> . . . were also entertained with the sight of a curious gun, made by Mr. [John] Pim of Boston,—a curious piece of workmanship,—which though loaded but once, yet was discharged eleven times following, with bullets, in the space of two minutes each of which went through a double door at fifty yards' distance.[77]

The principle on which Pim's gun operated is not known, but it could well have been that patented in London by Abraham Hill in 1664. Hill's mechanism was copied by several other English gunsmiths of his own time, notably John Cookson and John Shaw and by a host of others throughout the 18th century. Another John Cookson (1701-1762), probably a lineal descendant of Hill's contemporary, was a gunsmith in Massachusetts, active after about 1720, and he advertised in the *Boston Gazette* of April 12 and April 26, 1756 that he could make a repeating arm similar to those made by Hill and his forebear. Thus this type of repeating flintlock, popular in England from the third quarter of the 17th century, was known and manufactured in Massachusetts early in the 18th century and is therefore a likely candidate for the type made and used by Pim.[78]

The interrelationship of Hill and the Cooksons is worthy of some slight elaboration because of the misconceptions that have been prevalent in America

[215]

for the past quarter of a century. Because the first example of a gun built on the Hill system which achieved widespread notice in America had been made by John Cookson of London, his name was applied to all such guns by the majority of American collectors. Thus the Hill became known as the "Cookson type" repeating flintlock in this country. The picture was further complicated because the first specimen described here had had its date of manufacture altered so that it appeared to have been made a century before it actually was. Since the date it bore was obviously wrong, and since a John Cookson who advertised that he could make such guns lived in Massachusetts, there has been a tendency to accept the American maker as the one and only Cookson. Some have even listed him as the inventor of the type. John Cookson of London, however, has long been known to students in England, and several of these repeating guns made by him and bearing late 17th century dates are preserved in Great Britain. Thus there were definitely two John Cooksons, probably directly related, who made the Hill type of repeating flintlock, one working in England and one in America.[79]

The mechanism of the Hill repeating flintlock was ingenious. The butt contained two tubular cavities, one above the other, which could be filled from the outside through openings with hinged or pivoted covers on the left side. The uppermost of these cavities was filled with balls, the lower with powder. Between these cavities and the barrel was a cylindrical breech block which pivoted on an axis perpendicular to that of the bore. This cylinder could be revolved by means of a lever attached to its left end. Bored in the side of this cylinder were two cavities which could be aligned either with the cavities in the butt or with the bore by moving the lever. Cut into the side of the breech block near the right end of the cylinder was a shallow depression which served as the bottom of the priming pan.

The method of loading was swift and simple. The tubular cavities in the butt were filled separately with powder and balls, and a small magazine in front of the cock was filled with priming powder. Then the muzzle of the piece was pointed up, and the lever was pulled backward revolving the breech cylinder one half turn. This aligned simultaneously the two cavities in the cylinder with those in the butt. The muzzle was then depressed, allowing a ball to fall into one cavity and enough powder for a charge into the other. At the same time the action cocked the piece and moved the hollow serving as the bottom of the pan under the priming magazine where it also was filled. As soon as these actions had been accomplished the lever was returned to its original position. As it revolved the cylinder back again it aligned first one and then the other of its cavities with the bore. The first to align with the bore was the one containing the ball. As it did so the ball rolled forward to the anterior end of the chamber

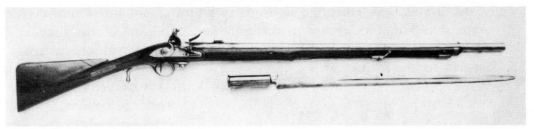

Plate 215. Officer's model Ferguson rifle and bayonet presented by Ferguson to Frederick De Peyster.

where a slight decrease in the diameter of the bore prevented it from going further. Next to align itself was the cavity containing the powder, and this also deposited its contents in the chamber. The same action returned the pan filled with powder to its proper place and pushed the frizzen into operating position. Thus with a simple forward and back movement of the lever the gun was loaded, cocked and primed.

The Hill was an efficient, fast-acting gun. Its great drawback was that it required many hours of work by a highly skilled gunsmith to produce one. Alignments had to be perfect, and the seal against the explosion in the chamber had to be secure or the powder in the magazine would also ignite. In the United States National Museum are preserved the remnants of one of these guns in which the seal was not adequate. Because of these factors the Hill was made by fine craftsmen in many countries for well over 100 years, but the expense of manufacture confined its use primarily to wealthy sportsmen.

Another type of repeating flintlock used in America was that invented by Joseph Belton of Philadelphia. Belton offered his gun to Congress, April 11, 1777, and his letter of that date is the only known surviving evidence of the operation of the piece.

To the Honorable Continental Congress
May it Please your Honors,

I would just informe this Honorable Assembly, that I have discovered an improvement, in the use of Small Armes, wherein a common small arm, may be maid to discharge eight balls one after another, in eight, five or three seconds of time, & each one to do execution five & twenty, or thirty yards, and after so discharg'd to be loaded and fir'd with cartrage as [useal?], which I am ready to prove by experimental proof, and can with eaquel ease fix them so as to discharge sixteen or twenty, in sixteen, ten or five seconds of time, which I have kept as yet a secret, thinking that in two or three Months we might have an armey thus equipt, which our enemy should know nothing of, till they should be maid to know it in the field, to their immortal sorrow—

[217]

And if you Gentlemen are desirous to enquire into this improvement, your Humble Servant, is ready to wait upon you at any time, or place, or he may be waited on at the Widow Ford's, in Walnut Street, between second & third Street.

from Your most Obedient
Humble Servant
Joseph Belton[80]

Philadelphia April 11th 1777

Congress acted swiftly and apparently put some of Belton's guns in service, for on May 3 they passed the following resolution:

> *Resolved,* That . . . Belton be authorized and appointed to superintend, and direct the making or altering of one hundred muskets, on the construction exhibited by him and called "the new improved gun" which will discharge eight rounds with once loading; and that he receive a reasonable compensation for his trouble, and be allowed all just and necessary expences.[81]

With only this meager description, it is impossible to determine exactly how the Belton improvement operated. The reference to predetermined timing of shots and the number of charges, however, would seem to indicate that a fuse or powder train was involved and that once the first charge was ignited, the rest followed automatically.

The only breech-loading arm that was used in any quantity as a military weapon during the period, however, was a rifle developed by Col. Patrick Ferguson of the British Army. In this arm, a plug operating on a screw passed vertically through the breech of the barrel. The lower end of this plug was attached to the trigger guard which acted as a handle. One revolution of the trigger guard in a clockwise direction lowered the plug until its top was flush with the bottom of the chamber in the breech. The plug being thus depressed left a hole in the top of the barrel which communicated directly with the bore. In order to load the gun the barrel was pointed slightly downward, the trigger guard revolved and the plug accordingly depressed. A ball was dropped into the hole in the top of the barrel where it rolled forward until stopped by the lands of the rifling at the end of the chamber. The ball was followed by a charge of powder which was measured simply by filling the cavity of the chamber behind the ball. The trigger-guard was then revolved in a counter-clockwise direction, closing the opening in the top of the barrel and forcing out any excess powder that might have been poured in. The pan was primed separately, and the piece was ready for firing.

The Ferguson rifle was a simple and efficient weapon. Its versatility, ac-

[218]

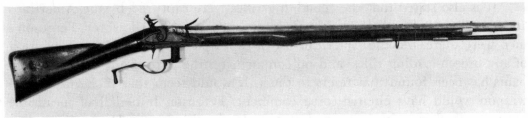

National Park Service

Plate 216. Enlisted man's Ferguson rifle with breech open.

curacy, and rapidity of fire were demonstrated by its inventor at Woolwich on June 1, 1776 before a board of distinguished army officers. A contemporary account declared that:

> . . . he made some experiments . . . with the rifle gun on a new construction which astonished all beholders. The like had never before been done with any other small arms. Notwithstanding a heavy rain and the high wind, he fired during the space of four or five minutes at the rate of four shots per minute, at a target two hundred yards distance. He next fired six shots in one minute, and also fired (while advancing at the rate of four miles an hour) four times in a minute. He then poured a bottle of water into the pan and barrell of the piece when loaded so as to wet every grain of the powder, and in less than half a minute he fired with it as well as ever without extracting the ball. Lastly, he hit the bull's eye lying on his back on the ground, incredible as it may seem to many, considering the variations of the wind and the wetness of the weather. He only missed the target three times during the whole course of the experiments.[82]

Despite the obvious excellence of the Ferguson rifle and its advantages over the standard British military arms, it was used by very few troops in the American Revolution. It is probable that only Ferguson's own company of light infantry in the 71st Regiment was armed with them, although there is a slight possibility that both light infantry companies of the 71st had them. At most, this would indicate a total of less than 200 Ferguson rifles in use.

The records of the use of these arms in America are very sketchy, but it would appear that their primary service was during the New Jersey campaign of 1777 and 1778. They were very definitely used at Brandywine, September 11, 1777, where Ferguson was seriously wounded. While Ferguson was recuperating from his wound, the rifles were retired from use. According to tradition he reassembled the rifle-corps upon his return to duty and used them in his famous engagement at Little Egg Harbor against the Pulaski Legion.

[219]

It is also stated that the remaining rifles were captured by the Americans at Stony Point July 16, 1779. This is by no means certain, however. Ferguson's men were there, but the American list of captured supplies makes no mention of any breech-loading rifles, and no comment on the part of any of the participants has been found that refers to them. It would seem that such an unusual weapon would have elicited some comment. Ferguson himself had meantime been detached from his corps and sent to the South with Sir Henry Clinton as Inspector-General of Loyalist troops. There he was killed on October 7, 1780 at the battle of Kings Mountain.[83]

The Ferguson rifle was not an entirely new invention. Rather it was an improvement over several existing systems. There had been guns with plugs that screwed out of the breech for many years. Some had even been attached to the trigger guard. A musket or rifle on this principle had been recommended for use by engineers in the British army many years before the American Revolution. In all of these systems, however, the plug passed through only one thickness of the barrel and had to be completely removed in order to load. Then it had to be inserted again. All this gave rise to several difficulties. There was the possibility of losing the plug while loading. Also there was the difficulty of aligning the threads of the screws correctly before the plug could be returned, no mean feat for a man under fire. Finally, these plugs had all been made with conventional threads which required several turns in order to remove the plug from the barrel.[84]

Ferguson's improvements over these systems were several. The breech plug passing entirely through the barrel left a hole at the top for loading while the plug remained in the lower thickness. Thus the plug was never removed, ran no risk of being lost or becoming fouled with dirt, and the threads were always aligned for a return to a closed position. Also the plug was made with a fast traveling thread that allowed it to be dropped its complete length in only one turn of the trigger guard. Ferguson further added ingenious channels cut in the thread which greatly reduced powder fouling, and he equipped his rifles with adjustable sights.

Two of the small group of Ferguson rifles used in America during the Revolution have survived the ravages of time. One is a typical private soldier's weapon with a standard government lock and the serial number 2. The other is a fine specimen of an officer's model made by Durs Egg, a well known English gunsmith who later produced many sporting rifles on the Ferguson system.

The private soldier's Ferguson, now preserved at Morristown National Historical Park, is patterned after the contemporary Brown Bess, but with a few notable exceptions. Aside from the breech mechanism and the sight, these dif-

Plate 217. Top of breech of enlisted man's Ferguson rifle showing opening, sight and sling swivel.

ferences include the method of fastening the barrel to the stock by keys instead of pins, the placement of the rear swivel on the side of the stock opposite the lock, and the placement of the bayonet stud underneath the barrel thus requiring a special bayonet. Finally, it had a wooden ramrod, and neither of the forward two ramrod thimbles were trumpet shaped.[85]

The officer's model Ferguson rifle is preserved in the United States National Museum. It is a particularly historic weapon in that it is the piece presented personally by Ferguson to Captain De Peyster, his second in command in the Southern Campaign. This piece differs from the contemporary officer's fusil in the same fashion as the private's weapon differed from the contemporary musket.

The bayonet which fitted these weapons differed considerably from the ordinary bayonet. As was noted above, the fact that the stud was on the underside of the barrel necessitated a bayonet with its slots on the opposite side of the socket from those on the regular infantry bayonets. There were, however, other differences. The blade was wide and flat, not triangular like the musket bayonets, and it was 25½ inches long—7½ inches longer than the musket bayonet.

These, then, were the principal firearms in a century which saw little change. The period began in 1689 with the muzzle-loading smooth-bore musket and pistol as the most popular weapons. In 1783, almost a hundred years later, the period ended with the same weapons still supreme, and without even any notable improvements in their design or construction. Breech-loaders and repeaters had appeared frequently on the scene but had made little impression upon it. The rifle had been developed and achieved considerable prominence as a sporting arm, but it still possessed drawbacks that prevented it from becoming an important military weapon. Changes, however, were not far off. In a few years the percussion cap would be invented, then the expanding bullet which made the rifle the supreme military arm, and finally the metallic cartridge which ushered in the era of the breech-loader and repeater. Change, when it came, was swift. The 18th century was the quiet prelude to these dramatic events.

NOTES—CHAPTER FIVE

1. There are many military texts and drill manuals of the period which are useful. The following is a selected list of some of the better volumes. *Fortification and Military Discipline*, London, 1688. Nicholas Boone, *Military Discipline*, Boston, 1701. *The Perfection of Military Discipline after the Newest Method as Practiced in England and Ireland, &c.*, 4th edition, London, 1702. William Brattle, *Sundry Rules and Directions for Drawing up a Regiment*, Boston, 1733. Humphrey Bland, *A Treatise of Military Discipline*, 4th edition, London, 1740. William Windham, *A Plan of Discipline Composed for the Use of the Militia of the County of Norfolk*, London, 1759. Timothy Pickering, Jr., *An Easy Plan of Discipline for a Militia*, Salem, Massachusetts, 1775.. Lewis Nicola, *A Treatise of Military Exercise Calculated for the Use of the Americans*, Philadelphia, 1776. M. de Lamont and the Chevalier de la Valliere, *The Art of War*, Philadelphia, 1776. Richard Lambert, 6th Earl of Cavan, *A New System of Military Discipline, Founded upon Principle*, Philadelphia, 1776. Col. David Dundas, *Principles of Military Movements Chiefly Applied to Infantry*, London, 1788. Friedrich Wilhelm August Heinrich Ferdinand, Baron Von Steuben, *Regulations for the Order and Discipline of the Troops of the United States*, editions of 1778, 1779, 1794, and others. Pickering's *Plan* is particularly useful to the beginner because it explains everything in minute detail. Windham and Bland were probably the two books most widely accepted in American military circles in the years just prior to the Revolution.

2. *Ibid.*

3. Thomas Simes, *The Military Medley*, London, 1768, 23.

4. Frederick Mackenzie, *A British Fusilier in Revolutionary Boston*, Allen French, editor, Cambridge, 1926, 28, 29. For Washington's attitude toward target practice with the musket see General Instructions to all Captains of Companies, July 29, 1757 in George Washington, *The Writings of George Washington*, John C. Fitzpatrick, editor, 39 vols., Washington, 1931-1944, II, 113. Also Washington to Maj. Andrew Lewis, April 21, 1758, *ibid.*, 180, 181.

5. Col. George Hanger, *To All Sportsmen and Particularly to Farmers, and Gamekeepers*, London, 1814, 205.

6. Order for a 100 Barrells of Powder and 200 muskets for Maryland, October 15, 1691, Browne, *Archives of Maryland*, VIII, 287. "Proceedings of the Council of Maryland, 1694-97," *ibid.*, XX, 40, 248. W. Shirley to Horatio Sharpe, April 24, 1756, *ibid.*, VI, 392. Godolphin to Col. Nicholson, August 20, 1702, Palmer and Fluornoy, *Calendar*, I, 80, 81. Col. Robert Hunter to the Lords of Trade, November 30, 1709, O'Callaghan, *Documents*, V, 113. "Minutes of the General Assembly," May 11, 1758, Hoadly, *Conn. Records*, XI, 123, 124. "Minutes of the Connecticut General Assembly, May, 1772," *ibid.*, XIII, 615, 616. Copy of Bond on the Part of Pennsylvania to the King for Arms, &c., 1755, Samuel Hazard and others, editors, *Pennsylvania Archives*, 17 vols., Philadelphia, 1852-1892, II, 300. "Journal of the House of Representatives," July 22, 1711, Nathaniel Bouton, and others, editors, *New Hampshire State Papers*, 40 vols., Manchester, New Hampshire, 1867-1941, XIX, 19, 20. "Records of the Council," May 20, 1712, *ibid.*, II, 634. Letter from the Earl of Egremont, December 12, 1761, *ibid.*, I, 811. Harold L. Peterson, "Committee of Safety Muskets," *The American Rifleman*, February, 1950, 26-28.

7. George, *Guns and Rifles*, 74, 75.

8. *Ibid.*

9. George, *Guns and Rifles*, 81, 106.

10. *Ibid.*, 80, 81, 113, 114, 173. Alm, *Eldhandvapen*, I, 323-325. Simes, *Military Medley*, in unpaged "Military Dictionary" under "Firelock." Lambert, *Military Discipline*, 18-23. "Firelock," George Smith, *An Universal Military Dictionary*, London, 1779. See also articles under the same heading in Charles James, *A New and Enlarged Military Dictionary*, 3rd edition, 2 vols., London, 1810; and William Duane, *A Military Dictionary*, Philadelphia, 1810.

11. Lawson, *Uniforms*, II, 42. Percy Sumner, "Morier's Paintings of Grenadiers, 1751," *Journal of the Society for Army Historical Research*, XVIII (1939), 215, 216.

12. Lawson, *Uniforms*, II, 45, 46.

13. George, *Guns and Rifles*, 149. Lawson, *Uniforms*, II, 46.

14. Percy Sumner, "Private, Light Troop, 11th Dragoons, c. 1760," *Journal* of the Society for Army Historical Research, XVIII (1939), 187. Major G. Tylden, "The Use of Firearms by Cavalry," *ibid.*, XIX (1940), 15.

15. This lock is now in the museum at Guilford Court House National Military Park, North Carolina.

16. Margerand, *Armement*, 21-43. Maurice Bottet, *Monographie de L'Armes A Feu Portative des Armées Françaises*, Paris, n.d., 1-11. James E. Hicks, *Notes on French Ordnance*, Mount Vernon, New York, 1938, 13-16.

17. Bottet, *Armes A Feu*, 6, 8.

18. *Ibid.*, 4, 5. Hicks *French Ordnance*, 15, 16.

19. An Act for Regulating the Militia, May, 1741, Hoadley, *Connecticut Records*, VIII, 380. Boone, *Military Discipline*, 73, 74. Governor Hardy to the Lords of Trade, June 16, 1756, O'Callaghan, *Documents*, VII, 3. An Act for the Better Regulating and Training the Militia, 1755, Henning, *Statutes*, VI, 536, 537. An Act for Settling the Militia, 1705, *ibid.*, III, 338. An Act for the better Regulation of the Militia, 1738, *ibid.*, V, 17.

20. Worthington C. Ford, editor, *Journals of the Continental Congress, 1774-1789*, 23 vols., Washington, 1904-1909, II, 188, 190, III, 322.

21. Peter Force, compiler, *American Archives*, 4th series, 6 vols., Washington, 1837-1846, III, 1496-1497.

22. *Ibid.*

23. Minutes of the General Assembly, April 1775, Hoadley, *Connecticut Records*, XIV, 420; May 1775, *ibid.*, XV, 17, 18.

24. Minutes of the General Assembly, October 1775, Hoadley, *Connecticut Records*, XV, 137; March 22, 1776, *ibid.*, 254, 255; May 1776, *ibid.*, 304, 305; June 1776, *ibid.*, 420, 421.

25. Proceedings of the General Assembly, March 18, 1776, John R. Barlett, editor, *Records of the Colony of Rhode Island and Providence Plantation*, 10 vols., Providence, 1856-1865, VII, 477, *et passim*.

26. Maj. Jonathan Child to Committee of Safety, July 14, 1776, Bouton, *New Hampshire Papers*, VIII, 304, 305; Committee in Moultonborough to Jonathan Moulton of Hampton, July 15, 1776, *ibid.*, 305; Committee of Safety to Washington, February 21, 1777, *ibid.*, 496, 497; *et passim*.

27. Proceedings of the Provincial Congress, June 30, 1775, O'Callaghan, *Documents*, XV, 13, 14.

28. Minutes of the Council of Safety, February 28, 1776, William H. Engle and others, editors, *Pennsylvania Archives*, 2nd series, 16 vols., Harrisburg, 1890, X, 498; July 3, 1775, *ibid.*, 282; March 6, 1776, *ibid.*, 506.

29. William Whitehead, and others, editors, *New Jersey Archives*, 39 vols., Newark, 1880-1946, *passim*.

30. "Journal and Correspondence of the Council of Safety 1775-76," Browne, *Archives of Maryland*, XI, 75.

31. Charles Beatty to Council, September 20, 1775, Browne, *Archives of Maryland*, XI, 81. Ewing to Council, February 12, 1776, *ibid.*, 155. Journal of the Council of Safety, August 17, 1777, *ibid.*, XVI, 219; July 29, 1777, *ibid.*, X, 320; August 16, 1777, *ibid.*, 335. Council of Safety to Richard Bond, November 15, 1776, *ibid.*, XII, 449; Council of Safety to Col. H. Holingworth, May 14, 1777, *ibid.*, XVI, 253. Benjamin Rumsey to Council of Safety, March 7, 1776, *ibid.*, XI, 211, 212. Council of Safety to Daniel Bowly, March 14, 1776, *ibid.*, 247. Council of Safety to the Commissioners of the Gunlock Manufactory in Frederick Town, July 30, 1776, *ibid.*, XII, 142.

32. Robert L. Miller, "Fredericksburg Manufactory Muskets," *Military Collector & Historian*, III, no. 3 (September 1951), 63-65.

33. September 28, 1776, H. R. McIlwaine, editor, *Journals of the Council of the State of Virginia*, 2 vols., Richmond, 1931, I, 177, 178.

34. Journal of the Council of Safety, January 2, 1776, Allen D. Candler, compiler, *The Revolutionary Records of the State of Georgia*, 3 vols., Atlanta, 1908, I, 85, *et passim*. Journal of the Council of Safety for the Province of South Carolina, 1775, (*Collections of the South Carolina Historical Society*) II, III, Charleston, 1858, 1859, 199-201, 213, 214, *et passim*. William L. Saunders, editor, *The Colonial Records of North Carolina*, 10 vols., Raleigh, 1886-1890, IX, X, *passim*.

35. Silas Deane to Secret Committee, August 18, 1776, Charles Isham, editor, *Deane Papers*, (*Collections of the New York Historical Society, 1886-1890*) 5 vols., I, 195-218. Henri Doniol, *Histoire de la Participation de la France à l'Établissement des États-Unis d'Amerique*, 6 vols., Paris, 1886, I, 133, 377, 482. Robert Morris to Council of Safety, December 23, 1778, Hazzard, *Pennsylvania Archives*, VII, 125, 126; May 10, 1779, *ibid.*, 386. Heads of an Agreement Made Between the Committee of Congress & Hodges & Bayard & Co., February 2, 1776, *ibid.*, IV, 708. Instructions to Captain Forsythe, January 1776, Browne, *Archives of Maryland*, XI, 98. William Lee to Governor Jefferson, September 24, 1779, Palmer and Flournoy, *Calendar of Va. State Papers*, I, 328, 331. Henry Laurens to Elisha Sawyer, January 19, 1776, *Journal of Council of Safety of South Carolina*, III, 199-201. Laurens to Capt. Joseph Darrell, January 24, 1776, *ibid.*, 213, 214. Harold L. Peterson, *Silas Deane in France*, typescript of Master of Arts thesis, University of Wisconsin, 1946, 21.

36. Peterson, *Silas Deane*, 21-45.

37. William Lee to Governor Jefferson, September 24, 1779, Palmer and Flournoy, *Calendar of Virginia State Papers*, I, 328-331. Peterson, *Silas Deane*, 27, 28.

38. January 30, February 1, February 14, February 24, 1777, Ford, *Journals of the Continental Congress*, VII, 74, 85, 119, 120, 151. Washington to Lt. Col. Benjamin Flower, March 31, 1777, Washington, *Writings*, VII, 341; to Gen. Alexander McDougall, April 17, 1777, *ibid.*, 424, 428. General Orders, Morristown, N. J., April 18, 1777, *ibid.*, 428. Washington to Gen. Samuel H. Parsons, April 23, 1777, *ibid.*, 457.

39. Of the two known specimens of the Prussian musket in America, one is in The West Point Museum. The other, originally found in New England, is now in the museum at Guilford Courthouse National Military Park, North Carolina.

40. Gustav Freytag, "The Citizen and His Shooting Festivals," reprinted in *The Gun Collector*, no. 37, 587-612. G. Charter Harrison, Jr., "The Kentucky Rifle Credo," *The Gun Collector*, no. 38, 617-626. John G. W. Dillin, *The Kentucky Rifle*, 3rd edition, New York, 1946, *passim*. Stephen V. Grancsay, "The Craft of the Early American Gunsmith," *Bulletin* of the Metropolitan Museum of Art, VI, No. 2 (October, 1947), 54-61.

41. Anonymous letter in Braddock's campaign, July 25, 1755, Stanley Pargellis, editor, *Military Affairs in North America, 1748-1765*, New York, 1936, 115.

42. Ford, *Journals of the Continental Congress*, II, 89, 90. John Adams to Abigail Adams, June 17, 1775, John and Abigail Adams, *Familiar Letters of John Adams and his Wife, Abigail Adams During the Revolution*, edited by Charles Francis Adams, New York, 1876, 65, 66.

43. James R. Bright, "The Rifle in Washington's Army," *The American Rifleman*, XCV, No. 8 (August 1947), 8. "Gazette," *Military Collector & Historian*, III, No. 2 (June 1951), 50, 51.

44. Hanger, *To All Sportsmen*, 122-124, 144.

45. *Ibid.*, 207-210.

46. Webster to Committee of Safety, June 21, 1775, Bouton, *New Hampshire State Papers*, VII, 526. Sullivan to Committee, July 19, 1775, *ibid.*, 565.

47. September 27, 1781, *Orderly Book for the Siege of Yorktown, from September 26, 1781 to November 2, 1781*, Philadelphia, 1865, 5.

48. Richard Peters to the Council of Safety, October 26, 1776, Browne, *Archives of Maryland*, XII, 405. Bright, "Rifle," 10. Washington to Morgan, June 13, 1777, Washington, *Writings*, VIII, 236. Wayne to Peters, February 3, 1778, Antony Wayne, *Papers*, Revolutionary Series, transcribed by Henry B. Dawson, 1860, from original manuscripts in possession of the Wayne family, 10 bound folios, Morristown National Historical Park, III.

49. John G. Simcoe, *Simcoe's Military Journal*, New York, 1844, 237.

50. Frank Moore, *Diary of the American Revolution*, 2 vols. New York, 1860, 349, 350.

51. Hanger, 199, 200.

52. *Ibid.*

53. Washington, *Writings*, IX, 78, 102.

54. Edward J. Lowell, *The Hessians and Other German Auxiliaries of Great Britain in the Revolutionary War*, New York, 1884, *passim*. Charles M. Lefferts, *Uniforms of the American, British, French and German Armies in the War of the American Revolution, 1775-1783*, New York, 1926, 261-278.

55. Harrison, *Kentucky Rifle Credo*, 617-626. Grancsay, *American Powder Horns*, 7, 8.

56. St. George Tucker, "St. George Tucker's Journal of the Siege of Yorktown, 1781," edited by Edward M. Riley, *The William and Mary Quarterly*, Third series, V, no. 3 (July 1948). 381.

57. "Blunderbuss," in "Military Dictionary" section of Simes, *Military Medley*. For a report on test-firing blunderbusses see Harold L. Peterson, "Did It Work," *American Rifleman*, February 1955, 20-23.

58. Washington to Board of War, April 4, 1779, Washington, *Writings*, XIV, 331.

59. Washington to Board of War, April 15, 1779, *ibid.*, 390.

60. George, *Guns and Rifles*, 73. Charles ffoulkes, *Arms and Armament*, London, 1945, 65. Lawson, *Uniforms*, II, 48. Herbert A. Sherlock, "Early British Grenade Launchers," *Military Collector & Historian*, III, No. 2 (June 1951) 44-46.

61. *Ibid.*

62. *Ibid.*

63. December 18, 1695, "Proceedings of the Council of Maryland, 1694-97," Browne, *Archives of Maryland*, XX, 446, 447. March 3, 1696/7, "Proceedings of the Council of Maryland, 1696/7-98," *ibid.*, XXIII, 75.

64. Saint Remy, *Memoires d'Artillerie*, I, 326.

65. Col. Lewis to Washington, February 4, 1776, *Washington Papers*, Manuscript Division, Library of Congress.

66. Miller, "Fredericksburg Manufactory Muskets," 63-65. The existing specimens of Rappahannock Forge wall guns are located at the following places: one at the United States Military Academy Museum, West Point, New York, one in the museum at the Springfield Arsenal, Springfield, Massachusetts, and two in the museum at Rock Island Arsenal, Rock Island, Illinois.

67. *Washington Papers*, Library of Congress.

68. George, *Pistols and Revolvers*, 38. Major G. Tylden, "The Use of Firearms by Cavalry," *Journal of the Society for Army Historical Research*, XIX (1940), 14.

69. George, *Pistols and Revolvers*, 43-56.

70. *Ibid.*, 50-52.

71. *Ibid.*

72. *Ibid.*, 52, 53.

73. Bottet, *Armes a Feu*, 4, 5.

74. *Ibid.* Hicks, *French Ordnance,* 80, 86.

75. *Ibid.*

76. George N. Hyatt, "The Kentucky Pistol," Dillin, *Kentucky Rifle,* 125-127.

77. Samuel Niles, *A Summary Historical Narrative of the Wars in New England with the French and Indians in the Several Parts of the Country,* Massachusetts Historical Society *Collections,* 4th series V (1861), 347.

78. George, *Guns and Rifles,* 69, 137, 138. Robert E. Gardner, *Five Centuries of Gunsmiths, Swordsmiths and Armourers, 1400-1900,* Columbus, Ohio, 1948, 25. *Boston Gazette,* April 12, 26, 1756. Stephen Van Rensselaer, *American Firearms,* Watkins Glen, New York, 1947, 55, 56.

79. *Illustrated Catalogue of United States Cartridge Company's Collection of Firearms,* Lowell, Massachusetts, n.d., 17-19. Metschl, *Nunnemacher Collection,* I, 84-87. George, *Guns and Rifles,* 69, 137, 138. L. D. Satterlee and Arcadi Gluckman, *American Gun Makers,* Buffalo, New York, 1945, 34.

80. *Papers of the Continental Congress,* Manuscript Division, Library of Congress, I, No. 41, 123, 124.

81. Ford, *Journals of the Continental Congress,* VII, 324.

82. *Annual Register,* XIX (1776), 148.

83. *Political Magazine, Naval, Military, and Literary,* January, 1781, 125. Dawson, *Wayne Papers,* V, VI, VII, *passim.* Henry P. Johnston, *The Storming of Stony Point,* New York, 1900, *passim.* George, *Guns and Rifles,* 148-152.

84. George, *Guns and Rifles,* 149. Metschl, *Nunnemacher Collection,* I, 87, 88. Lawson, *Uniforms,* II, 195, 196.

85. Harold L. Peterson, "The Private Soldier's Ferguson Rifle," *Military Collector & Historian,* II, No. 4 (December 1950), 60-62.

Chapter Six

Ammunition and Equipment

 N AMMUNITION, as well as in firearms, the period from 1689 to 1783 was characterized by gradual improvements on existing forms and a trend toward standardization. There were no revolutionary new developments. The composition of gun powder remained the same as it had been for the previous two centuries, and the spherical lead ball continued as the standard missile.

It continued to be the practice to load a musket with several balls, usually one regular full-sized ball and a few buck shot. The number of buck shot varied. One recruit in the "Standing Army" in 1777 mentioned having 64 rounds of ammunition with three buck shot each, a number which became standard in the next century. Washington, however, recommended that the men load for their first volley "with one musket ball and four or eight buck Shott, according to the strength of their pieces . . ." And General Henry Dearborn went still further as he reported in describing an incident during the American assult on Quebec, December 31, 1775.

> I Clapt up my Piece which was Charged with a ball and Ten Buck shott certainly to give him his due, But to my great mortification my Gun did not go off . . .

The heavy snowstorm during which the attack was made had apparently wet the priming powder in Dearborn's musket and thus saved his adversary from receiving a very lethal charge.[1]

Sometimes the balls were cut or otherwise mutilated, and sometimes other hard objects were used, thus giving rise to contemporary "atrocity stories." After the battle of Lexington and Concord, for instance, the British protested that the Americans had cut their musket balls so that they separated into four pieces upon firing, and a Boston surgeon who examined the wounded also reported the use of old nails and angular pieces of iron. Somewhat later, British General Howe wrote Washington:

Plate 218. Mutilated musket balls excavated from Revolutionary sites in and around New York City.

My Aid de Camp charged with the Delivering of this Letter will present to you a Ball cut and fixed to the Ends of a Nail, taken from a Number of the same Kind, found in the Encampments quitted by your

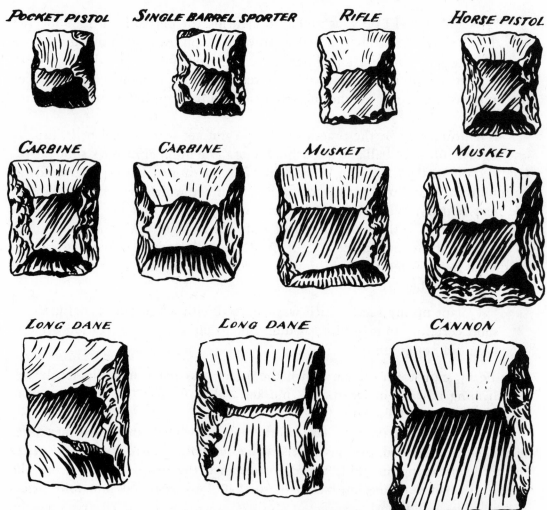

Plate 219. Flints chipped according to the traditional specifications by a modern knapper in England. The illustration is exact size. Drawing by Robert L. Miller.

Troops on the 15th Instant. I do not make any comments upon such unwarrantable and malicious Practices, being well assured the Contrivance has not come to your Knowledge.

General Howe was apparently just as ignorant of the fact that the same kind of missile was used by his own men, for several such balls were found in the excavation of a British camp at Inwood, New York, and are now preserved in the New York Historical Society's museum.[2]

The flints used in gun locks reached the full development of their form just as the period opened. Generally speaking, there were two major types of flints, the English and the French or, more accurately, the Continental Epropean. The English flint was normally black with straight bevels across point and heel produced by a single stroke of the knapping hammer. The Continental flints were almost always of a greasy gray or whitish color, and the heels were rounded with a gnawed effect produced by many strokes of the knapping hammer. Some of the whitish flints apparently made in the British fashion, however, are occasionally found. Many of these may have been made during the nineteenth century when French flints were frequently imported into England for finishing, but others come from apparently undisturbed eighteenth century sites. No flints were produced in America, and it is interesting to note that the great majority of all flints found in this country are of the Continental European type.[3]

According to tradition there were nine standard sizes of gun flints. These included sizes for the pocket pistol, single barrelled fowling piece, rifle, holster pistol, carbine, musket, long Dane (long Arabian pieces) and cannon. Of these, the last two would not be applicable to the period under consideration in America.[4]

Much has been written by modern writers concerning whether the flat or the chamfered side of the flint was usually placed uppermost by the men who originally used the flintlock. Actually, the truth is that there was never universal agreement at the time. Some men favored one position and some another. Often it was the practice to use a flint in one position until it no longer produced a good spark and then turn it over.[5]

The number of flints that a soldier was required to carry varied considerably. In 1701 Nicholas Boone recommended that each Massachusetts militia man carry 12 flints. In 1741 Connecticut required 12 flints for an infantry man and 20 for a trooper. On July 18, 1775 the Continental Congress recommended that the militia of the various states be furnished 12 flints each, but in 1779 Massachusetts cut that number in half.[6]

The methods of carrying and using ammunition showed some progression. The cartridge had been used in America for some time when the period opened, but it was not yet universal in the French army that served here during the

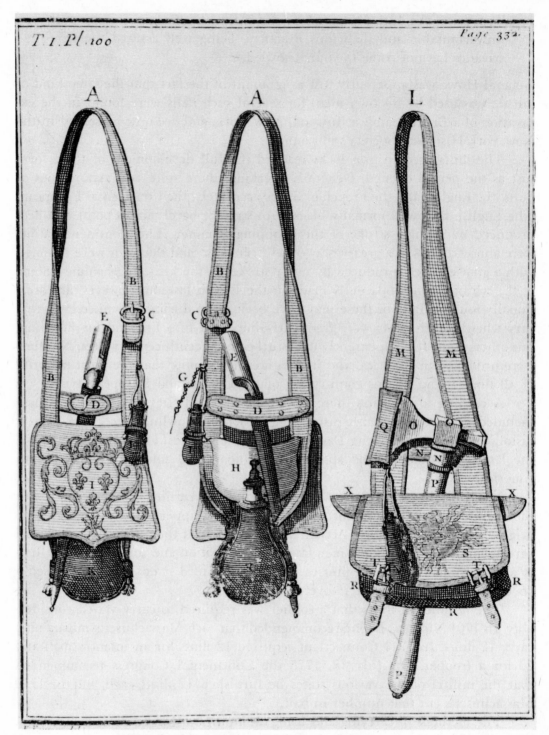

Plate 220. French cartridge boxes of 1697 from Saint Remy. The figures at left and center represent the front and back of the standard infantry box. The figure at the right is a grenadier's pouch.

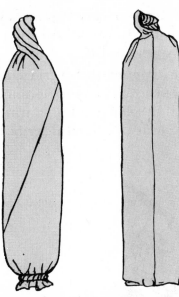

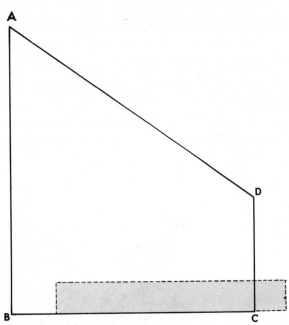

Plate 221. Left, British cartridge made according to Pickering's description. Right, French cartridge made according to the description of 1738.

Plate 222. Cartridge making diagram from Pickering's manual.

various wars for control of the Continent. In 1689 a regulation ordered these French troops to be equipped with a pouch which held seven or eight iron chargers, each containing enough powder for one load. Attached to this pouch also was a priming flask and a large regular powder flask. This latter flask served only to keep the powder it contained dry, for when the soldier had exhausted his measured charges he merely poured the powder from the flask into his pouch and proceeded to load his musket from that either with one of the iron chargers or, if pressed, with his hand.[7]

This practice was found to be most inefficient, and the trend toward the cartridge quickly followed. Some writers maintain that the French infantry began to use the cartridge between 1690 and 1700. Indeed, Saint Remy illustrates a musket cartridge with the ball attached by its sprue in the 1697 edition of his *Memoires d'Artillerie*. Nevertheless, it was not until 1702 that the King began to advocate the use of the cartridge for French troops, and then these cartridges were to contain the powder charge only. The balls were still carried separately as was the priming powder.[8]

It was not until 1738 that instructions were issued for making cartridges that contained both powder and ball. The cartridge described in these instructions was a cylinder of paper, folded flat and pasted at the ball end and along the edges. The upper end was either folded or twisted. It was probably almost 1750, however, before this cartridge became universally used in the French

[231]

Army. The Americans adopted this design during the Revolutionary War as they adopted the French musket and pistol. It continued unchanged in American service until about 1832 when a double-tied pattern superseded it.[9]

British troops were well ahead of the French in adopting the cartridge as standard and were using it widely when the period opened. The exact form of these first cartridges is not known, but that used by British soldiers at least during the greater part of the first half of the eighteenth century was well described

5th (Rifle) Battalion   Philadelphia Greens, Light   Battalion Companies, 3rd and 2nd Battalions
Infantry Company, 3rd Battalion

Associators of the City & Liberties of Philadelphia, 1775

Company of Military Collectors & Historians
Plate 223. Drawing by H. Charles McBarron, Jr. Note the battalion infantrymen with the regular cartridge boxes and bayonets worn on shoulder belts and the rifleman with the hunting bag and horn.

by Timothy Pickering who advised its continued use by American troops at the beginning of the Revolution. (See plates 221 and 222).

VII, the best method of making cartridges seems to be that used in the [British] army. It is this.—Take the soft brown paper called whitish

Captain   *Privates*

Glovers Marblehead or Marine Infantry, 1775-76
(14th Continental Infantry)

Company of Military Collectors & Historians
Plate 224. Drawing by H. Charles McBarron, Jr. This picture illustrates excellently the various items of equipment and the methods of wearing them.

brown, or wrapping paper, and cut it into pieces of the form represented in Plate I, figure 2, which is of these dimensions; the side *a b* measures about six inches, *b c* about five inches and a half, and *c d* about two inches. A piece of wood about six inches long is to be made round so as to fit exactly the size of the ball; this is called a *former:* make one end of it hollow to receive a part of the ball: lay the former upon the straight edge *b c* (as represented by the dotted lines) with its hollow end about an inch from the side *a b:* roll the paper around the former; then with the ball press in the corner of the paper so as to cover the hollow end of the former, and keeping fast the ball, roll on till the paper is all wrapped round the former; having before taken a piece of twine and fastened its two ends to something that will not easily be moved, and

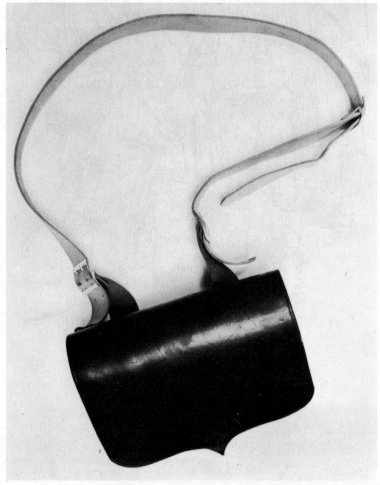

Colonial Williamsburg
Plate 225. Reconstruction of a British cartridge box and belt.

National Park Service
Plate 226. British waist cartridge box bearing the monogram of George II. This is made of a block of wood with the leather flap nailed at the back.

so far apart as to leave it slack, you are now to take with the twine a single turn around the paper, below the ball; then running in the end of your fore finger till it touches the ball, pull upon the string that it may girt the paper, and by turning round the former with one hand you will presently form a neck below the ball; which being afterwards tied with a piece of coarse thread will secure the ball from slipping out: then withdrawing the former, the cartridge is ready to be charged with powder; in doing which you must put in the more because part of it is to be taken for priming: having properly filled the cartridge, twist the top, and the work is done. The size of the paper above described will serve for an ounce ball: if your ball be less, the paper may be somewhat smaller. One thing should be remembered, that if the cartridge exactly fits your firelock when the barrel is perfectly clean, it will be too large, and difficult to be rammed down, when it becomes foul by firing; and 'tis dangerous firing when the ball is not rammed well home: for this therefore you are to make allowance.[10]

This resulted in a cartridge with the lower end tied below the ball only and the upper end simply twisted.

Cartridges were carried in pouches known as cartridge boxes or, colloquially, as cartouche boxes. At first these consisted of a relatively soft leather pouch with a large heavy leather flap, often decorated with regimental devices, and designed to protect the pouch from the weather. The cartridges were simply carried loose in them. A little later wooden inserts bored with holes, each large enough to hold a single cartridge, were added. These inserts were a considerable improvement, for they not only prevented the cartridges from bumping against each other and breaking, but they also offered further protection against the elements.

Author's Collection
Plate 227. American cartridge box. The pick and brush are probably post-Revolutionary.

West Point Museum

Plate 228. American cartridge cannister of the Revolution.

The number of holes in these boxes varied, but between 20 and 30 was standard. When filled the box might weigh five or six pounds.[11]

Infantry soldiers normally wore the cartridge box on a shoulder strap, and, according to Pickering,

> The pouch hangs on the right side, but so far behind as not to interfere with the right hand man when the files are close; and at such a height as is most convenient for taking out a cartridge with the right hand.[12]

Special troops and mounted men frequently carried the cartridge box, usually a smaller variety, on the front of the waist belt.

There was also one cheaper variant of the cartridge box used by both the British and Americans. This also was described by Pickering:

> . . . The British have for several years past, furnished their new levies with cartridge boxes made of close wood (as maple or beech) with no other covering than a good leather flap nailed to it at the back near the upper edge, and of sufficient breadth to cover the top & whole front of the box; they are fixed to the body by a waist belt, which passes through two loops that are nailed to the front of the box . . . .[13]

[237]

Actually, American troops in the field during the Revolution were often equipped with cartridge boxes much worse than those just described. The following two complaints give some picture of the situation.

Sir, the 300 cartouch boxes, that I informed you I understood were on the road coming from Virginia, are just come in. I have received

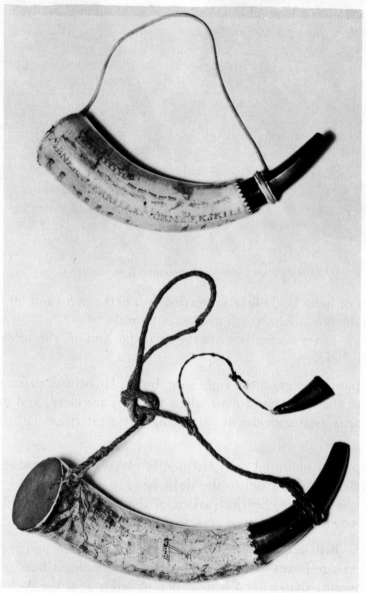

Author's Collection

Plate 229. American engraved powder horns. The upper one was made by Abner Merrill during the Revolution. The lower one, which retains its original thong and charger, was made by Capt. Nathan Deventer in 1759.

them and can assure you they are not worthy of the name. Numbers of them are without any straps, others without flaps, and scarce any of them would preserve the cartridges in a moderate shower of Rain— What straps there are to the boxes are of linen.[14]

* * * *

The arms in general are good but the cartouch boxes bad, many of the old construction and wore out. Some with waist belts, others without any belts at all slung by pieces of rope or other strings—I could there-fore . . . wish that a quantity of British arms and accoutrements not exceeding 600 stands may be sent me.[15]

In addition to the regular and variant cartridge boxes, American troops during the Revolution also used tin cartridge cannisters. References to these cannisters begin to appear in the fall of 1777 by which time they were already in the hands of troops in the field. Fortunately, one specimen of these cannisters is known to have survived, made almost exactly according to the specifications contained in a detailed description prepared by the Board of War in the spring of 1778.

The recommendation to provide cartridge boxes and tin cannisters for cartridges is given, because of the almost total want of them in the public stores, and the impossibility of making a number of them in any degree equal to the demands of the army, in public manufactories, where workmen are few, and it is impossible to encrease them: agree-able to the direction of congress, the board [of war] give the following description of the tin cannisters.

They are to be six inches and a half deep, or long; three inches and three quarters of an inch broad (this breadth receiving the cartridges lengthways, as they lie in a horizontal position) and two inches and seven eighths of an inch thick; (this thickness admitting four cartridges, to lay side by side) a box of these, in the clear, will well contain thirty six cartridges with ounce balls. A wire is to be fixed in all the edges at the top and then each side turned down (outwards) a full half inch and soldered. The cover is to be a full half inch deep, so that when fixed on the cannister the edges shall come close down to the ledge formed by the inclosed wire. This cover at one end turns on a hinge an inch and a quarter long, the wire (fixed as above mentioned) being laid naked, that space, for the purpose; and a piece of tin is run under-neath the wire, doubled together, and soldered on the inside of one end of the cover. The soldier carries a cannister by a shoulder belt, as he does a cartridge box: and for this reason the cannister has fixed to it three loops of tin, each half an inch wide, with the edges turned back, to be smooth and strong; one of them is placed underneath the middle of the bottom, and one on each of the narrowest sides, the latter at four inches distant from the bottom to their lower edges. The loops

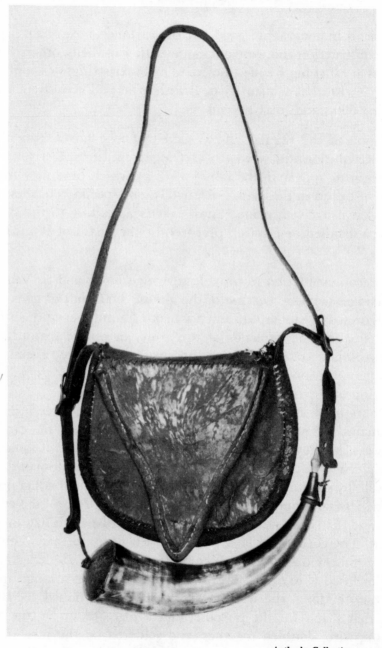

Author's Collection

Plate 230. Hunting bag and powder horn of the type carried by riflemen and some militia.

Author's Collection

Plate 231. Brass bullet mould with four cavities of different sizes. It belonged to Brig. Gen. Seth Pomeroy, famous gunsmith and soldier, and bears his name and the date 1760.

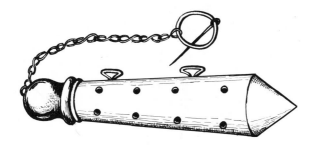

Plate 232. Grenadier's match case.

are to be sent down at each end and very well soldered, leaving a space to admit a leathern belt full one inch and a half wide, and nearly an eighth of an inch thick. The cover opens against one part of the belt, which causes it to fall down, after a cartridge is taken out, by wch means the rest are secured from accidental fire. If possible, the cannisters should be japanned, or painted, to preserve them from rust; and all fixed to belts.

The board are of the opinion that these cannisters are preferable to cartridge boxes, as they will infallibly secure the cartridges from rain, and their weight is so trifling as to be no burthen to the Soldier. And seeing leather is so scarce they will be a most excellent substitute for cartridge boxes.[16]

Despite the fact that the cartridge had become the preferred method for transporting and handling ammunition among both the British and Americans by the very beginning of the period, the powder horn and flask by no means disappeared. Accoutrements purchased by individual colonies or supplied by Great Britain during the early eighteenth century for the use of local troops almost always included cartridge boxes rather than flasks or horns, but the magazine at Williamsburg, Va., included a hogshead of powder horns in its inventory in 1775. Most militia laws listed cartridge boxes preferentially among the items of equipment it was necessary for each eligible citizen to possess. They almost always allowed horns as a substitution, however, and many colonists were happy to avail themselves of this loophole. A man could make a powder horn himself without much difficulty, and it was also more universally useful around the home than the strictly military cartridge box. Consequently the majority of individual citizens undoubtedly used horns for muster day drills, and when wars broke out they took these horns with them. Today the engravings on many of these horns attest the campaigns in which they were used. And finally, it should be noted that during the Revolution, when supplies of cartridge boxes

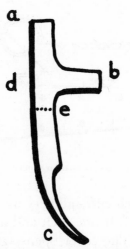

Plate 233. All-purpose tool invented
and described by Timothy Pickering.

and cannisters ran low, it was the practice to issue powder horns and shot pouches as an emergency measure.[17]

It should be remembered, too, that there were some arms with which cartridges could not be used. The largest category of these arms was, of course, the American rifle, but there were also the blunderbuss, the amusette, and the Ferguson rifle. Consequently, the men who carried these arms were of necessity forced to carry powder horns or flasks and shot pouches. Finally, some cannoneers carried horns with which to prime their guns, and officers were apt to use small horns or flasks to load their personal pistols, particularly those with screw barrels.

Bullet moulds, while not usually considered as part of the personal equipment of the individual soldier, must be considered in any discussion of ammunition and accoutrements. For military purposes gang moulds were preferred. Maryland specified brass moulds that would cast 12 bullets on one side and as many buck shot as possible on the other. A ratio of one mould to every 80 muskets was called for. Virginia specified that its bullet moulds should cast 16 bullets and established a ratio of one mould to every 40 muskets. Some of these gang moulds, however, were made of slate or soapstone as well as metal.[18]

Individual bullet moulds must not be overlooked either. Many men, particularly among the militia, brought their own moulds with them, and it was a common practice among riflemen. Two individual moulds were found in excavations of British and German campsites in New York City and are now preserved in the collection of the New York Historical Society. These single-cavity moulds were similar in every respect to those used during the next century, and it is almost impossible to differentiate between an eighteenth and a nineteenth century mould.[19]

There was also one other article slightly associated with ammunition that should probably be considered here. This was the match case which grenadiers of the British army wore on their cartridge box belt. This match case was a vestigial relic of the case with which musketeers armed with matchlocks had protected the lighted ends of their match from the weather. In the very first years of the period under consideration the grenadiers actually used them in all probability to protect the match from which they lit the fuses on their grenades. When the grenadiers ceased to perform their traditional functions, however, the case was carried on as one of the distinguishing features of the grenadier dress.[20]

In construction these cases were very simple. Usually they consisted of a perforated cylinder of brass or white metal, depending upon the color of the buttons of the regiment, with a wooden stopper attached to a chain in the upper end. Both tube and chain were fastened separately to the belt. The practice of wearing this case was continued by some regiments throughout the entire period.[21]

In addition to his ammunition and the accoutrements related thereto, the soldier also needed several small items of equipment with which to care for his firearms. First of all there were still the scourer and the worm that fitted on the ramrod and which the soldier used to clean the bore of his musket and withdraw wet charges. Then there were the priming wire or pick and brush. The pick was used to open the touch hole when it became stopped, and the brush was used to clean the pan. In the early years of the eighteenth century, at least through 1750, these items were attached to thongs on the loose end of the cartridge box belt below the buckle in the center of the chest. Thereafter, each was usually fastened to a short brass chain and hooked to the front of one of the shoulder belts.[22]

Timothy Pickering devised an all-purpose tool combining the pick, screw driver and a small hammer. In discussing it, he also describes the standard screw driver of the period (See plate 233):

> It is extremely convenient to have something to turn a screw, and break the edge of a bad flint when a better is not at hand to supply its place. The screw-driver used in the army has three blades, each of which is fitted to turn a screw, the blades are united at a common

M. H. de Young Memorial Museum
Plate 234. Portrait of a British officer by John Singleton Copley C. 1768-1774. Note the gorget, saber, waist cartridge box and fusil with sling.

Dragoons   *Officer*

Maryland Dragoons, Circa 1695

Company of Military Collectors & Historians

Plate 235. Drawing by H. Charles McBarron, Jr. Note the very wide band on the musketoon sling and the large cloth flaps on the holsters.

center, and disposed at equal distances so that three lines touching their extremities would form a triangle. But I believe the steel instrument represented in plate I, figure 1, will be much more useful: *a, b,* are screw drivers, *c,* is a picker, and serves instead of a priming wire to clear the touch-hole, and at *d* the back is near a quarter of an inch thick, and serves for a hammer, the whole length of it from *a* to *c* is four inches, and from *d* to *b* is about an inch and a quarter. As the tapered end will seldom be used, a leathern case may inclose it up to *e*; which will render the instrument fitter to be carried in the pouch, and more easy to use as a screw-driver.[23]

Some of these small items of equipment were concerned primarily with protecting the gun from the weather. These included tompions or plugs of wood to stop the muzzles of the muskets, and smaller plugs to close the touch holes and thus keep the powder charge dry. Leather covers for the gun lock were also recommended. These covers usually wrapped around the entire gun at the breech and laced or buckled on the left side. They were, thus, as effective as any device could be in protecting the charges of soldiers who had to be outside in inclement weather. For those arms that were stored in special tents, or bells of arms as they were called, leather covers for the frizzens only were recommended in 1750 by General Wolfe. In this case, however, it was as a safety

Company of Military Collectors & Historians

Plate 236. Bland's Continental Dragoons. Note the helmets and suspensory equipment. Drawing by Col. Frederick P. Todd.

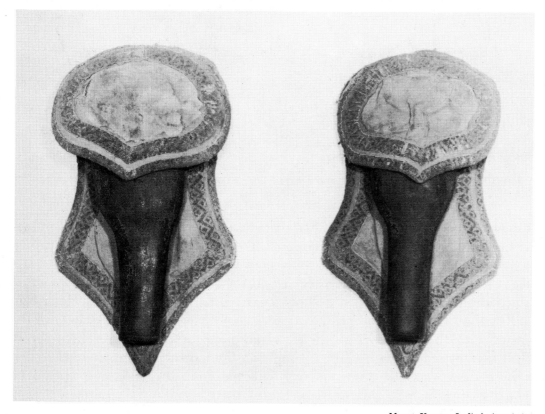

Plate 237. Pistol holsters which belonged to George Washington. The holsters are black leather and the cloth housings are trimmed with scarlet braid.

measure to prevent accidental discharges rather than to keep the arms dry.[24]

Finally, the colonial soldier also needed various items of carrying or suspensory equipment in order to support his weapons. Among these were gun slings, carbine belts, holsters and sword and bayonet belts. The first of these, the gun sling, was a simple affair as compared to its more complex modern counterpart. Usually it was made of buff leather although occasionally cloth, especially linen, was used. One end was passed up through the lower swivel, doubled back and tied with a thong. The other end was passed up through the upper swivel, doubled back and fastened with a buckle or slide. This gun sling is excellently depicted in a portrait of an unidentified pre-Revolutionary British officer attributed to John Singleton Copley and now in the M. H. de Young Memorial Museum, San Francisco.[25]

There were two principal means of carrying the true carbine or musketoon. One was by belt and swivel; the other by boot and strap. The first of these was a broad buff leather belt that was worn over the left shoulder with a buckle in front and a sliding snap on a swivel. The snap was attached to the ring on

[247]

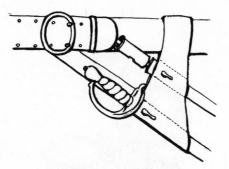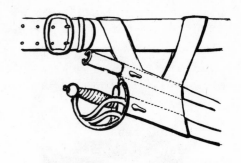

Plate 238. British infantry enlisted men's sword belts illustrating on the left one of the types popular about 1735-1742 and on the right one found frequently in Morier's paintings of 1751.

the swivel bar of the carbine. When dismounted the carbine hung thus on the right side, muzzle down. When mounted, the muzzle of the carbine was turned up, and the butt was put in a carbine boot which hung from the horse equipment just in front of the rider's leg. When the carbine was carried by boot and strap, the butt was placed in a boot exactly similar to the one just described, and the barrel was supported by a strap that came over from the vicinity of the pommel of the saddle. This strap is indicated in numerous contemporary paintings, passed through a ring or staple on the left side of the pommel. When carried thus the carbine was entirely detached from the soldier. It should be noted that mounted soldiers frequently carried a full musket rather than a carbine, and when they did so it was worn on the rider's back with the usual musket sling or carried in the boot and strap arrangement.[26]

For most of the period holsters for a mounted man's pistols remained the same. They consisted of tubes, usually leather, flaring out at the top to receive the trigger guard and the lock of the pistol. Usually there was a metal cap at the barrel end. Around all this was a cap or skirt of cloth decorated in military specimens with regimental devices. This skirt could be pulled up and folded over the butts of the pistols to keep out rain when necessary.

By the middle of the eighteenth century an important development in holster design had made its appearance. Caps of fur were added to the holsters in addition to the cloth caps. These fur caps were left always over the openings at the tops of the holsters when the pistols were in them, thus reducing the older caps to mere skirt-like decorations, which soon disappeared. In other instances, a cloth cover was used and a vestigial form of the older cap was attached to the under side of the holster.

The belts on which soldiers carried their swords and bayonets were of two principal varieties: waist belts and shoulder belts. Of these, the waist belt was more popular for infantry use throughout the greater part of the period. In both the British and French armies these belts consisted of relatively heavy waist bands with a buckle in front and a double frog, for sword and bayonet, on the left side. They were almost always made of buff leather and were worn inside the coat. It should be noted that there were exceptions, and some infantry soldiers wore shoulder belts from the very beginning. In the British army the advantages of having the sword and bayonet always outside the coat were gradually perceived, and some regiments adopted the expedient of wearing the waist belt over the shoulder. By 1774 the principle of the crossed cartridge box and bayonet belts was generally accepted, and it was standard for British troops during the Revolution although some regiments still used the older waist belts. It should be noted, also, that the warrants of 1768 forbade privates in the line companies to wear swords, and so these belts were equipped with only one frog. The French adopted the shoulder belt in 1776.[27]

Americans in general followed the British pattern, although somewhat more slowly. Among the militia, of course, there were no regulations, and a man carried his sword or bayonet (he was not usually required to have both) as best he could. During the Revolution the shoulder belt was most prevalent also among American forces. Since the tomahawk was a popular weapon in this country, however, these belts were sometimes made with double frogs so that both could be carried.[28]

Bayonet belts and scabbards were in short supply, and so it was not unusual for an American soldier to be without one. At one point, in fact, the scarcity was so acute that Washington issued a standing order to his troops to adopt the practice of keeping the bayonet fixed to the musket at all times except when the piece was being cleaned. Also because of these shortages the materials from which the belts and frogs were made were subject to variation. Thus linen and harness leather belts are found as well as the standard buff leather specimens.[29]

The belts on which officers wore their swords followed the same evolution as those of the men. At first it was the practice to wear a waist belt, sometimes

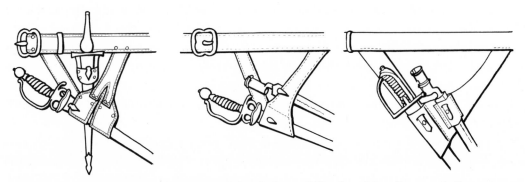

Plate 239. French infantry enlisted men's belts. Left: c. 1697 after Saint Remy and Bottet; center: sergeant of infantry. c. 1767 after Bottet; right: sergeant of infantry c. 1776 after Bottet.

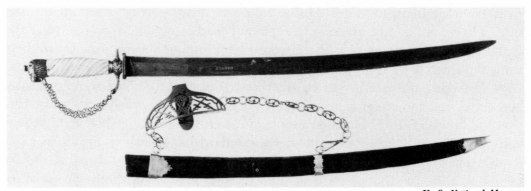

240. Hunting sword of Brig. Gen. Richard Montgomery with its scabbard, chains and hanger for attachment to a waist belt.

under and sometimes over the waistcoat. Such belts were made of cloth or buff leather as a rule. About 1768 British officers began to carry their swords on a shoulder belt of buff leather with a buckle in the center of the chest, worn under the coat. Gradually, however, the practice developed of wearing this belt outside the coat, and the buckle was changed to an oval or sometimes rectangular plate, gilt or silver depending upon the buttons of the regiment. By 1776 this was standard in the British army, and that year it was also adopted for the French officers.[30]

American officers of the Revolution used both the waist belt and the shoulder belt. Contemporary portraits and paintings show both, thus substantiating the existence of a situation that would be expected because of the shortages that forever plagued the American troops. Both black and white shoulder belts are shown.

When the sword was carried on a shoulder belt, it was almost always attached by a frog. When it was worn on the waist belt it could also be attached by a frog, but two other methods were also used. One of these was an arrangement of two straps suspended from the belt which snapped to rings on the scabbard. The other was a hook or hanger, a metal frame which hooked over the belt and from which two chains with snaps provided the means of attachment for the scabbard.

Mounted troops were sometimes equipped with waist belts, sometimes with shoulder belts. Throughout the period British dragoons wore waist belts while the horse and light horse troops used shoulder belts. American cavalry used both during the Revolution although the shoulder belt seems to have been more prevalent. French cavalrymen used the waist belt throughout the period.[31]

These, then, were the standard items of ammunition and equipment which a soldier used to care for and supplement his weapons during the years from 1689 to 1783. There were some changes from the previous patterns but none of them were radical or important. The only real advance lay in the gradual adoption of the cartridge by almost all military forces. Otherwise the period was static with no major advances and no steps backward. The big changes caused by the invention of fulminate of mercury which led to the percussion cap and then to the internally primed cartridge were still almost half a century away and completely unsuspected.

NOTES—CHAPTER SIX

1. Samuel Blakeslee, "Narrative of Colonel Samuel Blakeslee," Buffalo Historical Society *Publications*, VIII (1905) 428. General Orders, Head Quarters, New York, June 29, 1776, Washington, *Writings*, V, 198. Henry Dearborn, *Revolutionary War Journals of Henry Dearborn, 1775-1783*, edited by Floyd A. Brown and Howard H. Peckham, Chicago, 1939, 69.

2. Frank Moore, *Diary of Revolution*, I, 67, 68, 100, 101. Howe to Washington, September 21, 1776, Washington, *Writings*, VI, 74n. William L. Calver and Reginald P. Bolton, *History Written with Pick and Shovel*, New York, 1950, 75, 76.

3. Robert Donkin, *Military Collections and Remarks*, New York, 1777, 189. Arthur Woodward, "Some Notes on Gun Flints," *Military Collector & Historian*, III, No. 2 (June 1951), 29-36.

4. Woodward, "Gun Flints," 32-36.

5. Woodward, "Gun Flints," 32. Donkin, *Military Collections*, 189.

6. Boone, *Military Discipline*, 73. An Act for Regulating the Militia, May 1741, Hoadly, *Connecticut Records*, VIII, 380, July 18, 1775, Ford, *Journals of the Continental Congress*, II, 188. Broadside order, 1779, Ralph Gabriel, editor, *Pageant of America*, 15 vols., New Haven, 1925-1929, VI, 187.

7. Margerand, *Armement*, 62. Saint Remy, *Memoires d'Artillerie*, I, 332.

8. Margerand, *Armement*, 62-68. Saint Remy, *Memoires d'Artillerie*, I, 142.

9. "*Instructions sur les Cartouche dont les Troupes Doivent se Servir*," Margerand, *Armement*, 69.

10. Pickering, *Easy Plan*, Part I, 2, 3 and Plate I.

11. Resolution, March 19, 1778, Hazard, *Pennsylvania Archives*, VI, 375. Samuel Chase to Daniel of St. Thomas Jennifer, February 9, 1776, Browne, *Archives of Maryland*, XI, 150, 151. September 24, 1694, "Proceedings of the Council of Maryland, 1694-1697," *ibid.*, XX, 140, 248. Thomas Paine to Benjamin Franklin, 1778, *Pennsylvania Magazine of History and Biography*, II, 2. Gabriel, *Pageant of America*, VI, 187. July 18, 1775, Ford *Journals of the Continental Congress*, II, 188. General Orders, Head Quarters, Perkiomy, October 8, 1777, Washington, *Writings*, IX, 341, Pickering, *Easy Plan*, Part I, 1, 2. For a discussion of metal cartridge box ornaments, see Calver and Bolton, *Pick and Shovel*, 156-182.

12. Pickering, *Easy Plan*, Part I, 1, 2.

13. Pickering to Governor Jefferson, July 3, 1780, Palmer and Flournoy, *Calendar of Virginia State Papers*, I, 364, 365.

14. Edward Stevens to General Gates, July 21, 1780, *ibid.*, 367.

15. Col. Christian Febiger to Col. Davies, December 3, 1781, *ibid.*, II, 636.

16. Gen. Horatio Gates, to Thomas Johnson, March 28, 1778, "Journal and Correspondence of the Council of Maryland, 1777-78," Browne, *Archives of Maryland*, XVI, 558, 559. For references to the issuance of cannisters in the field, see General Orders, Head Quarters, Perkiomy, October 8, 1777, Washington, *Writings*, IX, 341; General Orders, Headquarters Towamensing, October 13, 1777, *ibid.*, 363, 364; Washington to Gen. Knox, May 27, 1779, *ibid.*, XV, 158; Resolution, March 19, 1778, Hazard, *Pennsylvania Archives*, VI, 375.

17. An Act for Settling the Militia, "Province Laws [1692-1702]," Bouton, *New Hampshire State Papers*, III, 178. Proceedings of a Special Convention, June 7, 1755, *ibid.*, I, 396, 397. An Act for Regulating the Militia, May 1741, Hoadly, *Connecticut Records*, VIII, 380. June 13, 1775, *Journals of the House of Burgesses of Virginia, 1773-1776*, XIII, 223, 224. An Act for Regulating the Militia, May 1777, Henning, *Statutes*, IX, 268, 269, General Orders, Headquarters Towamensing, October 13, 1777, Washington, *Writings*, IX, 363, 364.

18. August 30, 1775, "Journal and Correspondence of the Council of Safety, 1775-76," Browne, *Archives of Maryland*, XI, 75. September 28, 1776, H. R. McIlwaine, *Journals of the Council of Virginia*, I, 177, 178.

19. Calver and Bolton, *Pick and Shovel*, 74-77.

20. Lawson, *Uniforms*, II, 1-48.

21. *Ibid.*

22. August 30, 1775, "Journal and Correspondence of the Council of Safety, 1775-76," Brown, *Archives of Maryland*, XI, 75. An Act for Regulating the Militia, May 1741, Hoadly, *Connecticut Records*, VIII, 380. July 18, 1775, Ford, *Journals of the Continental Congress*, II, 188. Gabriel, *Pageant of America*, VI, 187. Boone, *Military Discipline*, 73.

23. Pickering, *Easy Plan*, Part I, 1, 2, and plate 1.

24. Washington to Col. Henry Bouquet, July 12, 1758, Washington, *Writings*, II, 243, 244. "Extracts from the Orders of the Late General Wolfe," Pickering, *Easy Plan*, 162.

25. Lawson, *British Uniforms*, II, *passim*. For an interesting analysis of the Copley portrait see Frederick P. Todd, "Major Patrick Campbell," *Military Collector & Historian*, III, No. 4 (December 1951) 88-90.

26. Godolphin to Col. Nicholson, August 20, 1702, Palmer and Flournoy, *Calendar of Virginia State Papers*, I, 80, 81. Lawson, *Uniforms*, II, 107-161

27. Margerand, *Armement*, 58-75. Maurice Botet, *L'Arme Blanche de Guerre Française au XVIIIe Siècle*, Paris, 1910, 58-62. Lawson, *Uniforms*, II, 1-48. Lefferts, *Uniforms*, 178, 181, 185, 186, 193, 194. Calver and Bolton, *Pick and Shovel*, 156-166, 176-180.

28. Samuel Chase to Daniel of St. Thomas Jennifer, February 9, 1776, Brown, *Archives of Maryland*, XI, 150, 151.

29. General Orders, Headquarters Peekskill, August 2, 1780, Washington, *Writings*, XIX, 304.

30. Bottet, *L'Arme Blanche*, 60. Lefferts, *Uniforms*, 193, 194. Calver and Bolton, *Pick and Shovel*, 156-166, 176-180.

31. Lawson, *Uniforms*, II, 107-150. Bottet, *L'Arme Blanche*, 59, 60.

Chapter Seven

Edged Weapons

THE PERIOD from 1689 to 1783 is an especially interesting era to students of edged weapons in America. During these years a wide variety of such arms were employed here. There were many improvements in design, and there was a gradual trend toward the standardization of types. More important, however, were two broad movements. The first was the emergence of the bayonet as the principal auxiliary weapon of the foot soldier and the corresponding disappearance of the infantry sword. The second was the paradoxical rise to prominence of the pole arm in American armies at the same time that European troops were abandoning such weapons as useless encumbrances.

At the beginning of the period the sword was regarded as an essential item in the armament of every foot soldier. The changeover to the bayonet came slowly, and for a long period many soldiers carried both. This was particularly true of the British and French infantry, American militia laws usually requiring either one or the other but not both.

The swords carried by the British infantry and artillery were of a wide variety of patterns. The choice of design usually fell to the colonels of the individual regiments who purchased the swords for their men from an allowance each was granted for the equipping of his troops. There were even differences within regiments, for frequently the grenadiers wore different swords from the privates in the line companies.[1]

There were certain boundaries to this variation, however, and the British infantry sword can be readily recognized by the student. All had short, single-edged cutting blades. The majority were slightly curved with a single relatively narrow fuller at the back. There were two principal hilt types. One was a basket hilt of pierced iron. The other was a combination of a simple knuckle-bow,

Plate 241. British infantry sword 1742.

Plate 242. British infantry sword 1751.

sometimes with one or two branches, and a shell counterguard. The basket hilts were most often worn by grenadiers, the simpler hilts by line companies.

Among these swords with brass knuckle-bow and counter-guard hilts, two general patterns were so popular that modern collectors have given them informal "model" designations. The first of these has been called the "model" 1742 because it is so clearly delineated in the *Representation of the Cloathing of His Majesty's Household, and of all the Forces upon the Establishments of Great Britain and Ireland,* which was compiled for the Duke of Cumberland in that year. Actually, this sword was probably in use much earlier. A typical specimen has a slightly curved single-edged blade with a single fuller. The hilt is of cast brass and consists of grips moulded in a spiral pattern, a large globular or urn-shaped pommel with a capstan rivet, a simple knuckle-bow which expands to form a heart-shaped counter-guard, and a downturned quillon that terminates above the blade in a slightly bulbous finial. The principal variations of this type include straight blades, wooden grips wrapped with wire, and grips with the crests of the regiments cast upon them.

The second general pattern is often called the "model" of 1751 because it appears in a series of paintings of British grenadiers that were made by David Morier at that time. This pattern differs from the previous only in that it has one or two branches connecting the knuckle-bow and counter-guard on the obverse side, thus forming a half-basket guard. It is also subject to the same variations in the construction of the grips and blade. The scabbards for both

Plate. 243. Scottish basket-hilted broadsword.

U. S. National Museum

Author's Collection

Plate 244. American infantry sword of the Revolution.

of these patterns were of black leather with brass tips and a brass stud for attachment to a frog on the obverse side near the throat. Almost all British infantry swords found in America with histories of use here are of one or the other of these two patterns.

In addition to the types described above. there was one other distinctive sword carried by British infantry soldiers. This was the basket hilted broadsword, the traditional sidearm of the highland regiments. Often mistakenly called a "claymore" today, it was a much larger weapon than the standard infantry sword. The blade was straight, and sometimes it was double-edged. The grips were wood, usually covered with leather and wrapped with wire, although sometimes fish skin was used. The pommel was normally flat, and the large iron basket guard was pierced with open-work decorations, featuring the heart and St. Andrew's cross motives.[2]

The beginning of the abandonment of infantry swords by British forces began with the Braddock expedition against Fort Duquesne in 1755. On April 19 of that year General Braddock wrote of his men:

[255]

"I have lighten'd them as much as possible, and have left in store their Swords and the greatest part of their heavy Accoutrements."

This order, however, did not apply to the sergeants who were specifically instructed to retain their swords. Four years later, an order dated Albany, May 5, 1759, stated: . . .

> . . . sergeants to carry firelocks, instead of halberts, with cartouche box and bayonet instead of sword, the soldiers no swords nor sword belt, if they can carry their bayonet securely without them; . . . the Grenadiers to take their swords into the field. . . . The Royal Highland Regiment [42nd or Black Watch] and the 77th Highlanders are excepted in the order of no swords. The C.O. of each of those regiments may do as he thinks best.[3]

The Royal Warrant of 1768 applied this order to all the infantry regiments of the British establishment as it proclaimed:

> All the Serjeants of the regiment, and the whole grenadier company, to have swords. The Corporals and private men of the battalion companies (excepting the regiment of royal highlanders) to have no swords.
>
> All the drummers and fifers to have a short sword with a scimitar blade.[4]

The American Revolution brought the complete abandonment of the sword by infantry privates among the British soldiers who fought here. The Black Watch landed on Staten Island in 1776 completely equipped with their broadswords, but they laid them aside in the campaigns of that year and did

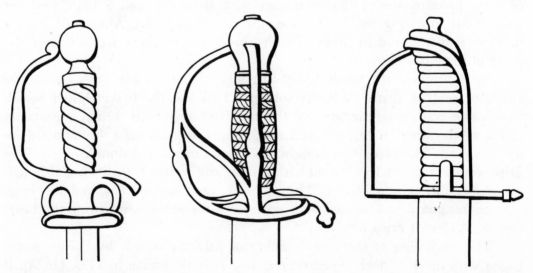

Plate 245. French infantry swords. Left: type prior to 1750; center: 1750-1767; right: grenadier's bricquet, 1767.

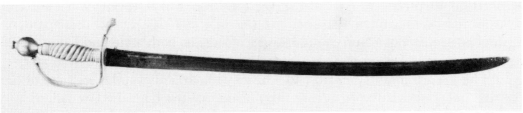

U. S. National Museum

Plate 246. German infantry sword. Note the close resemblance to the British.

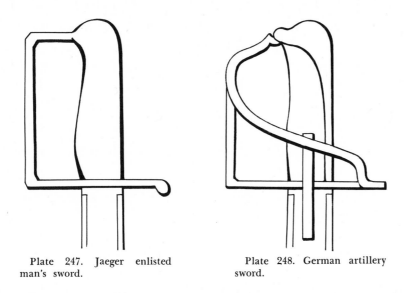

Plate 247. Jaeger enlisted man's sword.

Plate 248. German artillery sword.

not resume them again in this country. The grenadiers of the various regiments abandoned their swords gradually, but by the end of the war almost all were gone, and the sergeants alone among enlisted men retained the traditional weapon.[5]

In America, the local militia tended generally to follow the British pattern. At first all men subject to militia duty in infantry regiments were required to own either a cutting sword or a hatchet. Then the regulaions were modified to specify either a sword or hatchet or a bayonet, and in some colonies the laws finally specified the bayonet alone. The laws of Virginia and Connecticut serve as typical examples. In 1705 Virginians were required to have a sword. In 1738 either a bayonet or sword was acceptable; and in 1755 the sword was omitted for all but corporals and sergeants and the bayonet became mandatory. In Connecticut the sword only was acceptable until 1758. In that year the bayonet was allowed, and in 1775 only the bayonet was required.[6]

It should be noted, however, that the changeover to the bayonet was not universal by the beginning of the Revolution. Congress in 1775 sent a recommendation to the states concerning their militia which specified a sword or hatchet in addition to the bayonet. And as late as 1779 Massachusetts still required both weapons. Non-commissioned officers of both state and Continental troops were required to wear swords when obtainable throughout the war.[7]

The French infantry sword had a history remarkably similar to those of the British and American types during this period. At first both the Grenadiers and battalion companies carried straight double-edged swords with brass hilts similar to those on the contemporary small sword. Sometimes the grips were cast brass, but often they were wood wrapped with cord or covered with leather. About 1750 the pas d'anes began to disappear and a hilt very like the British "model" 1742 developed. The counter-guard, however, was normally bilobate rather than heart-shaped, and the blade remained straight. Sometimes branches were added on the obverse side and half-basket hilts resulted. On April 20, 1736 a royal ordinance standardized the blade length for infantry swords at 26 *pouces* (27 inches). Previously the length had varied greatly, sometimes running as long as 32 inches.[8]

The adoption of a distinctive grenadier sword, the ancestor of the briquet, became official in 1747. Prints of a few years before, however, reveal that some grenadier companies had been equipped with the distinctive weapon at least ten years earlier. This new grenadier sword differed from the standard infantry sword only in its blade, which was single-edged, slightly curved, and by the terms of the ordinance, no longer than 32 inches. There were no definite regulations for the hilts, and thus a variety of patterns were used, some of the small sword type, some resembling the British infantry sword, and some with half-basket hilts.[9]

Plate 249. British light cavalry saber.

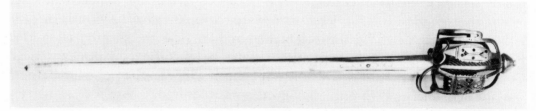

Maryland Historical Society

Plate 250. Basket-hilted broadsword carried by Captain Nicholas Ruxton Moore of the 4th Continental Dragoons.

These variations in the grenadier sword hilt, however, were greatly curtailed by the ordinance of January 25, 1767, which brought into being the true briquet. The specifications called for a single-edged, slightly curved blade 22 *pouces* (22.8 inches) long. The hilt was to be of brass with a simple knuckle-bow and quillon. The pommel was to be helmet-shaped or a simple bird's head. In general the earlier examples of this briquet are found with the hilt made in two pieces: one comprising the grips and pommel, the other the knuckle-bow and

Harry D. Berry, Jr. Collection
Plate 251. American stirrup-hilted saber.

quillon. Sometimes, however, hilts cast in a single piece are found, and sometimes wooden grips are encountered. The scabbard was of black leather with a brass throat and tip. There was a ball finial on the tip, and the throat had a staple and strap for attachment to a frog.[10]

Like their British counterparts, the French infantry swords also began to disappear during the French and Indian War (1755-1763). There had been grumblings about their uselessness by the soldiers as early as 1705, but until that conflict high officials had always insisted on their retention. They were officially abandoned except for sergeants, musicians and grenadiers March 20, 1764. The latter groups continued to wear their swords throughout the American Revolution and consequently until after the end of the period under consideration.[11]

The final group to carry infantry swords in America during the years from 1689 to 1783 were the German auxiliaries of the British during the Revolution, and their weapons were almost indistinguishable from the British "model 1742."

[259]

Officer and Sergeant of Grenadiers   *Officer and Trooper of Hussars*

The Lauzun Legion, French Navy, 1780-1783

Company of Military Collectors & Historians
Plate 252. Drawing by Col. Harry C. Larter, Jr

The differentiation is made particularly difficult by the fact that some of the swords used by British infantry during the first half of the century were made in Germany and so bore German marks. Prior to 1744 the blade length for German infantry swords was about 30 inches. In that year it was reduced to 24 inches. The scabbard was of brown leather with a brass throat and tip. The tip was completely covered by the leather except for a ball finial. A stud for attachment to a frog was fastened to the throat.[12]

Among the German infantry units there was one special group with distinctive swords, the jaegers. These men carried a short straight bladed, double-edged

Plate 253. Brunswick dragoon private's sword.

Plate 254. Brunswick dragoon private's sword. Note the crude lion's head pommel. All mountings are brass.

sword. The hilt was cast brass and consisted of a smooth grip, simple bird's head pommel, a rectangular knuckle-bow and quillon. At the time of the Revolution the blade was usually about 22 inches long. The scabbard was brown leather with a brass throat and rounded tip, with stud. Jaegers were an elite corps, however, and it was not unusual for them to wear swords quite at variance with the accepted pattern.[13]

In addition to the infantry privates, it was often the practice for the enlisted men of the artillery to carry swords. In the British, American and French armies these swords were the same as those carried by the infantry, but the German troops had a special artillery sword or "pallasch" as it was generally called. This was a short weapon with a straight, double-edged blade about 29½ inches long and a brass half-basket hilt. There were several minor variations in this hilt. Usually it consisted of solid smooth grips and a stirrup-shaped knuckle-bow with langets on the quillon and a single branch on the obverse side. Sometimes, however, the grips were ribbed, and, as in the case of the Hesse Hanau model of 1776, the grips were wood covered with leather. The scabbard was of brown leather with a brass frog stud near the throat.[14]

Unlike the infantry side-arm, the importance of the horseman's sword remained undisputed throughout the entire period. Troopers frequently carried other weapons also, it is true, but neither the musket nor the musketoon, the carbine nor the pistol seriously challenged the supremacy of the sword. Firearms might serve their purpose when the cavalryman was on picket duty or when he was dismounted; but once he was ahorse and in formation he had no use for them. William Washington, gallant commander of the 3rd Continental cavalry, called the sword the "most destructive and almost the only necessary weapon a Dragoon carries," and Henry Lee, the famous "Light Horse Harry" of the Revolution expressed himself forcefully on the subject:

> ". . . the fire of cavalry is at best innocent, especially in quick action . . . The strength and activity of the horse, the precision and celerity of evolution, the adroitness of the rider, boot-top to boot-top, and the keen edge of the sabre, with fitness of ground and skill in the leader, constitute their vast power so often decisive in the day of battle." [15]

Perhaps the best summary of contemporary attitude, however, was made

Plate 255. Brunswick dragoon believed to have been drawn by a participant in the Burgoyne campaign.

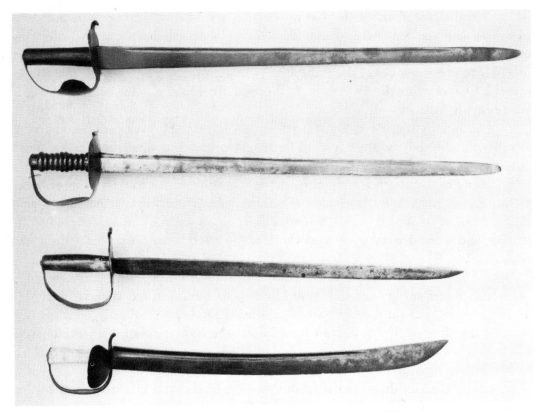

Chicago Historical Society, Hermann W. Williams, Jr. and Author's Collection

Plate 256. American cutlasses of the 18th century. Top to bottom: Revolutionary cutlass copied directly from the British; the same but with turned wooden grips; Revolutionary cutlass by Richard Gridley; early 18th century cutlass with shell guard and bone grips.

by Epaphras Hoyt, a cavalry captain from Massachusetts who became famous after the Revolution for his military treatises:

> It is generally agreed by experienced officers, that fire arms are seldom of any great utility to cavalry in an engagement, while they are drawn up in regiments, squadrons, or other considerable bodies: Indeed there is little hope of success from any who begin their attack with the fire of carbines or pistols; numerous examples could be cited from military history to show their inefficiency. It is by the right use of the sword they are to expect victory: This is indisputably the most formidable and essentially useful weapon of cavalry: Nothing decides an engagement sooner than charging briskly with this weapon in hand. By this mode of attack, a body of cavalry will generally rout one that receives it with pistols ready to fire.[16]

At the beginning of the period the typical horseman's sword in Great Britain, and consequently in America, was a heavy basket-hilted weapon. It was a lineal descendant of the Cromwellian basket-hilted broadsword and was identical with the Scottish broadsword which also descended from the same ancestor. Both the *Representation of Cloathing* of 1742 and Morier's paintings of 1751, referred to above, show these hilts in unmistakable detail; and a schedule of 1705 refers to the swords of Killigrew's dragoons as "Baskethilted Highland Scotish broadswords." [17]

In 1756 a light horse troop was added to each dragoon regiment, and a new sword was adopted for their use. The new weapon was described as "a short cutting sword 34 in. long with light hilt without basket." Since these sabers were provided by the colonels also, there was some variation within this prescription, but generally they had iron stirrup hilts, sometimes with langets, and either straight or slightly curved blades. The grips were of wood covered with leather and wound with wire; and there was a back strap terminating in a flat pommel.[18]

In America, the British patterns were closely followed. Thus, for instance, Maryland specifically requested "250 Horsemens basket hilted swords" in 1742, and an inventory of public arms at Annapolis in 1768 recorded 70 broadswords.[19]

By the time of the American Revolution the lighter saber with the curved blade was widely popular in this country. The commonest type had the iron-mounted stirrup hilt similar to that used by the British light cavalry but without langets. Usually there was no fuller on the blade, and as a rule, the blades tended to be somewhat longer than the British. Some surviving specimens have blade lengths of 36½ inches, 36 inches, 34 inches, and 32½ inches. Often the tang of the blade was secured at the pommel by a nut instead of being riveted. Epaphras Hoyt's own saber, now preserved in Memorial Hall, Deerfield, Massachusetts, was of this pattern, and similar sabers are shown in William Mercer's painting of the battle of Princeton which he finished before the end of the war. Also, it was this pattern which the newly formed United States Army adopted as its official cavalry saber in 1798.[20]

The only French cavalry to see any considerable service in what is now the United States were the Hussars and lancers of Lauzun's Legion who arrived in

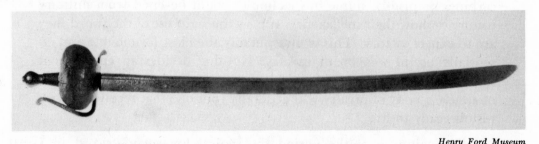

Henry Ford Museum

Plate 257a. Cutlass with shell guard. Normally this type is considered late 17th-early 18th century, but the specimen illustrated was made just prior to 1750.

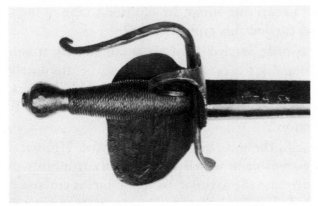

Plate 257b. Close-up view of shell guard.

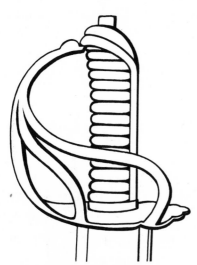

Plate 258. French cutlass of the late
Revolution.

Mable Brady Garvan Collection, Yale University
Plate 259. American silver-hilted small
sword attributed to John Coney, c. 1722.
Note the large pas d'anes and shells.

1780 to take part in the actions around New York and in the siege of Yorktown.
These horsemen carried the typical French hussar sabers with stirrup guards
and slightly curved blades. Both iron and brass mounted specimens survive in
French museums, and although there is no definite proof, it is the general belief
of students that Lauzun's Legion was equipped with iron mounted ones. A
particularly interesting feature of these sabers was the metal tip of the scabbard
which extended up more than half-way to the throat. Suspension rings on the

[265]

throat and tip provided attachment to carrying slings. In addition to the French, the cavalry of Pulaski's Legion also carried this type of saber.[21]

Surviving specimens of the swords carried by German mounted troops during the Revolution are exceptionally scarce. In fact, only three absolutely authenticated specimens are known; one, an officer's sword, and the others, privates' swords. All were used by the Brunswick dragoons who were practically annihilated at the battle of Bennington.[22]

One dragoon privates' sword is in the museum of the New York Historical Society. It has a straight, double-edged blade which tapers evenly from hilt to point. The grip is wrapped with wire, and the asymmetrical pommel is embossed on the obverse side with a crown. The knuckle-bow is almost of the reverse-P shape, and there is a branch on the obverse side which joins a large oval plate bearing the embossed figure of a running horse. A solid plate and an additional branch on the reverse side complete the counter-guard. All mountings are brass. The second enlisted man's weapon is a basket hilted broadsword, similar to the officer's sword, which is preserved in the State House in Boston and described below in the section on officers' swords.

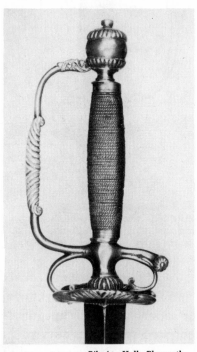

Pilgrim Hall, Plymouth
Plate 260. American silver-hilted small sword c. 1725 carried by Capt. William Basset in the Revolution. Note the upturned ends of the pas d'anes.

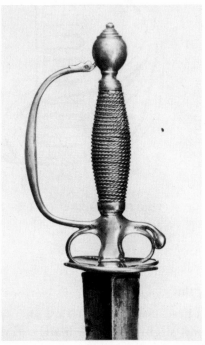

Mable Brady Garvan Collection, Yale University
Plate 261. American silver-hilted small sword by Jacob Ten Eyck, c. 1740.

There is one further source for the design of the swords carried by the Brunswick dragoons. This is an early print of one of the dragoons which is believed to have been taken from a drawing by a participant in the Burgoyne campaign. In it the dragoon is shown carrying the long straight sword with a brass basket hilt. The scabbard is wood covered with leather and it is attached to a frog.[23]

The final type of sword carried by enlisted men was the naval cutlass. The term was still used loosely during much of the period to denote any short cutting sword, but nevertheless distinct naval patterns were developing.

At the beginning of the period the design of the British and therefore also of the American cutlass was quite fluid. Individual captains selected the weapons for their particular vessel. By the first quarter of the eighteenth century, however, the older version with the large turned-up shell counter-guard and the up-curving quillon forming a knuckle-bow that stopped short of the pommel had been considerably modified. The shell was still there, but it was smaller. The pommel was smaller, usually only a flat cap, and there was a true knuckle-bow. As the century progressed the shell became flatter, and it was joined by a similar plate on the reverse side, thus forming a flat roughly circular counter-guard.

By the time of the American Revolution, the British had developed a standard design, and the Americans copied it closely. In this arm, the blade was straight and single-edged with a single fuller near the back. The hilt was entirely of iron. The grips were a simple cylinder, sometimes covered, sometimes bare. The pommel was a flat cap and the guard was cut from a sheet of iron. It began as a single knuckle-bow, then expanded into an elliptical lobe, contracted into a narrow neck, and expanded again to form an elliptical counter-guard. The quillon terminated above the blade in a simple roll. There is some disagreement among students concerning whether all the British grips were smooth at this period or whether the ribbing and corrugations which were characteristic of a slightly later period had already begun to appear. American specimens can be distinguished from British ones only by the quality of the workmanship. Some American cutlasses have turned wooden grips instead of the iron cylinders.

The French boarding cutlass of the late Revolution was quite different from the British and American version. The blade was exceptionally wide and slightly curved with one broad and one narrow fuller. Often there was an anchor stamped on the obverse side of the blade. The hilt was cast with grips and pommel resembling the briquet but with a half-basket guard consisting of a knuckle-bow and two branches on the obverse side. Usually the hilt was brass, but browned iron was also used. The scabbard was the same as that for the briquet.[24]

[267]

Hermann W. Williams, Jr. Collection
Plate 262. American silver-mounted small
sword by Jonathan Otis c. 1770. Note the
boat-shaped counter-guard.

In addition to the swords carried by enlisted men there were, of course,
those worn by the officers of all branches of the service. Often these were similar
to those carried by enlisted men, differing only in the quality of workmanship
and decoration. In other instances, however, they were entirely different in
design.

American officers probably carried a greater variety of these swords during
the period under consideration than the officers of all the other nations who
served here combined. Some wore purely civilian swords, some the semi-military
types, and some carried strictly military weapons. These were the products of
local smiths, importations from Europe, family heirlooms, and captured arms.

During the first part of the period particularly, and indeed through the
Revolution, the most popular single type of officers' arm was the small sword.
It was the standard civilian arm and was thus available to many who were not
able to obtain a strictly military piece.

The small sword developed just before 1689 and so was described in an
earlier chapter. Its essential elements remained the same throughout the eighteenth century also, but there were certain modifications which occurred from
time to time and which assist the student in determining the date of a given

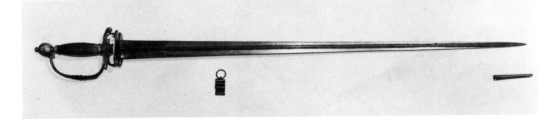

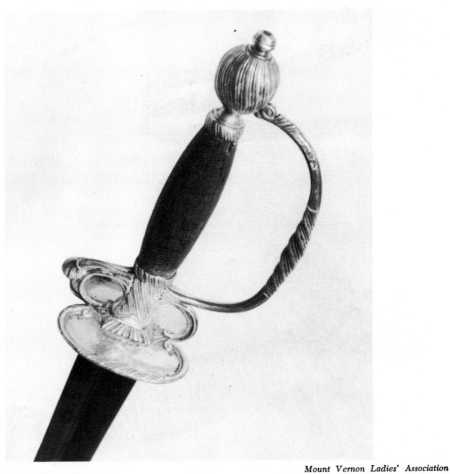

Mount Vernon Ladies' Association

Plate 263. French silver-mounted small sword of 1753-1754 carried by George Washington on the Brad-dock expedition.

specimen. During the years from 1700 to 1720 the shells of the counter-guard became smaller as did the pas d'anes. The latter were still large enough for the fingers, but on some the distal end of the bars turned upwards inside the rings, thus making it impossible to pass a finger through. It may be that this was done in a conscious effort by swordsmiths to support contemporary fencing masters who were attempting to discourage the practice. In any event these internal

[269]

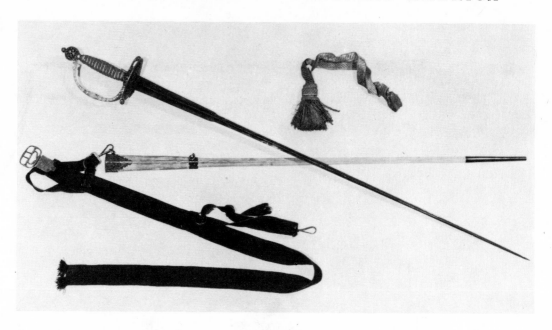

Mount Vernon Ladies' Association

Plate 264. British silver-mounted small sword with colichemarde blade, c. 1760-1770 used by George Washington. According to tradition he favored this sword for state occasions.

Plate 265. American silver-mounted hunting sword by William Moulton.

projections are normally found only on swords made between 1700 and 1725. The pommel lost its globular shape and became ovoid, and the knuckle-bow began to assume more graceful curves. The earlier military and Biblical decorations disappeared, and absolutely plain hilts became fashionable. Finally brass joined steel and silver as an acceptable metal for mountings.[25]

The next decades brought a few more changes. After 1720 the two sides of the counter-guard became equal in size, the plain hilts gave way to rococo decoration, and the quillon ceased to project beyond the counter-guard. About 1760 blued steel joined the hilt metals. Heart or boat-shaped counter-guards began to appear, and with them the quillon on the side of the knuckle-bow often returned. The pas d'anes were reduced to semi-circles, and after 1770 they became truly vestigial. About that time also, the hexagonal and colichemarde blade, which had disappeared from all but military specimens as early as 1720, were abandoned entirely and only the slender even-tapered triangular blades were left.[26]

Another form of sword which was popular among American officers toward the latter part of the period was the hunting sword. This side arm was designed primarily for the chase as its name implies, and it had little to recommend it as a weapon. For this reason it seems principally to have been worn by high-ranking officers who had little expectation of active personal conflict.

These hunting swords were short, cut and thrust weapons. The blade was normally slightly curved and usually less than two feet long. The grips were horn, bone or ivory, frequently carved and sometimes colored. The guard consisted of simple straight or S-curved quillons. The pommel was sometimes a flat cap and sometimes in the form of an animal or bird's head. Frequently it was connected to the quillon by a chain. Brass and silver were the most popular metals for the mountings.

Closely akin to the hunting sword was a form of light saber carried by some officers. The blades of these weapons were often exactly the same as those of the hunting swords. The hilts, however, had a more substantial guard. Usually this took the form of a knuckle-bow with one or more branches forming an open work counter-guard. Sometimes both branches were on the obverse side, but most often there was one on either side with connecting crossbars. The grips were frequently wood covered with fish skin instead of the horn and ivory found on the hunting swords, and iron mounts are encountered as well as brass and silver.

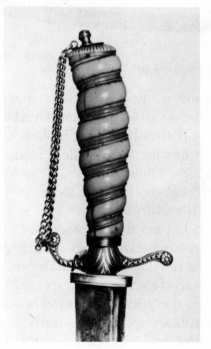

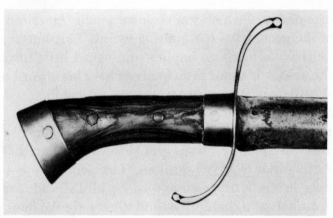

John Scofield, Massachusetts Historical Society, and Author's Collection
Plate 266. Silver mounted hunting sword hilts. The one at the right belonged to Gen. Artemas Ward; the one below was made by C. Chouso.

Author's Collection
Plate 267. Officer's short saber with lion's head pommel.

The most efficient military sword, however, was probably the heavy saber, and next to the small sword it was the most widely used type. Both mounted and foot officers carried such swords. Indeed, they were almost mandatory for the mounted officer who expected to become personally involved in a hand-to-hand conflict, for none of the other types were practical for use on horse back.

The individual variations among sabers in this category are infinite; yet they all have certain features in common which make the type readily recognizable. The broad blade is normally slightly curved and about 30 inches long. It is sometimes flat, but more often there are three narrow fullers, with the one nearest the back shorter than the other two. The grips are most often of plain wood, sometimes smooth, sometimes carved in a spiral pattern. Bone and ivory grips are occasionally found, however. The standard metal for mounts is brass. The pommels are of many designs, lion head, dog head, ball, urn, ovoid, balluster and some unclassifiable shapes. The guards are sometimes cast but more frequently cut from a heavy sheet of brass. The simple separated guard with a knuckle-bow and one branch on either side is most common, but there are several variations of the half-basket on existing specimens. Much depended upon the ingenuity and ability of the individual smith. The scabbards, few of which survive, are almost always of leather with brass throat and tip and a stud for attachment to a frog.

It should be noted also that many officers carried sabers that cannot be distinguished from those used by enlisted men. This was particularly true of

[273]

cavalry officers who customarily equipped themselves for the field from the same supply of sabers as their men.

In the British army there was somewhat more homogeneity than among the Americans, but standardization was by no means complete. As long as individual colonels continued to furnish the swords for their regiments they tended largely to wear swords of their own chosing themselves. This situation persisted throughout the entire period under consideration. As late as 1768 the Royal

Plate 268. American officer wearing a short saber on a shoulder belt. From a drawing believed to have been made by a participant in the Burgoyne campaign.

Warrants required only "The swords, sword-knots and sword belts of the officers of each regiment to be uniform." [27]

In actual practice the standard British infantry officers' sword of the first half of the eighteenth century was some form of the small sword. Sometime after 1750 and before the outbreak of the Revolution a modification of the type appeared and gained such widespread approval that it was made mandatory in 1786. This new sword had a straight single-edged blade that could be used for both cut and thrust. The hilt somewhat resembled the small sword, but the pas d'anes were gone, and the shells were larger and flat. At this period the shell on the reverse side was not yet hinged. Those hilts which were not steel were either gilt or silver according to the lace of the regiments. The grips were wood, sometimes plain and sometimes wrapped with wire, and the pommel was urn-shaped.[28]

A minority of officers carried other swords. Contemporary portraits reveal cutting swords with half-basket hilts of a variety of patterns. One is illustrated in the portrait of a British officer attributed to John Singleton Copley illustrated in the previous chapter, and of course, the Highland officers carried the basket hilted broadswords of their regiments. Cavalry officers also normally carried swords similar to those worn by their men, although some portraits reveal swords

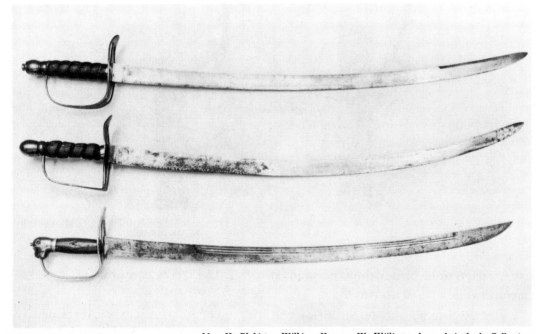

Mrs. H. Blakiston Wilkins, Herman W. Williams, Jr. and Author's Collection

Plate 269. American Revolutionary sabers showing typical blade types and proportions. Top: officer's saber by James Potter which belonged to Maj. Benjamin Tallmadge of the 2nd Continental Dragoons; center: enlisted man's saber by Potter; bottom: brass mounted saber with lion's head pommel.

[275]

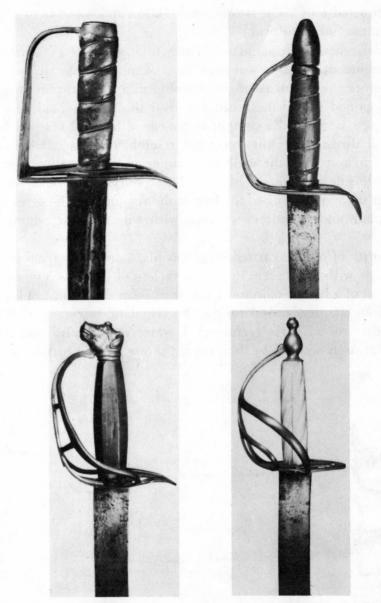

Hermann W. Williams, Jr. and Author's Collection
Plate 270. Some American saber hilts of the Revolution.

which seem to be either the true small sword or the later cut-and-thrust development of it described above.[29]

In the French Army uniformity among officers' swords was prescribed by the ordnance of April 25, 1767. Prior to that time the choice had been left to the individual commanders, and the small sword design had predominated. The ordinance of 1767 continued that design but restricted its materials. All officers

[276]

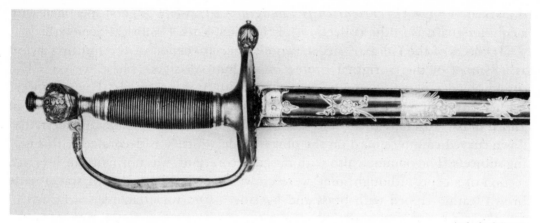

Plate 271. British infantry officer's sword. This specimen is post-Revolutionary as indicated by the blade decoration, but the same form was used during the war.

of infantry, both mounted and foot, were to wear swords *"à la mousquetaire"* with guards of gilded brass and silver grips. There are a number of swords of this type in the *Musée de l' Armée,* and a fine specimen, reputedly presented by Lafayette to an American officer, is preserved in the museum at Morristown National Historical Park. The blade is straight, diamond-shaped in cross-section and about 27 inches long. The hilt is that of a typical small sword of the period but with no decoration except ribbing on the pommel and ricasso and engraved or raised follow lines. The pommel is ovoid, and the grips are wrapped with braided wire.

Despite these regulations, many if not most officers of grenadiers and fusiliers continued to wear sabers of the same pattern as their men but of a better quality. Officers of hussars, such as those in Lauzun's and Pulaski's Legions, also wore sabers similar to those of their enlisted men.[20]

Although the German officers who fought in America came from a variety of different states, there was a remarkable uniformity among their swords. Both mounted and foot officers of infantry and artillery (and also frequently dragoon officers when dismounted) wore a straight sword which resembled the comparable British sword in most respects. It had a straight blade, diamond-shaped in cross-section. The hilt was of gilded brass with a simple knuckle-bow, slightly cupped shell counter-guard and a short quillon. The grips were normally wood wrapped with silver wire. The pommel shapes normally varied among urn, ball, crown, lion and eagle heads. Other variations included the presence or absence of a thumb ring and counter-guard and the quillon. The scabbard was normally brown leather with gilded brass throat and tip and a stud for frog attachment. An excellent specimen of such a sword with an urn pommel and without a counter-guard is preserved at Morristown National Historical Park. The blade

[277]

is marked "F^{II} L Z H" *(Friedrich II Landgraf Zu Hessen).* A good specimen with a counter-guard is in the collections of the New York Historical Society.[31]

Officers of the German jaegers wore a special version of the hunting sword as a symbol of their original profession as hunt masters. These weapons had straight blades, about 22 inches long etched with hunting motifs. The grips were leather covered and wrapped with wire, and the pommel and guard were of gilded brass. Normally this guard consisted of an S-curved quillon and a circular down-curved counter-guard on the obverse side which was decorated with hunting subjects. The pommel, also with raised decorations, was normally an inverted section of a cone, although some were crown-shaped. The scabbard was usually brown leather tipped with brass and bearing a stud for attachment to a frog.[32]

As was mentioned above, there exists in America one sword carried by an officer of the Brunswick dragoons. This sword was captured at the battle of Bennington and presented by General Stark to the colony of Massachusetts. It is an interesting specimen particularly because it is of the cuirassier pattern rather than the standard dragoon type. This may indicate that it was worn by a former officer of cuirassiers or that the officers of that unit as a whole preferred the cuirassier pattern. It has a straight double-edged blade 36¼ inches long. The basket hilt is brass with a crown and "C" device. There is a thumb ring, and the grip is covered with leather and wrapped with wire. The scabbard is wood covered with leather and reinforced with an iron throat and a tip that extends up over half its length. Four rings are provided for suspension slings, and in this it differs from the dragoon scabbard which had a stud for a frog.

In addition to the swords, a second major category of edged weapons comprised the pole arms, that is, those arms in which the handle or haft exceeded

National Park Service

Plate 272. French infantry officer's sword reputedly presented by Lafayette to an American officer.

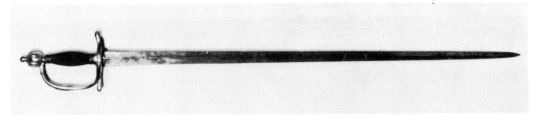

New-York Historical Society

Plate 273. German officer's sword with counter-guard.

the length of the blade. In this group were the halberd, the spontoon, the pike and its close relatives the trench and boarding spears, and, technically speaking, even the tomahawk. Some of these were mere badges of rank that were abandoned as the period progressed. Others were both symbols of rank and practical weapons, and finally there were those designed purely for utilitarian purposes. Both of these latter groups persisted throughout the period and even gained in popularity in some quarters.

Of all the types of pole arms, the halberd was the one which was most often purely a symbol of rank. At one time it had been a fighting weapon, but early in the preceding period it had come to be the symbol of a sergeant in almost all armies. Gradually its usefulness decreased, and it became more and more a mere symbol. Such was its status in 1689 when the present period begins, and as such its years were numbered. Nevertheless it should be noted that even well into the eighteenth century American made specimens are found with sharp edges and a workmanlike and practical design, indicating that some smith or some sergeant intended to have a badge of office that could still be used as a weapon.

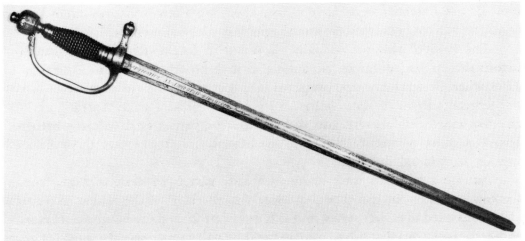

National Park Service

Plate 274. German officer's sword without counter-guard.

State House, Boston

Plate 275. Brunswick dragoon officer's sword captured at Bennington.

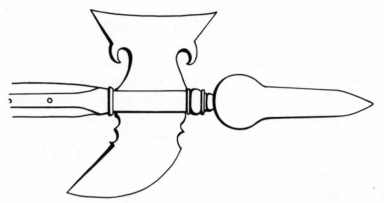

Plate 276. British halberd.

In the British army the sergeant's halberd varied little in design throughout the entire period. It consisted of a double-edge spear point with a slight median ridge at the end of a cylindrical iron shaft. This shaft was pierced with a slot, and through this slot passed the sheet of iron which formed the blade and beak. The whole assemblage was fastened to a wooden haft about seven feet long by two long iron straps which were pierced for frequent rivets or nails. The butt end was shod with an iron cone. No edges were sharpened, and the whole construction was weak. It could never have served any purpose as a weapon. Although most British halberds were made of iron there are a few brass specimens known which must have been used by some regiments with yellow lace.[33]

The halberd was not officially abolished in England until 1791, but well before that it had disappeared among British troops serving in America. In 1759, when General Amherst prepared for his campaign to the north, he ordered the sergeants to leave their halberds in Albany. The Royal Warrant of 1768 again specified that all sergeants of battalion companies were to carry halberds, but it is quite apparent that once the Revolution broke out the regiments quickly abandoned them.[34]

American halberds were made in a wide variety of designs. Many copied the contemporary British model as closely as the skill of the maker permitted. Others reverted to earlier styles, and still others produced the handsomely pierced and decorated arms that are so much prized by collectors today. In most instances the blade and beak were cut from a single flat sheet of metal and passed through a vertical slot in the metal shaft of the head. Sometimes this piece was riveted in place, but more often it was merely put in loose and held in place by the friction of a tight fit. In some instances blade and beak were forged instead of cut, and a serviceable weapon was produced. In these instances they were usually either fitted with a collar through which the shaft passed or else both they and the shaft were notched to form a locking joint and then securely riveted. Attachment to the wooden shaft was provided in a number of ways. Some had the conventional straps, some a socket, some a combination of both, and some a tang which was driven into the end of the shaft. The length of these halberds

Company of Military Collectors & Historians

Plate 277. Independent Company of Cadets, Massachusetts, 1772-1776. Drawing by H. Charles McBarron, Jr. Note the officer with a spontoon and the sergeant with a halberd.

also varied somewhat, but most of them ranged between seven and eight and a half feet.[35]

In America halberds were carried by sergeants, just as they were in the British Army. But they were also frequently carried by corporals, court officials and governors' attendants on ceremonial occasions. Some idea of the quantities

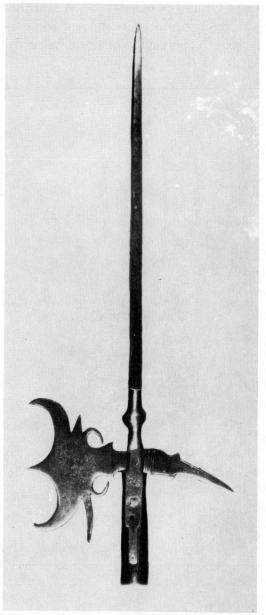

C. O. v. Kienbusch Collection
Plate 278. American halberd c. 1700 from Pennsylvania.

Joe Kindig, Jr. Collection
Plate 279. American halberd c. 1700-1725 from Pennsylvania.

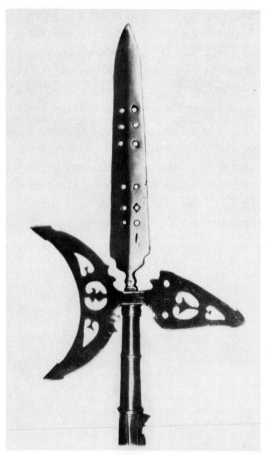

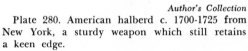

Author's Collection
Plate 280. American halberd c. 1700-1725 from New York, a sturdy weapon which still retains a keen edge.

C. O. v. Kienbusch Collection
Plate 281. American halberd c. 1720 from Maine, pierced but heavily forged by an expert armorer.

of halberds in America can be obtained from a Maryland inventory of 1736 which listed 74 of them belonging to the colony; a list of arms in the council chamber at Annapolis in 1768 which noted the presence of 23, and an inventory of the powder magazine in Williamsburg which contained 19 halberds in 1775. These arms were required for military duty throughout the colonies until the outbreak of the Revolution, and some may have been used at the very beginning of that conflict. Soon thereafter they were abandoned for military use and replaced by the fusil and bayonet. They continued to be carried by court officers and for ceremonial purposes, however, until well after the close of the period under consideration.[36]

The French halberd was considerably different in appearance from the British and the American versions. It was, in fact, a type that would be today denoted a partisan. That is, it had a central spear point with symmetrical lateral branches at the base. Such a weapon is illustrated as a "halberd" in Saint Remy's *Memoires d'Artillerie* in all editions (1697-1747), and early prints such as those by Hermand in 1721 show the sergeants holding arms of that type. In 1683 and again in 1703 the length of the halberd was set at six feet nine inches "because two halberds are 13½ feet, which is the distance which must exist between each rank when they are formed for battle." [27]

The French also were quicker to abandon the halberd than either the British or the Americans. In 1703 sergeants of grenadier companies were allowed to arm themselves with muskets and bayonets, and thereafter there was considerable agitation to extend this practice to the sergeants of the line companies as well. In fact, the practice was well begun long before official sanction was given on October 1, 1758. An ordinance of March 20, 1764 ordered the return of the

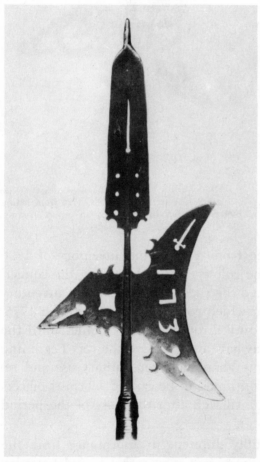

C. O. v. Kienbusch Collection
Plate 282. American halberd dated 1739 from Connecticut.

C. O. v. Kienbusch Collection
Plate 283. American halberd c. 1750 from Connecticut.

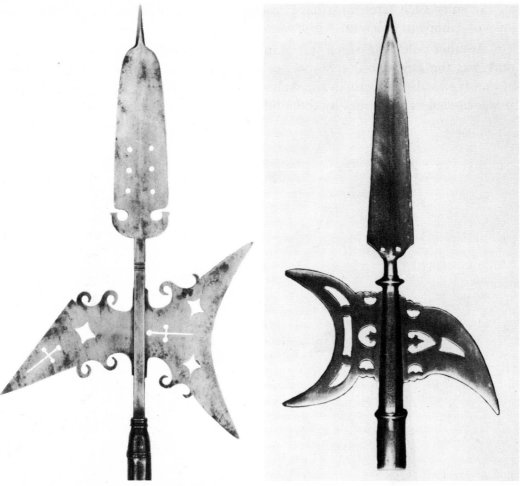

Author's Collection
Plate 284. American halberd c. 1750 from Maryland.

C. O. v. Kienbusch Collection
Plate 285. American halberd c. 1760 probably from New England.

halberd for line companies, but this was rescinded January 1, 1766, and the weapon disappeared completely from the French army.[38]

The German halberds greatly resembled those of the French. In fact, some of the plain ones of the Hesse Hanau and Hesse Darmstadt type are almost indistinguishable from them except that the spear points are shorter and wider than most of the French specimens and the sockets are faceted instead of round as was more common with the French.

There has been considerable doubt that many of these German halberds were used in America during the Revolution. No direct documentary evidence that they were carried has yet been found, but there are two surviving specimens known. Both are the heads of Brunswick halbreds. One is now preserved in the Valley Forge museum. The other is in Johnson Hall, Johnstown, N. Y. Thus

[285]

at least some such arms must have reached this country even if they were used only by troops in garrison.

Another pole arm which was akin to the halberd in that it was a badge of rank was the espontoon, spontoon or half pike. It differed from the halberd in that it was also, at least in the American army, designed for use as a weapon. It was carried in all armies by those officers who performed their duties on foot.

West Point Museum
Plate 286. American halberd c. 1750-1760 probably New York or Pennsylvania.

West Point Museum
Plate 287. American halberd c. 1750-1760 probably New York or Pennsylvania.

[286]

The British spontoon normally consisted of a simple point with a bulbous base and a crossbar or toggle below. As such it closely resembled and is sometimes mistaken for the sergeant's pike of 1800. The pike, however, lacked the bulbous base and almost always was attached to the shaft by a simple socket without the straps which are often found on the spontoons. There seems to have been some attempt on the part of some contemporary writers to differentiate between the spontoon and the half-pike, the latter term referring to the simple types described above and the former denoting a more decorative form more closely resembling the earlier partisan. Most of the military men of the time, however, used the terms synonomously.[39]

The spontoon remained the official arm of the British foot officer until April 17, 1786. In actual practice it had been gradually abandoned by most troops for combat some years earlier. Braddock ordered his officers to leave their spontoons in store when they left Alexandria in 1755. In 1768 Simes noted in his *Military Medley* that the officers were to carry espontoons or fusils "which ever is the appointment of the regiment." During the Revolution almost all regiments abandoned them for active field service.[40]

As was the case with the halberd, American spontoons were made in an infinite variety of patterns. Here, too, the current British design was the most popular, and various approximations of it are found. But there were also many patterns which were apparently the inventions of the individual smiths or supervising officers. In 1778 an attempt was made to standardize spontoons, and a general council of brigade commanders recommended that:

> ". . . the Quartermaster General be directed to cause spontoons or pikes made for officers, the staff six feet long and one inch and one quarter diameter in the largest part, and that the iron part to be one foot long."

Washington approved the recommendation and ordered it put into effect. It should be noted, however, that this order applied primarily to the regular regiments, and so there was still room for variation among the others. Also, with the general shortage of arms, it is unlikely that all spontoons that did not conform were discarded.[41]

Unlike the British, the Americans did not abandon their spontoons during the Revolution. Some military men, such as Timothy Pickering, advocated their abandonment at the outbreak of the war, but Washington was a firm believer in the use of pole arms, as were Wayne, and many others. Thus, throughout the war one finds frequent general orders to the effect that all platoon officers who did not have spontoons were to apply to the quartermaster immediately, and that no such officer or any other officer who was performing his duties on

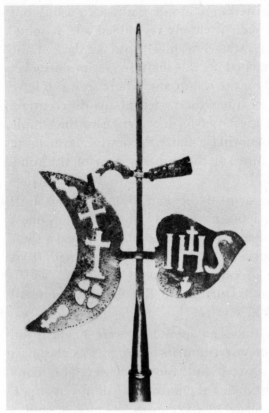

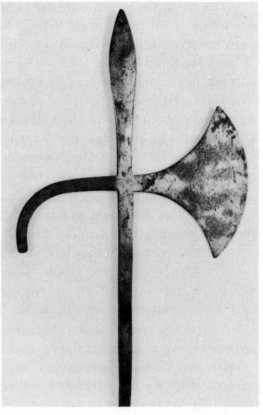

Plate 288. American halberd c. 1770 from Pennsylvania.

Plate 289. American halberd made for the Indian trade, early 18th century.

foot was to appear with his men without being so armed. Apparently there was no shortage of these weapons since all orders assumed that the quartermaster could supply them.[42]

The American spontoon was usually a weapon intended for use in combat, not just a symbol of authority. In stating his reasons for arming his officers with them, Washington wrote:

> As the proper arming of officers would add considerable strength to the Army, and the officers themselves derive great confidence from being armed in the time of action, the General orders everyone of them to provide himself with a half pike or spear as soon as possible—fire-arms, when made use of, withdrawing their attention too much from their men, and to be without either, has a very awkward and unofficer-like appearance.[43]

Wayne emphasized the fact that they were to be used in action when he wrote Washington stating that his officers had no means of defense in close fighting and asking for 50 spontoons as soon as possible so that the officers could practice with them before the impending attack on Stony Point. The arms were sent promptly, and in that famous assault, Wayne himself, who commanded his men on foot, carried a spontoon.[44]

In the French army the espontoon was a subject of much controversy throughout most of the period. An ordinance of May 10, 1690 required all officers to carry such a weapon between seven feet three inches and eight feet long. On December 1, 1710 another ordinance repeated the same dimensions for the spontoon, but restricted its use to colonels, lieutenant colonels, and captains. Other officers were to be armed with muskets and bayonets. The French *Archives de la Guerre,* however, are full of letters indicating that the regulations were being ignored and arguing either for or against the spontoon. It was abandoned in 1758, resumed in 1764, and finally abandoned for good with the regulations of January 1, 1766.[45]

None of the orders or regulations established a definite pattern for these spontoons. Only the length was controlled. In practice, however, there were two types, the so-called French pattern and German pattern. The French spontoon possessed a slender leaf-shaped point with a median ridge, a socket, and straps for attachment to the shaft. It was a direct descendant of the pike. The "German" pattern had a much broader blade, frequently barbed at the base, a toggle, and a socket without straps.[46]

As might be expected, many of the spontoons carried by the German soldiers who fought in the American Revolution closely resembled the "German" pattern spontoons carried by some French officers at an earlier period. The blades were broad, cut out decoratively at the base, and frequently pierced with cross, arrow, and crescent designs. There was often a decorated toggle in a highly developed faceted socket. Long straps provided the means for securing the head to the haft. The usual overall length for these arms was about seven feet, seven inches.[47]

No specific documentary evidence has been found concerning the use of these arms by German troops in America, but two different specimens survive in museums here.

In addition to the pole arms carried by officers, there were also some varieties used by enlisted men. The navies of all nations used boarding pikes, but during the Revolution, it was apparently only the American Army which made extensive use of the pike in land warfare. Great interest in these weapons was manifested by both the Continental Congress and the individual colonial governments, and large contracts were placed for them. Pennsylvania and Maryland, for instance, ordered theirs in lots of one thousand.[48]

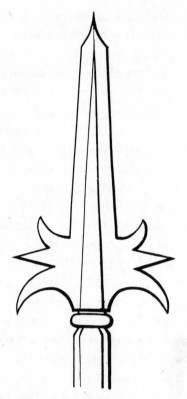

Plate 290. French halberd after Saint Remy.

Plate 291. Brunswick halberd drawn from specimens at Valley Forge and Johnson Hall

The exact use for which all of these pikes were intended is not always ascertainable. In 1775, the Pennsylvania Council of Safety approved a recommendation that they be used by infantry in line of battle, with the following resolution:

It has been regreted by some great Soldiers, particularly by Marshal Saxe, that the use of Pikes was ever laid aside, and many Experienc'd Officers of the present time agree with him in opinion, that it would be very advantageous in our Modern Wars to resume that Weapon, its length reaching beyond the Bayonet, and the compound Force of the Files (every Man laying hold of the presented Pike) rendering a charge made with them insupportable by any Battalion armed only in the common manner. At this time, therefore, when the Spirit of our People supplies more Men that we can furnish with Fire Arms, . . . the use of Pikes in one or two Rear Ranks is recommendable to the Attention & consideration of our Battalions. Every Smith can make these, and therefore the Country may soon be supplied with plenty of them. Marshal Saxe's direction is, that the Staff be fourteen feet in length, and the Spear eighteen inches, thin and light, the Staff to be made of Pine, hollowed for the sake of lightness, and yet to retain a degree of stiffness; the whole not to weigh more than seven or eight pounds. When an Army is to encamp, they may, he observes, be used as Tent Poles, and save the trouble of carrying them. The Committee of Safety will supply samples to those Battalions who are disposed to use them. Each Pikeman to have a cutting sword, and where it can be procured, a Pistol.[49]

Some pikes may well have been used in this manner by American troops. Certainly there are records of the issuance of large numbers of pikes to certain battalions without any comment on their purpose. Most such pikes, however, were probably used for defending fortifications. These were the "trench spears" and "spears for defending the works" that are so frequently encountered in Revolutionary records. One order for the issuance of these weapons, dated December 15, 1775, indicates the manner in which they were to be used:

Colonial Williamsburg
Plate 292. British spontoon.

Author's Collection
Plate 293. American spontoon c. 1760-1770 from New York-Pennsylvania border, purely a badge of rank.

[291]

Every colonel will appoint thirty men that are bold, active and reso-
lute, to use the spears in defense of the lines instead of guns; to form
in the center of the rear of the regiments and to stand ready to push
the enemy off the breastworks.[50]

Spears also were used in attacking fortifications. Thus it was that a council
of war held by American officers before the walls of Quebec in 1775 reported
that:

"A majority . . . was for Storming the Garrison of Quebec as soon
as the men are well equip'd with good arms, Spears, hatchets, . . .&c."

The attack was delayed until Captain Hanchet and his six smiths could
make those spears which they considered so necessary.[51]

A special and unusually interesting type of spear was that devised in 1777
for Morgan's Riflemen. The lack of a bayonet, which was one of the principal
drawbacks of the rifle as a military weapon, worried Washington considerably,
and he turned to the spear as an auxiliary weapon. On June 13, 1777, he wrote
Morgan:

I have sent for Spears, which I expect shortly to receive and deliver
you, as a defence against Horse; till you are furnished with these, take
care not to be caught in such Situation as to give them any advantage
over you.[52]

By June 20 the spears had arrived, but although they had a folding joint
in the haft, they were not exactly what Washington desired, and so he wrote
the Board of War:

The Spears have come to hand, and are very handy and will be useful to the Rifle Men. But they would be more conveniently carried, if
they had a sling fixed to them, they should also have a spike in the but
end to fix them in the ground and they would then serve as a rest for
the Rifle. The Iron plates which fix the spear head to the shaft should
be at least eighteen inches long to prevent the Shaft from being cut
through, with a stroke of a Horseman's Sword. Those only, intended
for the Rifle Men, should be fixed with Slings and Spikes in the end,
those for the Light Horse need neither. There will be 500 wanted for
the Rifle Men as quick as possible.[53]

The Board of War referred the letter to Col. Benjamin Flower, who was
in charge of the manufactory at Philadelphia. Flower prepared a sketch [see
cut, page 300] and returned it to the Board with the following comment:

[292]

Below is a drawing of a Rifleman's Pike intended to be seven feet long and the manner of slinging it agreeable to your request, which if you approve of, I will give directions and have the five hundred made as soon as possible. . . . The Letters and explanations show the different parts of the Pike

Viz.—

A. The Hinge

B. The Sliding Band that supports the Joints

C. The Hook that keeps the two parts together

D. The Sling

E. The Socket & Spear

F. The Spring to keep the band in place

G. A pin to keep the Band from sliding too far

H. Are Iron plates on both sides the spear from the end to prevent its being cut by a stroke of the Horseman's Sword.[54]

The sketch met with approval all along the line, and Washington asked that they be sent forward as quickly as possible. Unfortunately there is no evidence to indicate whether Morgan's men carried these spears at Saratoga a few months later.[55]

As was noted above in Washington's letter about the riflemen's spears, he also contemplated arming the light horse with a similar weapon, without sling and ground iron. Unfortunately, there is again no positive evidence as to whether any of the Continental light horse actually used them. There is, however, a Virginia ordinance of May, 1776 stating that each horseman was to be supplied by the colony with a carbine, a pair of pistols, a tomahawk and a spear. Thus there is some possibility that for at least a short time there were some American lancers during this period.[56]

The final major category of spears used by enlisted men during the Revolution was the boarding pike. It would be almost impossible to distinguish a Revolutionary boarding pike from any other spear used by American enlisted men that was less than nine feet in length and made without a ground iron. In fact the records seem to indicate that once a colony had a supply of pikes on hand, the same stock was used to supply both trench pikes and boarding pikes.

There is no question that these boarding spears were used widely. Records of their issue to boat and ship crews are numerous, and the *Pennsylvania Evening Post* of May 28 and June 1, 1776 describes an encounter between the American privateer schooner *Franklin* and several small boats manned by the British. The Americans defended themselves with firearms, spears, and cutlasses, and the account declares, "Great execution was done by the spears. One man, with that weapon, is positive of having killed nine of the enemy."[57]

One other weapon, which in a technical sense, was also a pole arm, was the hatchet or tomahawk. Long a standard side arm for American militia men, it was probably the most widely used pole-arm of the period. All colonies from well before the beginning of the era under consideration until the outbreak of

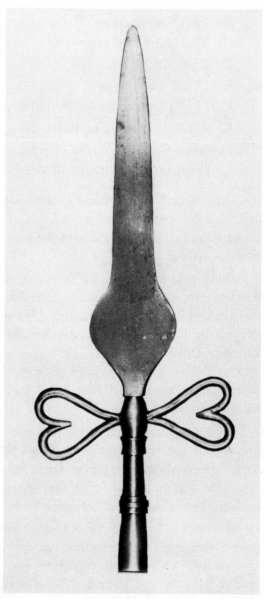

C. O. v. Kienbusch Collection
Plate 294. American spontoon c. 1750 from Maine carried by Richard Shepleigh of Kittery.

C. O. v. Kienbusch Collection
Plate 295. American spontoon c. 1750-1770 from Massachusetts.

[294]

the Revolution, called for either a bayonet, a sword or a tomahawk for each soldier. Even after the sword was no longer required, many colonies still called for the tomahawk which was to be carried in a frog on the same shoulder belt as the bayonet. For riflemen who never had bayonets, the tomahawk remained standard throughout the period.[58]

The Americans were not the only ones to carry tomahawks or hatchets,

C. O. v. Kienbusch Collection

Plate 296. American spontoon c. 1750 from Massachusetts.

C. O. v. Kienbusch Collection

Plate 297. American spontoon c. 1750-1770 from New Hampshire.

[295]

however. The French in America also used them during the colonial period, although it appears that the regular French regiments of the Revolution did not. The British light infantry also adopted the weapon at least as early as 1759, and they carried it throughout the Revolution.[59]

These hatches were normally small copies of the standard felling axe. The

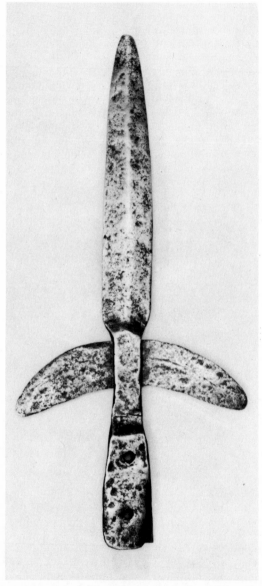

Author's Collection
Plate 298. American spontoon c. 1775-1780 from New York, crude but a serviceable weapon.

National Park Service
Plate 299. American spontoon by Lewis Prahl, probably part of his pike contract of 1775, a sturdy weapon.

[296]

head was single-bitted with no beak opposite. Sometimes there was a flat poll. but more often the iron encircling the eye or hole for the handle was left rounded. The handle was normally a straight round stick without any shaping. Specimens have been recovered from almost every major campsite or fortification of the Colonial and Revolutionary periods at which archeological work has been done, and thus there are several major collections to which the student can turn for comparisons.[60]

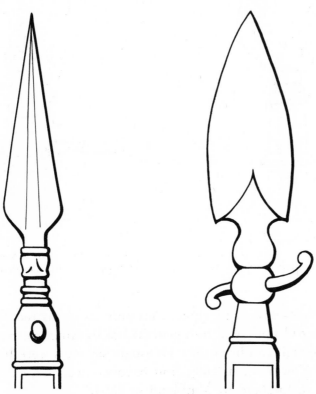

Plate 300. French spontoons, the "French pattern" on the left and the "German pattern" on the right. After Bottet and Margerand.

In addition to the sword and pole arm, there was, of course, one other major type of edged weapon—the bayonet. In many ways it was probably more important than either of the other categories, for it finally supplanted both. Much has been said about the bayonet already in the chapters on firearms and in the earlier sections of this chapter in which its inter-relationships with the swords and pole arms were discussed. Thus there remains the necessity only of a brief history of the weapon and some general comments on particular national designs.

The history of the origin of the bayonet is lost in obscurity. According to tradition, it was developed early in the seventeenth century in Bayonne, France,

Valley Forge Museum
Plate 301. German spontoon used in America.

Plate 302. German spontoon of the type carried by troops of Hesse Hanau and Hesse Darmstadt.

from which town it derived its name. Certainly its use is recorded in France as early as 1640. It did not come into general use in America, however, until the beginning of the eighteenth century, although bayonets were listed in an inventory of arms in New York in 1689, and bayonets were included in a group of arms purchased in England by Maryland in 1694.[61]

The first bayonets used in America were undoubtedly of the type known today as the plug bayonet. That is, the bayonet was fitted with a tapering wooden handle which was inserted into the muzzle of the musket. The Maryland purchase referred to above, in fact, specified "Bayonets fit for the Bore of these fusees . . ."[62]

The defects of such a device were obvious from the start. The bayonet could not be attached until the gun had been fired, and in order to reload it was necessary to remove the bayonet. Also, unless the bayonet were very firmly driven into the barrel, it was apt to be pulled out when the user tried to recover his weapon after delivering a stroke. Attempts to correct this situation were soon forthcoming, and eventually the socket bayonet was evolved. It was this

[298]

latter form of bayonet which was adopted by all of the armies of western Europe about 1700 and which consequently saw the most widespread use in America.

As was noted in the chapter on firearms, the adoption of the bayonet in the British Army was a gradual process which was not completed until well into the eighteenth century. Interestingly enough, the British bayonet underwent no major changes throughout the period. It had a triangular blade, flat on the top but grooved on the two under sides. The blade was cut square at the base, and the elbow curved sharply up to the socket. There was a heavy ring around the base of the socket, and since the bayonet stud on British muskets was on top of the barrel, the locking groove began on the bottom of the socket, made a right angle turn to the right, and then another right angle turn to the front. The only differences that one can notice between the bayonets of the early part of the century and those of the Revolution is that the latter tend to have a longer socket and a slightly narrower blade. As a rule, the blades throughout were sixteen inches long.[63]

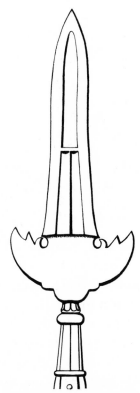

Mohawk-Caughnawaga Museum
Plate 303. A spontoon head probably German, excavated on the De Graf Flats near Amsterdam, New York.

Plate 304. American pikes and trench spears idealized from excavated specimens. All four types were found in some quantity. Left to right: from a trash heap near the site of Fort Washington, New York City; from Fort Ticonderoga; from Fort Ticonderoga; from West Point.

[299]

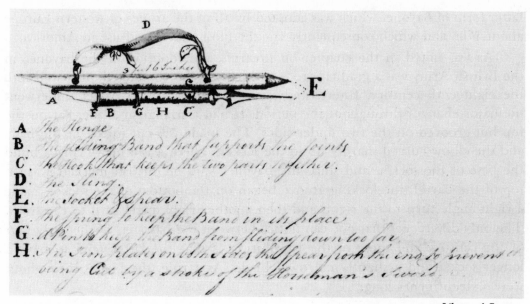

A. *The Hinge*
B. *The sliding Band that supports the joints*
C. *The Hook that keeps the two parts together.*
D. *The Sling.*
E. *The Socket & Spear.*
F. *The Spring to keep the Band in its place*
G. *A Pin to keep the Band from sliding down too far.*
H. *An Iron Plates on both the sides the Spear from the end to prevent its being Cut by a stroke of the Horseman's Sword.*

Plate 305. Col. Flower's original drawing of the pikes to be made for Morgan's Riflemen, 1777.

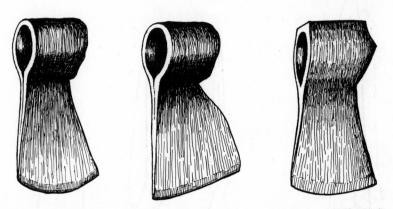

Plate 306. Some typical 18th century tomahawk heads.

American bayonets at first were patterned after those of the British. This practice continued up through the first years of the Revolution as the musket contracts let by the various Committees of Safety and quoted in the chapter on firearms called for bayonets with sixteen-inch blades similar to those used by the British. As the war progressed, and French muskets became more common in the American Army, the French pattern bayonet also began to appear from the shops of American smiths.

Unlike the British and American bayonets, those used by the French army underwent several changes in design. The first regular model was adopted for use with the model 1717 musket. It had a fourteen-inch triangular blade, flat on all three surfaces, and the socket was made without a collar at the base and with only one turn in the slot. In 1746 a second turn was added to this slot, but otherwise the bayonet remained unchanged. Sometime between 1746 and 1763 the blade was grooved, and then in 1763 came the first of the major changes in the locking system on the socket. In that year, the socket was made with a collar at the base and a single straight slot. A turning ring prevented the stud on the musket from slipping out. In 1766 the turning ring was replaced by a flat spring,

Memorial Hall, Deerfield

Plate 307. French plug bayonet taken from an Indian who was using it as a knife in 1675. This is the earliest known recorded use of a bayonet in America. Bayonets did not come into general use here until much later.

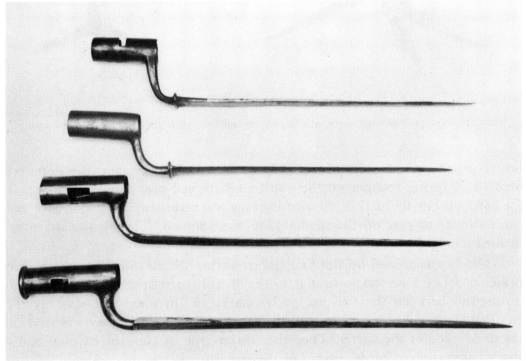

Author's Collection

Plate 308. Eighteenth century socket bayonets. Top to bottom: German, German, French, British.

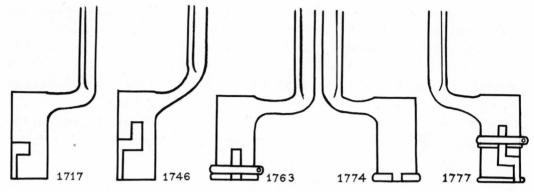

Plate 309. Development of the French bayonet.

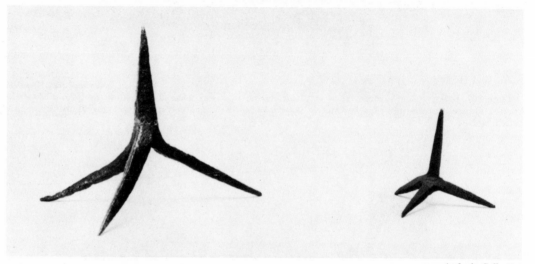

Author's Collection

Plate 310. Caltrops. The large specimen is forged; the smaller one is cut from a sheet and bent.

but returned again in 1768. In 1774 both the turning ring and the slot were omitted. A spring retainer on the gun barrel slipped over the collar and held the bayonet. Finally in 1777 the turning ring was returned, and a slot with two turns similar to that on the model 1746 was adopted. This final pattern remained standard until well after the close of the period.[64]

The bayonets used by German troops during the Revolution were of two principal types. One was so similar to the British pattern that it is difficult to distinguish between the two except by marks, or, in some instances, by the fact that the slot in the socket is made for a musket with the bayonet stud on the under side of the barrel. The other major type of German bayonet had a short, flat two-edged blade instead of the more usual triangular one.

Finally, there was one other implement of warfare which must technically be classed as an edged weapon. This was the caltrop. A contemporary dictionary defined this device as:

> a piece of iron having 4 points, all disposed in a triangular form; so that three of them always rest upon the ground, and the 4th stands upwards in a perpendicular direction. Each point is 3 or 4 inches long. They are scattered over the ground and passages where the enemy is expected to march, especially the cavalry, in order to embarrass their progress.[65]

An implement that was known to the Romans and which is still in use today, the caltrop is linked to colonial America through a list of arms desired in New York in 1689, the recent recovery of one large specimen at Jamestown, Virginia and some small ones from the site of a colonial fort at Sunbury, Pennsylvania, and the discovery of a large cache of mixed sizes near Harrisburg, Pa.[66]

This, then, was the history of edged weapons in America from 1689 to 1783. The principal development was the emergence of the bayonet which replaced the sword as the standard sidearm for infantry. Perhaps more interesting, however, was the reversion of the Americans to the use of the pole arm while European armies attempting to adapt themselves to American conditions abandoned them. Thus, if an effect on the evolution of armament is to be claimed for the American environment in this period, its agents must be the European troops and not the Americans.

NOTES—CHAPTER SEVEN

1. Charles ffoulkes and C. E. Hopkinson, *Sword, Lance & Bayonet*, Cambridge, England, 1938, 71-75. Lawson, *Uniforms*, II, 34. Simes, *Military Medley*, 6.

2. Lawson, *Uniforms*, II, 56, 58, 66-68, 73, 74. ffoulkes and Hopkinson, *Sword*, 74, 75. James Drummond, *Ancient Scottish Weapons*, Edinburgh and London, 1881, *passim*.

3. Braddock to Robert Napier, April 19, 1755, Pargellis, *Military Affairs*, 83. Lawson, *Uniforms*, II, 45, 46.

4. Lefferts, *Uniforms*, 186.

5 *Ibid.*, 164.

6. An Act for Settling the Militia, "*Province Laws,*" Bouton, *New Hampshire State Papers*, III, 178. Report of Committee to Inspect Arms, June 9, 1768, "Proceedings and Acts of the General Assembly of Maryland, 1766-1768," Browne, *Archives of Mary-*land, XXIX, 363, 364. Godolphin to Col. Nicholson, August 20, 1702, Palmer and Fluornoy, *Calendar of Virginia State Papers*, I, 80, 81. An act for Settling the Militia, 1705, Henning, *Statutes*, III, 338. An Act for better regulating and training the Militia, 1755, *ibid.*, VI, 536, 537. An Act for the better Regulation of the Militia, 1738, *ibid.*, V, 17. An Ordinance for raising and embodying a sufficient force, for the defense and protection of this colony, 1755, *ibid.*, IX, 31. An Act for Regulating the Militia, 1741, Hoadly, *Connecticut Records*, VIII, 380. Minutes of the General Assembly, March, 1758, *ibid.*, XI, 110. Minutes of the General Assembly, May 11, 1758, *ibid.*, XI, 23. Minutes of the General Assembly, April, 1775, *ibid.*, XIV, 418, 419.

7. July 18, 1775, *Journals of Continental Congress*, II, 188. Gabriel, *Pageant*, VI, 187. General Orders, TeaNeck, New Jersey, August 31, 1780. Washington, *Writings*, XIX, 478. Von Steuben, *Regulations*, 5.

8. Saint Remy, *Memoires*, I, 335. Margerand, *Armement*, 49-52. Bottet, *L'Arme Blanche*, 26-28.

9. Margerand, *Armemend*, 53-56. Bottet, *L'Arme Blanche*, 28-30.

10. *Ibid.*

11. *Ibid.*

12. Oberleutnant Deiss, "Blank-und Schutzwaffen Preussens vom 18 Jahrhundred ab," *Zeitschrift für Historische Waffenkunde*, Band V (1909-11), 324-330. Notes compiled by Col. Harry Larter from specimens in German museums and the paintings of Richard and Herbert Knoetel, Menzel, and C. Rochling.

13. *Ibid.*

14. *Ibid.*

15. Major Richard Call to Jefferson, March 29, 1781, Palmer and Flournoy, *Calendar of Virginia State Papers*, I, 605. Henry Lee, *Memoirs of the War in the Southern Department*, New York, 1869, 91n.

16. Epaphras Hoyt, *A Treatise on the Military Art*, Brattleborough, 1798, 101. For other dicta on the same subject see page 133.

17. ffoulkes and Hopkinson, *Sword*, 45-48. Lawson, *Uniforms*, II, 107-150.

18. ffoulkes and Hopkinson, *Sword*, 48-50. ffoulkes and Hopkinson, "Swords of the British Army," *Journal* of the Society for Army Historical Research, XII (1933), 152-158. Percy Sumner, "Private, Light Troop, 11th Dragoons, c.1760," *ibid.*, XVIII (1939), 187-189.

19. Proceedings of the Council of Maryland, 1742, Browne, *Archives of Maryland*, XXVIII, 292. Report of Committee to Inspect Arms, June 9, 1768, Proceedings and Acts of the General Assembly of Maryland, 1766-1768, *ibid.*, XXIX, 363, 364.

20. Harold L. Peterson, "The American Cavalry Saber of the Revolution," *Military Collector & Historian*, II, no. 3 (September 1950), 33-36.

21. Bottet, *L'Arme Blanche*, 46-50. Tench Coxe to Henry Dearborn, October 29, 1807, James E. Hicks, compiler, *Notes on United States Ordnance*, 2 vols., Mount Vernon, New York, 1940, II, 142.

22. Deiss, "Blank-und Schutzwaffen," 324, 330 contains a general description of German horsemen's swords.

23. This print is reproduced, among other places, in Charles Snell, *Saratoga National Historical Park*, Washington, 1949.

24. Bottet, *L'Arme Blanche*, 29, 30.

25. Aylward, *Small Sword, passim.* Dean, *Court Swords, passim.*

26. *Ibid.*

27. Lefferts, *Uniforms*, 178.

28. Lawson, *Uniforms*, II, *passim.* ffoulkes, *Sword*, 62, 63.

29. Lawson, *Uniforms*, II, *passim.* ffoulkes, *Sword*, 42-62.

30. Bottet, *L'Arme Blanche*, 38-40, 46-49.

31. Deiss "Blank-und Schutzwaffen," 324-330. Notes compiled by Col. Harry C. Larter, Jr. on specimens in German museums and paintings by Richard and Herbert Knoetel, Menzel, and C. Rochling.

32. *Ibid.*

33. ffoulkes, *Sword*, 115-117. Stephen H. P. Pell, "American Pole Arms or Shafted Weapons," *Bulletin* of the Fort Ticonderoga Museum, V, no. 3 (July 1939), 66-103.

34. ffoulkes, *Sword*, 115-117. Lawson, *Uniforms*, II, 46. Lefferts, *Uniforms*, 184, 208. Pell, "Pole Arms," 88.

35. Bashford Dean, "On American Polearms, Especially those in the Metropolitan Museum of Art," *Metropolitan Museum Studies*, I, (1928), 32-48. Pell, "Pole Arms," *passim.* Carl Otto v. Kienbusch, "A Footnote on New England's Colonial Halberds," *Journal* of the American Military Institute, IV, no. 2 (1940), 121-124.

36. *Ibid.* Assembly Proceedings, May 20-June 8, 1717, Browne, *Archives of Maryland*, XXXIII, 14, 15; March 19, 1733/34, *ibid.*, XXXIX, 158; May 6, 1736, *ibid.*, 463, 464. Report of Committee to Inspect Arms, June 9, 1768, "Proceedings and Acts of the General Assembly of Maryland, 1766-1768, *ibid.*, XXIX, 363, 364. June 13, 1775, *Journals of the House of Burgesses of Virginia, 1773-1776*, XIII, 223, 224. An Act for the better regulating and training the Militia, 1755, Henning, *Statutes*, VI, 536, 537. An Ordinance for raising and embodying a sufficient force, for the defence and protection of this colony, *ibid.*, IX, 31. General Orders, Tea Neck, August 31, 1780, Washington, *Writings*, XIX, 478, Von Steuben, *Regulations*, 5.

37. Margerand, *Armement*, 101-103. Saint Remy, *Memoires*, I, 331.

38. Margerand, *Armement*, 101-104.

39. ffoulkes, *Sword*, 114, 115. Pell, "Pole Arms," *passim.* Lawson, *Uniforms*, II, 18, 38, 45, 195, 211, 226. Lefferts, *Uniforms*, 184, 208.

40. *Ibid.* Simes, *Military Medley*, 17. Lawson, *Uniforms*, II, 45. ffoulkes, *Sword*, 115.

41. General Orders, Valley Forge, January 17, 1778, Washington, *Writings*, X, 311; January 18, 1778, *ibid.*, 314. Pell, "Pole Arms," *passim.* Dean, "Polearms," 42-45, *et passim.*

42. Pickering, *Easy Plan*, Part I, 4. General Orders, Valley Forge, December 22, 1777, Washington, *Writings*, X, 190; January 17, 1778, *ibid.*, 311; January 18, 1778, *ibid*, 314; March 23, 1778, *ibid.*, XI, 133. General Orders, Moore's House, October 12, 1779, *ibid.*, XVI, 458. General Orders, Morristown, April 4, 1780, *ibid.*, XVIII, 215. Von Steuben, *Regulations*, 5.

43. General Orders, Valley Forge, December 22, 1777, Washington, *Writings*, X, 190.

44. Wayne to Washington, July 10, 1779, *Wayne Transcripts*, V. General Claiborne to Wayne, July 11, 1779, *ibid.* Wayne to Major Posey, August 28, 1779, *ibid.*

45. Margerand, *Armement*, 81-97. Bottet, *L'Arme Blanche*, 66, 67.

46. *Ibid.*

47. Notes and sketches compiled by Col. Harry C. Larter on specimens in German museums. Deiss, "Blank-und Schutzwaffen," 324-330.

48. March 20, 21, 1776, Ford, *Journals of the Continental Congress*, IV, 215, 224. September 26, 1776, Journal and Correspondence of the Committee of Safety, Browne, *Archives of Maryland*, XII, 301. September 27, 1776, *ibid.*, 303, 307. General Orders, Cambridge, July 23, 1775, Washington, *Writings*, III, 357. General Orders, New York, May 17, 1776, *ibid.*, V, 51; June 6, 1776, *ibid.*, 99; June 7, 1776, *ibid.*, 105; June 8, 1776, *ibid.*, 106; August 12, 1776, *ibid.*, 421; August 14, 1776, *ibid.*, 436. Robert W. Bingham, "The American Military Pike of '76," *Miscellany of Arms and Armor*, 39, 40.

49. July 18, 1775, Minutes of the Council of Safety, *Minutes of the Provincial Council of Pennsylvania*, 10 vols., Philadelphia, 1852, X, 322.

50. John W. Wright, "Some Notes on the Continental Army," *William and Mary College Quarterly*, Second Series, II, nos. 2 and 3 (April and July 1931), 12. General Orders, Cambridge, July 14, 1775, Washington, *Writings*, III, 338; July 23, 1775, *ibid.*, 357; February 29, 1776, *ibid.*, IV, 362. George P. Keeports to Governor Lee, Journal and Correspondence of the Council of Maryland, Browne, *Archives of Maryland*, XLV, 11. Pell, "Pole Arms," 76.

51. Dearborn, *Journal*, 64. Matthias, Ogden, *Journals of Major Matthias Ogden*, Morristown, New Jersey, 1928, 13. Captain Simeon Thayer, "Journal," Kenneth Roberts, compiler, *March to Quebec*, New York, 1940, 264. Return J. Meigs. "Journal," *ibid.*, 187.

52. Washington, *Writings*, VIII, 236.

53. June 20, 1777, Washington, *Writings*, VIII, 272. Washington to Maj. Gen. Thomas Mifflin, June 10, 1777, *ibid.*, 222.

54. Benjamin Flower, Commissary General of Military Stores to Richard Peters, Secretary of War Office, June 23, 1777, *The Papers of George Washington*, Manuscript Division, Library of Congress, XLIX, 112.

55. Washington to Board of War, July 7, 1777, Washington, *Writings*, VIII, 367.

56. An ordinance to supply certain defects in a former ordinance of this convention for raising six troops of horse, May 1776, Henning, *Statutes*, IX, 142.

57. George Henry to Council, February 11, 1779, Hazard, *Pennsylvania Archives*, VII, 190. June 26, 1776, McIlwaine, *Journals of the Council of the State of Virginia*, I, 45. June 27, 1776, *ibid.*, 48. December 2, 1778, *ibid.*, II, 200. June 27, 1780, Journal and Correspondence of the Council of Maryland, Browne, *Archives of Maryland*, XLIII, 206. November 9, 1780, *ibid.*, 355. November 18, 1780, *ibid.*, XLV, 187. November 19, 1780, *ibid.*, 218. Moore, *Diary*, I, 245, 246.

58. An Act for Settling the Militia, Province Laws, Bouton, *New Hampshire Documents*, III, 178. Minutes of the General Assembly of Connecticut, May 11, 1758, Hoadly, *Connecticut Records*, XI, 123. July 18, 1775, Ford, *Journals of the Continental Congress*, II, 188. Gabriel, *Pageant*, VI, 187. An Act for regulating and disciplining the Militia, May, 1777, Henning, *Statutes*, IX, 268, 269. Proceedings of the Provincial Congress, February 18, 1776, O'Callaghan, *Documents*, XV, 67; July 23, 1776, *ibid.*, 117; August 10, 1776, *ibid.*, 123. September 24, 1694, Proceedings of the Council of Maryland, 1694-97, Browne, *Archives of Maryland*, XX, 140. Enclosure in Samuel Chase to Daniel of St. Thomas Jennifer, February 9, 1776, *ibid.*, XI, 150, 151. John J. Henry, "An Accurate and Interesting Account of the Hardships and Sufferings of that Band of Heroes who Traversed the Wilderness in the Campaign Against Quebec in 1775," Hazard, *Pennsylvania Archives*, XV, 65.

59. O'Callaghan, *Documents*, X, 79, 80. Lawson, *Uniforms*, II, 47. Lefferts, *Uniforms*, 195, 196. Arthur Woodward, "The Metal Tomahawk," *Bulletin* of the Fort Ticonderoga Museum, VII, no. 3 (January 1946), 30-32.

60. Woodward, "Tomahawk," *passim.* The best collection of these axes by far is at Fort Ticonderoga.

61. Margerand, *Armement*, 45-47. Grose, *Military Antiquities*, I, 112n, 162, 163. Lt. Gov. Leisler and Council to the Bishop of Salisbury, January 7, 1689, O'Callaghan, *Documents*, III, 656. September 24, 1694. Proceedings of the Council of Maryland, 1694-97, Browne, *Archives of Maryland*, XX, 140.

62. *Ibid.*

63. Charles ffoulkes "Notes on the Bayonet," *Journal* of the Society for Army Historical Research, XVIII (1939), 190-198.

64. Margerand, *Armement*, 48, 49. Hicks, *French Ordnance*, 70, 72. Bottet, *L'Arme Blanche*, 67, 68.

65. Smith, *Military Dictionary*, unpaged.

66. Lt. Gov. Leisler and Council to the Bishop of Salisbury, January 7, 1689, O'Callaghan, *Documents*, III, 656.

Chapter Eight

Armor

IT WOULD BE IMPOSSIBLE to select any period of 100 years in American history in which some form of armor was not used in warfare. The era from 1689 to 1783 was no exception.

Although the practice of wearing body armor had been almost completely abandoned, some forms of it were still in use, and defenses for the head continued to be popular, especially among mounted troops. These later head pieces differed considerably from the earlier varieties, it is true, but nevertheless they were a form of armor.

At the beginning of the period there was still much armor in America remaining from the earlier times when it was a highly desired article of equipment. Thus, for instance, the armory at New York was found by a French observer to contain a supply of cuirasses in 1692. Some of the mounted troops also continued to wear the breast and back plates that had been requisite a few years earlier, and British heavy cavalry troopers wore such cuirasses until the early years of Queen Anne's reign (1702-1714). Thereafter cavalry armor disappeared in the British army until it was revived for a few years after 1758.[1]

Most true body armor was confined to heavy suits used by engineers and special assault forces that operated within the range of an entrenched enemy. Such armor for British engineers was mentioned as late as 1754, and in the French service it remained popular still later. A list of military necessities for the French in Canada in 1758 contained an item of 100 "Cuirasses or complete armor" evidently for such purposes, and there is reason to believe that some of the engineers in the American Revolution were so equipped. In 1776, in fact, the Chevalier de Valliere recommended such suits for any force that was sent against a fortified enemy in daylight.[2]

The backplate from one of these suits of engineer's armor that was used

[307]

in America is still in existence. It was found a few years ago by workmen who were repairing one of the walls at Fort Ticonderoga that had been built in 1755, and is now preserved in the museum there. It had apparently been placed in the wall by the original builders in accordance with a superstitious practice of the time.

Engineers were highly skilled soldiers who frequently found it necessary to expose their persons to enemy fire from a distance. For this reason it was highly logical that they should have had the protection of armor. For the same reason armor was recommended for ship captains. Bourdé de Villehuet expressed contemporary thought on the subject as follows:

Every one allows that a Captain is the soul of his ship: the whole crew fix their eyes upon him and examine him in all perilous circumstances.

Fort Ticonderoga
Plate 311. Backplate from engineer's armor found during the repair of a wall at Fort Ticonderoga.

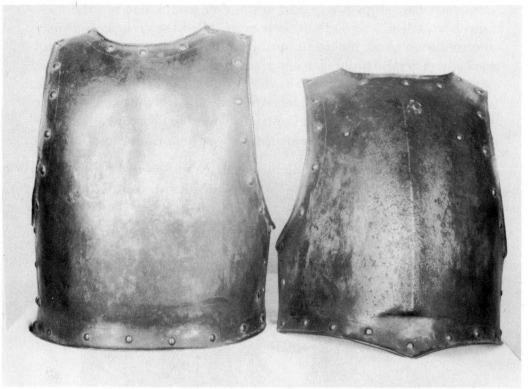

Plates 312. Back and breast plates worn by John Paul Jones.

He alone is the true mover of the actions of each individual, especially in an engagement, when every thing good or bad is charged to his account. It would therefore, methinks, be very essential that such a principal man at least should be a little more sheltered against the blows than any other Officer or soldier who has nothing but his own person to answer for, and whose loss is not of so dangerous tendency for the remainder of the crew. I could then wish that the Captains of ships should, during an engagement, be covered with a good armour musketproof, which would be a great advantage, for they would then have hardly anything else to fear but the great shot. This armour could not be cumbersome to them, because they are not exposed to leap on board the adversary as those of the crew who are under their command; they are bound never to quit the deck on which they are acting, and they are not to go from one place to the other; thus, an armour could not hinder a Captain from executing with ease all the motions necessary in the course of an engagement. The utility and advantages resulting from such a precaution can therefore not be denied; for, how

[309]

frequently have ships been taken, who never would, had not the Captains been killed, and had not their death filled the crew with dismay and confusion! And, indeed, it must be allowed that, in such a circumstance, a general discouragement seizes on the minds of all the crew, who no longer make any but false manoeuvres: the fire is badly served, and the end is always a surrender. After all, it is less for one's self than for others and the State, that a Captain is bound to take care of himself: therefore, he should not be ashamed of wearing armour. . . .[3]

It is not known how widely Villehuet's advice was heeded by naval officers, but at least one of the most famous ship captains of the Revolution agreed in principle with him. In the museum of the United States Naval Academy at

Plate 313. George Washington as a colonel of Virginia militia, 1772. From the original portrait by Charles Willson Peale which now hangs at Washington and Lee University.

Annapolis is preserved a corselet consisting of back and breast plates that John Paul Jones said he wore during his famous fight with the *Serapis,* and which he may well have worn in other naval actions in which he participated.

There was also one vestigial form of body armor that was widely worn by commissioned officers throughout this entire period. This was the gorget. A diminutive remnant of the piece of armor that once protected the throat, these crescentic plates, suspended about the neck by a ribbon, had already become the badge of a commissioned officer on duty when the period opened. In the British army there was some variation in materials and design at first, but the draft regulations of the 1740's and the warrants of 1768 specified that they should be either silver or gilt according to the regimental buttons and lace and that they should have the royal arms and the number of the regiment engraved upon them. Sometimes a regimental crest was added, and sometimes the royal cypher

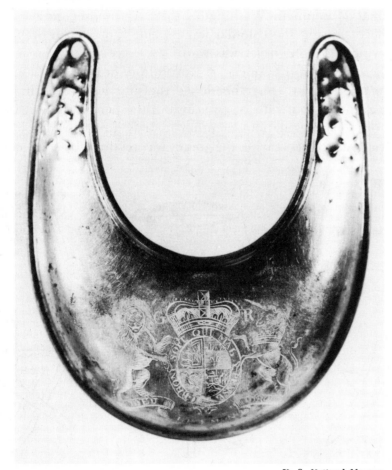

U. S. National Museum

Plate 314. British gorget worn by Lt. Col. Adam Stephen prior to the Revolution.

was used instead of the arms, although the cypher was not authorized for this purpose until 1796.

French officers wore gorgets of gilded copper with the Royal Arms in the center in silver. Officers of some German troops in the Revolution wore gorgets. Others did not. There were variations in the design of the gorgets that were worn just as there were in the weapons that these troops used, but the typical German gorget of the period was very large, made of silver with the arms of the kingdom or principality in gilt and enamel. It was worn sometimes over and sometimes under the coat.[4]

The gorget was also worn by some American officers during the French wars and perhaps by a few early in the Revolution. The painting of George Washington as a colonel of Virginia Militia done in 1772 by Charles Willson Peale clearly indicates the gorget, which bears the arms of the colony of Virginia. It is preserved today in the Massachusetts Historical Society. In the United States National Museum in Washington there is another gorget worn by an American officer during the colonial wars, Lieut. Col. Adam Stephen. In this instance, a typical British gorget was worn.

With the coming of the American Revolution, however, it is apparent that the officers of the regular army abandoned the practice of wearing the gorget. None of the authentic portraits or paintings of the period show it, and none of the general orders or regulations mention it. It is quite possible, on the other hand, that the practice of wearing the gorget was retained by some of the militia

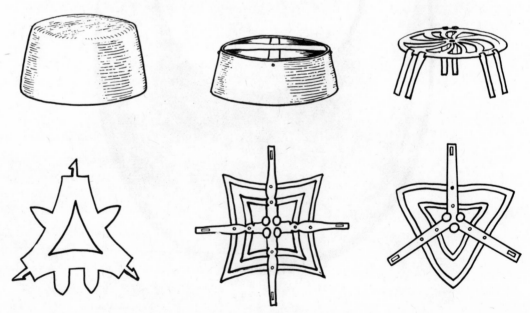

Plate 315. French calottes based on Bottet. Upper row: early 18th century types. Bottom row: for a tricorne 1754, for a square hat, 1776, for a tricorne 1779.

Plate 316. Helmet of the British 17th Light Dragoons.

officers. Two silver gorgets bearing Revolutionary devices and inscriptions are still in existence. One bears the coiled rattlesnake and the other a trophy and the motto "Libertas Potior Vita." Both are ascribed to officers of South Carolina troops. Also, there is preserved in Fort Ticonderoga a gorget that has been attributed to Gen. Henry Knox. In this interesting specimen the royal arms have been effaced, and the arms of Massachusetts superimposed, thus indicating that it is definitely post-colonial. It might have been used by Knox early in the War or it could be post-revolutionary when the regular army as well as many militia units returned to the practice of wearing gorgets.[5]

Except for the gorget, which was at best only a vestige, the wearing of body armor was confined to a very small number of men during most of the period. The helmet, however, was widely used by mounted troops. Of these cavalry helmets there were two principal types, the skull cap of iron or brass worn under the regular cocked hat, and the light cavalry helmet.

The skull cap or calotte was worn throughout the entire period. It is probable that the British cavalry troopers wore them from the very beginning of the period although no specific reference to them has been found before 1758. They are indicated for French troopers, however, in Saint Remy's *Memoires d'Artillerie*, in 1697, and specified in the regulations of 1733, 1750, 1767, 1776 and 1779.[6]

There was considerable variation in the design of these skull caps. Some were hollow hemispheres of brass or light iron. Other and heavier ones were made of musket-proof iron or steel. On some, the top was round in true hemispherical shape. On others it was flattened. Still others were made of a lattice work of metal straps which formed a sufficient defense against sword cuts and reduced the weight load to a minimum.[7]

The most striking helmet type of the period, however, was that of the light cavalry. This distinctive headgear appeared in Great Britain in 1756 when it was decided to add a light troop to each regiment of dragoon guards and dragoons. In specifying the helmet desired, the warrant of April 14, 1756 stated:

> . . . instead of hats the men are to have jockey caps ornamented in the front with H. M.'s cypher and crown in brass, and the number or rank

Detmar H. Finke Collection
Plate 317. Illustration from the *Kalender oder Jahrbuch* . . ., Berlin, 1784, showing at the left a member of Washington's mounted lifeguard wearing a leather helmet with a foxtail crest.

Yale University Art Gallery
Plate 318. Capt. Thomas Seymour by John Trumbull. The collar of the uniform is incorrectly shown, but the helmet and the colors are accurate.

of regiment. The crest is likewise to be covered with brass, out of which is to be a tuft of stiff horsehair, coloured half red and the other half of the facing colour.[8]

The use of the term "jockey cap" should not be interpreted in the light of the headgear worn by modern jockeys. These helmets had a visor fastened permanently upright. There was often a turban or a high band of leather around the body of the helmet, and there was a crest passing along the center of the crown from front to back. Usually these helmets were made of black japanned boiled leather with mountings of metal. Sometimes the entire helmet was made of metal. The 17th Light Dragoons which served in America during the Revolution wore such helmets made entirely of brass.[9]

The American cavalry during the Revolution seem to have preferred a helmet which more closely resembled the modern conception of the jockey cap. These helmets were made of black boiled leather and possessed the long visors that are so noticeable on the modern cap. Frequently there was a half crest of horsehair or a fox tail for decoration. The William Mercer painting of the battle of Princeton indicates the former, and a print of Washington's Life Guard which appeared in a German yearbook in 1784 depicts the latter. Both the cavalry of Lee's Legion and Moylan's Fourth Continental Regiment of Light Dragoons are referred to as wearing "tall caps draped with bearskin," and Col. Theodorick Bland's Virginia Light Dragoons wore leather helmets with white horsehair crests before they acquired metal helmets from France.[10]

The typical French metal helmet of the period is well illustrated in two pictures by John Trumbull. One is a drawing of Major Benjamin Tallmadge, and the other is a miniature of Capt. Thomas Seymour. Both men were officers of the 2nd Continental Light Dragoons, and both are pictured wearing brass helmets of the French Pattern with white horse hair plumes and bound around the edge with blue scarves.

In addition to being decorative, these light cavalry helmets offered valuable protection. Although neither the metal nor the leather helmets were proof against bullets, they served well against sword cuts. And it should be remembered that the sword was considered the principal weapon for cavalry, many leading horsemen even stating that the pistol and carbine were futile and ineffective. Even the decorative features of the helmets were designed to augment the natural strength of the boiled leather or metal in stopping a blow. The crest raised an obstacle above the crown that had to be crushed before the helmet itself could be reached, and the turban of cloth or the bearskin binding provided additional padding around the circumference of the bowl.

It should be noted that some infantry companies and at least one artillery organization, the Rhode Island Train of Artillery, wore caps of boiled leather.

[315]

These, too, since their purpose was at least partially for protection, must be considered as armor. In general design they differed from the cavalry helmet by being either conical or close-fitting over the skull and bearing a large up-turned plate in front on which the designating device of the organization was painted. They lacked both plume and turban.[11]

Thus the wearing of armor was continued through the period even though some of its forms were vestigial. The next few years brought the practice to its nadir, but with the American Civil War an upward trend began that brought armor once more into prominence. World War I saw the helmet as standard equipment, and World War II added flak suits, sniper's aprons, and defences for engineers until once more a goodly proportion of the combat forces of the world are equipped with some protective covering, some form of armor.

NOTES—CHAPTER EIGHT

1. Lamonthe, Cadillac, "Memoir on Acadia, New England, New York and Virginia, 1692," OCallaghan, *Documents*, IX, 548. Lawson, *Uniforms*, II, 144, 145.

2. Statement of What is Indispensable to send from France, by the first ships, for the service of the Artillery of the Colony, O'Callaghan, *Documents*, X, 864. Lawson, *Uniforms*, I, 167, 173, 174, II, 192. *Bulletin* of the Fort Ticonderoga Museum, VI, 115. Dean, *Helmets and Body Armor*, 52-54. M. de Lamont and the Chevalier de Vallière, *The Art of War*, Philadelphia, 1776, 240.

3. Bourdé de Villehuet, *The Manoeuverer or Skilful Seaman*, translated by the Chevalier de Sauseuil, London, 1788, 218.

4. Stephen H. P. Pell, "The Gorget," *Bulletin* of the Fort Ticonderoga Museum, IV, no. 5 (September 1937), 126-141. Lawson, *Uniforms*, II, 4, 17, 185, 211. Lefferts, *Uniforms*, 183, 242, 273, 274.

5. Pell, "Gorget," 126-141.

6. Lawson, *Uniforms*, II, 144, 145. Bottet, *L'Arme Blanche*, 70.

7. *Ibid*.

8. Lawson, *Uniforms*, II, 147.

9. *Ibid*. Lefferts, *Uniforms*, 150, 201.

10. *Historisch-genealogischer Calendar oder Jahrbuch*, Leipzig, 1784. Thomas Boyd, *Light-Horse Harry Lee*, New York, 1931, 61. Lefferts, *Uniforms*, 18, 64, 86. *The Pennsylvania Packet*, (Philadelphia), April 3, 1779.

11. Lefferts, *Uniforms*, 14-145.

Appendix

"THE COMPLEAT SOULDIER"

The foregoing chapters have traced the evolution of the various forms of arms and armor that appeared in America between 1521 and 1783. Since the discussion of these arms was organized in such a way that each type was carried through its evolution by itself, it was not possible properly to indicate the relationships of the various weapons and accoutrements to each other. For this reason a selected group of contemporary statements, lists, and regulations have been compiled here to give a more rounded picture of what the average individual settler or soldier and the standard colonial arsenal would have possessed at a given time.

CORONADO EXPEDITION, 1540-1542

On February 22, 1540 a muster roll of the expedition was made, listing the men and the personal arms and equipment they were taking with them. Below are some sample entries:

Lope de Samaniego, maestre de campo, swore that he is taking sixteen or seventeen horses, two buckskin coats, one coat of mail with its accoutrements, some native cuirasses and weapons . . .

Don Lope de Gurrea [Urrea], five horses, native weapons Castile armor, headpiece, and buckskin coat.

Don Tristan de Arellano, captain, eight horses, one coat of mail with sleeves and breeches, native weapons, some plate armor, one sallet [celada] with beaver, one harquebus, two crossbows, one double-edged sword, three swords and other arms for himself and his followers.

Francisco Rodríguez, one horse, native weapons, one sallet.

Jorge Páez, two horses, native weapons.

Luis Hernandez, two horses, one coat of mail, one gorget, one beaver, native weapons.

Cristóbal Caballero, two horses, some cuirasses, one helmet with beaver, native weapons.

Infantry

Lorenzo Ginovés, one harquebus, native weapons.

Francisco de Godoy, one sword and shield, native weapons.

Juan de Duero, harquebus, sword, dagger, native weapons.

Roque Alvarez, crossbow, sword, buckskin coat.

Galiveer, buckskin coat, sword, corselet.

Francisco Gómez, harquebus, helmet, native weapons.

In addition to the arms declared, the horsemen carried "lances, swords, and other weapons."

—Hammond, *Coronado Narratives*, 87-104.

FLORIDA, 1578

When Alvaro Flores made an inspection of the forts in Florida, he left detailed notes in his reports concerning the public arms and ordnance stores at various locations in the different posts and also lists of the arms carried by the individual soldiers. Some sample entries of both types are given below:

He found likewise, at the door which is the principal door whereby one enters this platform and the fort, twenty-five arquebuses, primed and loaded, laid on a long table, and the said table is fixed and placed there for that purpose.

Also, secured against the wall of the guard-room, outside and inside of it, on the platform, three dozen pikes hung on some nails . . . and in the sentry-box . . . two pikes and his arquebus . . . with its fuse lighted . . .

And above each *cadalecho* there are two nails where were [hung] the arquebuses of the soldiers, and a few muskets among them.

The said *visitador* was present to see the supplies landed . . . [including] forty *escaupiles* [cotton armor] and thirty pikes . . .

Andres Calderon, soldier . . . appeared with his arms, which are an arquebus, a sword, powder-flasks and bullets.

Adrian Laurel, master gunner . . . with his sword, linstocks, and powder horns.

[318]

Hernando de Segovia, barber . . . with his sword, buckler, and case of instruments for making cures.

Domingo Lopez de Basurto, soldier, . . . with his arquebus, sword, dagger, powder-flasks, and bullets.

—Connor, *Records of Florida,* II, 117-203.

NEW MEXICO, 1597, 1598

Don Juan de Oñate who was appointed leader of an expedition to explore, pacify and settle New Mexico offered to supply the following military materiel as an aid to outfitting the command:

Six light cavalry saddles
Six troopers' saddles
Six leather shields
Six lances
Twelve halberds
Six coats of mail [*cotas*]
Six thigh pieces [*escarcelas*]
Six helmets with beavers [*celadas con sus vistas*]
Six sets of horse armor
Six arquebuses
Six swords and daggers
Two complete corselets
Two stands of arms
Six buckskin jackets

—Statement of what Don Juan de Oñate and Don Pedro Ponce de León offer for the exploration, pacification, and settlement of New Mexico, Hackett, *New Mexico Documents,* I, 280-283.

NEW MEXICO, 1597, 1598

A captain on Oñate's expedition listed the following among the goods he was taking into New Mexico:

. . . three complete suits of armor [*ternos de armas*], to arm himself and two other soldiers in coats of mail with thigh pieces [*cotas con escarzelas*], beaver [*sobrevista*], and helmet, all complete with nothing lacking.

. . . Three wheel lock arquebusses [*arcabusses De rrueda*], with their large and small powder horns . . . bullet screws, moulds, and all the rest that pertain to each one.

... three sets of horse armor of buckskin, lined with undressed leather, for the flanks, foreheads, breasts, necks—all without anything lacking.

... A halberd, garnished with yellow velvet and purple tassels, and all studded with nails, which he bought for his sergeant to carry.

... A sword and a gilded dagger with their waist belts stitched with purple, yellow, and white silk.

... One horseman's broadsword with shoulder belt, and two shields for defense against arrows.

> —Manifest made by Captain Don Luís de Velasco of the goods, arms, and horses which he is taking to serve his Majesty in the expedition to New Mexico, of which Don Juan de Oñate goes as governor and captain general, May 19, 1597, Hackett, *New Mexico Documents,* I, 428-433.

New Mexico, 1602

The arms which the *maestre de campo,* Vincente de Zaldívar y Mendoza, intends to take for the expedition to New Mexico:

Seventy harquebuses.
Thirty muskets.
Fifty leather jackets or skins for making them.
One hundred coats of mail. [*Cien Cotas*]
One hundred cuishes. [*Cien escarzelas*]
Fifty steel helmets with beavers. [*Cinquenta moriones con sus sobre-
    bistas*]
One hundred swords and daggers.
Fifty leather jackets or skins for making them.

> —The Council of the Indies to the president of the Casa de Contractación, June 12, 1602, Hackett, *New Mexico Documents,* I, 403.

Virginia, 1609

When Captain John Smith left Jamestown in the fall of 1609, he reported that the colony had on hand:

... 24 peeces of ordinances, 300 muskets snaphanches and fire lockes, shot powder and match sufficient; curats [cuirasses], pikes, swords. and moryons more than men; ...

> —Simmonds, "Proceedings," 197.

THE FRENCH WARS AND THE REVOLUTION

VIRGINIA, 1611

Hee [the Governor] shall not suffer in his Garrison any Souldier to enter into Guard, or to bee drawne out into the field without being armed according to the Marshals order, which is, that every shot shall either be furnished with a quilted coate of Canuas, a headpeece, and a sword, or else with a light Armor, and Bases quilted, with which hee shall be furnished: and every Targiteer with his Bases to the small of his legge, and his headpeece, sword and pistoll or Scuppet provided for that end. And likewisee every Officer armed as before, with a fire-locke, or Snaphause, headpeece, and a Target, onely the Serieant in Garrison shall vse his Halbert, and in field his Snaphaunse and Target.

The Gouernour shall have a Principall care, that he vse his Garrison to the dayly wearing of these Armors, least in the field, the souldier do finde them the more vncouth strange and troublesome.

—"Instructions to the Marshall for the better inhabling of the Colonell or Gouernour, to the executing of his or their charges in the present Colony the 22. of June, 1611," Strachey, *Lavves,* 32.

VIRGINIA, 1618

The following is an abstract of the amount and costs of military goods it was thought necessary to provide for one hundred men who were to be sent from England to Smythe's Hundred:

20 muskets, 10 with "snapphammers, & 10 without" complete with moulds	16	13	4
40 swords and daggers	12	0	0
2 bbls. powder, (200 lbs.)	10	0	0
6 hundredweight of lead	2	13	4
20 breastplates at 6^s apiece			
36 headpieces at 2^s 6^d	10	10	0

—Meeting of a Committee for Smythe's Hundred, May 18, 1618, Kingsbury, *Records,* III, 96.

VIRGINIA, 1622

Prospective colonists were advised to bring with them these military goods:
suit of light armor (one for every two men is enough)
piece 5 or 5½′ long near musket bore
sword
belt
bandoleer
20 pounds powder
60 lbs. shot or lead, pistol and goose shot

> —Edward Waterhouse, "A Declaration of the State of the Colony and
> . . . a Relation of the Barbarous Massacre . . .," Kingsbury,
> *Records,* III, 578.

VIRGINIA, 1622

After the disastrous massacre, the Virginia colonists received the following
arms from the Tower of London:

brown bills—1000
bowes—400
sheafs of arrowes—800
callivers—700
short pistols with fire locks—300
arquebusses—300
skulls of iron—2,000
brigandines—100
plate coats—40
shirts and coats of mail—400

> —Warrant to the Lord Treasurer, September 1622, Kingsbury,
> *Records,* III, 676.

THE FRENCH WARS AND THE REVOLUTION

Virginia, 1624, 1625

In 1624, 1625 an attempt was made to take a complete military census of the Virginia settlers. It was not a complete success because some individuals and plantations failed to make returns and because there was some confusion in terminology. Nevertheless it provided much data for the modern student. A simple individual return and a modern tabulation of the results are given below.

Sir Francis Wyatt reported for his plantation at Pasbehaighs:

> . . . 8 snaphance Peices, 2 machlocks, 4 Armours, 1 Jack Coat, 2 Coats of mail, 1 steel coat, 1 corslett, 2 good head pieces, 10 lbs. powder and 60 lbs. shott

At his Jamestown residence there were:

> . . . 20 lbs. powder, 180 lbs. lead and shot, 6 snaphaunce pieces, 6 armors, and 6 swords . . .

Sir George Yeardley reported for his plantation and Jamestown residence combined:

> . . . 20 lbs. powder, 100 lbs. lead, 30 snaphance pieces, 40 Sword, 10 Armours . . .

George Sandys also combined his plantation and town house:

> . . . 20 pounds powder, 300 pounds lead and shott, 30 snaphaunce pieces, 1 piece of ordnance, 30 Armours, steel coats & coats of mail, 20 swords . . .

An old planter on a smaller scale than these, but in good circumstances, was one of the four John Smiths in the colony. He reported:

> . . . I pound powder, 30 pounds shot, 1 snaphaunce piece, 2 matchlocks, 1 armor, 1 coat of steel, 2 coats of mail . . .

—Brown, *First Republic,* 625, 626.

CENSUS OF ARMS, AMMUNITION, AND EQUIPMENT OF VIRGINIA SETTLERS, 1624, 1625.

Location	pop. M.	pop. F.	powder	shot	"pieces of ordnance"	"peeces fixit" & snaphaunces	matchlocks	pistols	petronels	armor complete	coats of mail & headpieces	quilted coats & buff coats	murderers	falconets	jackets, jack coats & corslets	swords
The College Land	20	2	12½	52	2	18	...	...	...	16	...	...	...	...	...	6
Neck of Land in Charles Cittie	25	19	46	248	...	28	...	2	...	12	15	...	...	...	...	16
West & Sherley (100)	44	16	65	507	...	46	...	1	...	14	16	1	...	...	...	...
Jordan's Journey	36	19	37½	704	...	37	...	...	1	10	26	...	...	...	...	...
Chaplain Choice & Truelove's Co.	13	4	20	340	...	14	...	2	...	7	5	...	5	1	2	...
Pierseys (100)	40	9	88	265	6	34	...	...	...	20	3	...	2	...	...	34
Pasbeayghs	35	8	19	60	...	25	2	...	...	16	3	...	...	...	2	7
The Maine	30	6	29	...	...	19	...	...	...	8	...	16	...	...	...	...
James Cittie	122	53	92	822	4	123	...	7	...	35	80	...	...	...	...	70
Neck of Land Near James Cittie	126	19	126	1,176	2	156	2	11	2	46	62	3	3	...	...	67
Hog Island	40	13	39	190	...	11	6	1	...	...	...	...	...	...	5	11
Martins (100)	20	7	84	366	1	26	26	...	...	19	13	...	...	...	...	31
Mulberry Island	25	5	52	...	...	37	...	...	...	22	...	...	...	...	...	42
Wariscoyack	8	...	10	...	...	13	...	...	...	9	...	...	...	...	...	...
Basses Choyce	16	3	33	300	...	20	...	4	1	...	11	...	1	...	11	12
Newportes Newes	20	...	200	200	3	16	...	...	...	20	19	...	...	...	...	20
Elizabeth Citty	198	59	154½	3,055	...	334	...	23	2	51	19	...	3	...	...	90
Elizabeth Citty beyond Hamptone River	78	20	72	711	2	90	11	3	...	14	3	...	...	...	...	20 plus one target
The Eastern Shore over the Baye	44	7	150¼	601	...	34	...	1	...	23	4	...	...	...	...	3
Totals	940	269	1,129¾	9,657	20	981	47	55	6	342	260	20	14	1	26	429

"Military Census," 364-367. Browne, The First Republic, 610-627.

THE FRENCH WARS AND THE REVOLUTION

MASSACHUSETTS, 1626

As the Massachusetts Bay colonists prepared for their voyage, they made a list of the public arms they intended to take with them.

Armes ffor 100 men:—

3 drums, to ech 2 pere of hedds;
2 ensignes;
2 partizans, for capten & lieftenant;
3 halberts, for 3 seriants;
80 bastard musketts, wth snaphances 4 ffote in the barrill, w^thout rests;
06 longe ffowlinge peeces wth muskett boare, 6 ffoote longe, ½;
4 longe ffowlinge peeces, wth bastard muskett boare, 5½ foote longe;
10 ffull musketts, 4 foote barrill, wth matchlocks and rests;
90 bandeleeres, for the musketts, ech wth a bullett bag;
10 horne fflaskes, for the longe fowlinge peeces, to hould a £ a peece, &
100 swoordes x and belts;
60 cosletts, & 60 pikes; 20 halffe pikes;
12 bbls powder, 8 barrills for the forte,
               4 ffor small shot;
   shott, 1 £ to a bandeleere
8 peecs of land ordnance for the forte, w^rof 5 alreddy ᵱuided;
   namely, 2 demie culverings 30 C. weight a peece
         3 sackers, ech weinge 25 C. w^t;
  to ᵱuide { 1 whole culveringe, as long as may bee,
          { 2 small peecs, iron drakes;
For great shott, a ffitt preporcon to the ordnance.

—Shurtleff, *Massachusetts Records*, I, 25, 26.

MARYLAND, 1635

A list of necessary provisions for each adventurer (copied from John Smith, *Generall Historie*) included:

In Armes.
For one man,
Item, one musket
Item, 10 pound of Powder

Item, 40 pounds of Lead, Bullets, Pistoll and Goose shot, of each sort
some.
Item, one sword
Item, one belt
Item, one bandeleere and flaske
Item, in. Match

"A Relation of Maryland," 94.

RHODE ISLAND, 1638

It is ordered that every Inhabitant of the Island shall be always provided of one muskett, one pound of powder, twenty bulletts and two
fademe of match, with Sword and rest and Bandeliers, all completely
furnished.

—Minutes of a General Meeting, March 13, 1638, Bartlett, *Records
of Rhode Island*, I, 54.

NEW HAVEN COLONY, 1639

Itt is ordered thatt every one that beares armes shall be compleatly
furnished wth armes (viz), a muskett, a sworde, bandaleers, a rest, a
pound of powder, 20 bullets fitted to their muskett, or 4 pound of
pistoll shott or swan shott att least . . .

—Proceedings of a General Court, November 25, 1639, Hoadly, *New
Haven Records*, 25, 26.

CONNECTICUT, 1640-1643

Inventories of estates listed in Connecticut provide an insight into the arms
possessed by individual settlers. Below are four sample entries:
James Olmstead, 1640—1 pike, 1 corselet, 3 muskets, 1 fowling piece,
3 pr. bandoleers, 1 sword, 1 rapier, 1 dagger, 3 rests, 2 pistols,
powder, shot, match.
Will Spenser—1 musket, bandoleers, 2 swords, 1 fowling piece.
Tho. Johnson—1 musket, sword, bandoleers, rest.
Thos. Scott, 1643—1 snaphance, 1 matchlock, 1 rapier, 2 bandoleers.

—Hoadly, *Connecticut Records*, I, 448, 449, 451, 453, 456.

THE FRENCH WARS AND THE REVOLUTION

PLYMOUTH, 1643

An act of the General Court required every able-bodied citizen to possess: a muskett, either firelock or matchlock . . . Also match, pair of bandoliers or pouch for powder and bullets, a sword and belt, a worm, scowrer, a rest and a knapsack.

—Proceedings of the General Court, October 10, 1643, Shurtleff and Pulsifer, *Plymouth Records*, II, 65.

VIRGINIA, 1644

The men who marched against Opecancanough were ordered to take with them:

4 lb. bullets (lead or pewter)
1 lb. powder
1 good fixed gunne
some defensive coat or armor and head piece
sword or cutlass

—"Acts, Orders and Resolutions of the General Assembly of Virginia," *loc. cit.*, 231.

NEW NETHERLANDS, 1656

List of the munitions of war required for 150 men, to be sent to the South River of New Netherlands (Delaware):

75 muskets, 75 firelocks or snaphances, 75 bandoleers, 75 cartridge boxes, 75 swords, 75 hangers, 75 sword belts, 75 saber belts, 2000 lbs. powder, 600 lbs. lead, 400 lbs. musket balls.

—O'Callaghan, *Documents*, I, 645.

NEW NETHERLANDS, 1660

Return of Goods for the Colonie in the Delaware River [New Amstel, formerly Fort Casimier]
800 lbs. powder
600 lbs. musket and snaphance bullets
 40 snaphances
  Worms, priming brushes and flints in proportion
  8 snaphance moulds
 40 cartridge boxes
  3 iron ladles to melt lead

O'Callaghan, *Documents*, II, 185.

MARYLAND, 1666

Voted necessary that there be 400 lb. Gunpowder 4200lb Shot or lead [140] Snaphance Musketts high Caluver bore 140 Cutlashes & Belts fifty Carabines for Horsemen two dozen Bullettmolds high Caluver bore & two dozen of Carabine Bullet Moulds to be equally distributed into the several Countys of this Province when purchased to remain there in the Charge & Custody of such Person or Persons as the Lieu^t General . . . shall appoint . . .

—Proceedings and Acts of the General Assembly of Maryland, April 17, 1666, Browne, *Archives of Maryland*, II, 19, 20.

CONNECTICUT, 1678

Each trooper to have a horse, sword, case of pistols and holsters, cartridge box or other means of carrying his ammunition.

—Proceedings of a Court of Election, May 9, 1678, Hoadly, *Connecticut Records*, III, 12.

CONNECTICUT, c.1687

. . . every foot soldier be provided with a well-fixed musket, the barrel not under three foot in length and the bore for a bullet of twelve to the pound, a collar of bandoliers or cartouch box with twelve charges of powder and bullets at the least, and a sword, or, if the officer so appoint, with a good pike and a sword . . .

—An Act for Settling the Militia, Hoadly, *Connecticut Records*, III, 430.

MARYLAND, 1694

The Council ordered the following to be purchased in England and sent to the Colony as soon as possible:

Twenty Dragoons Bridles & Sadles. Ten hand Mortars such as the two companys at Tangier had sent them when my Lord Dartmouth was there To inquire of Sr Henry Goodrich or some other officers at the Tower of the price and where they are to be had with one hundred hand Granadoes fit for those hand Mortars and ffuzces with proper Wadding and directions how to Use them.

Half a dozen Instrum^ts to try powder with an the rest of the 250lb to be laid out in Granadoes [Grenadiers] Arm's, Viz^t slung fusees [fusils] Sanguind or otherwise fited the best way to keep them from Rust & Byonets fit for the Bore of these fusees with large Cartouch boxes to hold betwixt two or three doz^n of carthrages and to Send good hatchets. The Cartouch box to goe upon one belt and the Hatchet & Bayonet in two hangers upon the Same belt and pouches to carry the Granadoes in.

—September 24, 1694, Proceedings of the Council of Maryland, 1694-97, Browne, *Archives of Maryland,* XX, 140.

NEW HAMPSHIRE, 1692-1702

. . . every soldier shall be provided [by himself] with a well fixed gun or fussee, Sword or Hatchett, Snapsack, Courtouchbox, horne, charger and flints, wth six charges of powder . . .

—An Act for Settling the Militia, Province Laws, Bouton, *New Hampshire Documents,* III, 178.

MASSACHUSETTS, 1701

Every foot soldier was to provide himself with:

a well fixt Firelock Musket of Musket or Bastard Musket bore; the Barrell not less than three foot and a half long, or other good Fire Arms, to the Satisfaction of the Commission Officers of the Company, a Snapsack, a Coller with Twelve Bandeleers or Cortouch box, one Pound of good Powder, twenty Bullets fit for his Gun, and twelve Flints, a good Sword or Cutlash, a Worm and Priming-wire fit for his gun . . .

Every trooper was to carry pistols, carbine with at least a 30 inch barrel, a sword, a flask or cartridge box, and a swivel and sling for his carbine.

—An Act for Regulating the Militia, Boone, *Military Discipline,* 73.

VIRGINIA, 1702

Queen Anne sent the following arms from the Tower to equip 1,000 foot and 400 horsemen:

Snaptice Musquets, 1000
Cartouch Boxes, 1,000
Carbines, 400
Belts with swivles for d^o., 400
Pistols, with Holsters, 400 pair

[329]

Swords $\begin{cases} \text{Horse, 400} \\ \text{Foot, 1,000} \end{cases}$

Belts for d° $\begin{cases} \text{Shoulders, 400} \\ \text{Wast 1,000} \end{cases}$

—Godolphin to Col. Nicholson, August 20, 1702, Palmer and Flournoy, *Calendar of Virginia State Papers,* I, 80, 81.

VIRGINIA, 1705

Every foot soldier to have a firelock, musket or fusee, a sword and cartouch box and six charges of powder. to have 2 lbs powder and 8 lbs shot at home and to bring that, too, when required.

horsemen to have a case of pistols, sword, double cartouch box and 12 charges of powder. Carbine with belt and swivel at home.

—An Act for settling the Militia, 1705, Henning, *Statutes,* III, 338.

CONNECTICUT, 1741

The following is an abstract of the arms and equipment required for the militia of Connecticut:

Infantry:

firelock, barrel not less than 3½ feet long, or other good firearms
to the satisfaction of the commission officers
sword or cutlass
worm
primer and priming wire
cartridge box
1 lb. powder
4 lbs. of bullets for gun
12 flints

Troopers:

carbine—barrel not less than 2½ feet with belt and swivel
a case of pistols
sword or cutlass
flask or cartridge box
1 lb. powder
3 lbs. bullets
20 flints
boots and spurs

—An Act for Regulating the Militia, May, 1741, Hoadly, *Connecticut Records,* VIII, 380.

THE FRENCH WARS AND THE REVOLUTION

MARYLAND, 1747

Maryland supplied the following items for its troops who were to take part in an expedition against Canada:

300 muskets with slings and bayonets
300 cartouch boxes with belts
  6 drums
  9 Half-pikes
  6 Halberds

—June 22, 1747, Assembly of Proceeding, Browne, *Archives of Maryland*, XLIV, 549.

VIRGINIA, 1755

The following arms were required for officers of the militia:

colonels, lieutenant colonels, majors, captains and lieutenants of horse
    to have cutting sword, pistols
colonels, lieutenant colonels, majors, captains, and lieutenants of foot—
    half pike or partisan and cutting sword.
colonels of horse: cutting sword and pistols
ensigns: cutting sword
corporals and sergeants: cutting sword and halberd

—An Act for the better regulating and training the Militia, 1755
Henning, *Statutes*, VI, 536, 537.

FRENCH (CANADA), 1758

Statement of what is indispensable to send from France, by the first ships, for the service of the Artillery of this Colony, vizt.:

* * *

Priming horns for cannon, taking care that they be large ..	400
Same, for Militia, containing 1 lb. of powder	8,000
Cuirasses or complete armor	100
Grenadier muskets, *à domino*, iron ring, furnished with their bayonet	6,000
Fowling pieces *(thules de chasses)* with their bayonets	6,000
Fowling pieces without bayonets, to arm the Indians	2,000
Clear and transparent flints for grenadier muskets	30,000
Flints for fowling pieces	600,000
Bullets 20 or 22 to the pound	250,000
Same, 28 or 30 ” ” ”	250,000

—O'Callaghan, *Documents*, X, 864.

MARYLAND, 1768

An inventory of the arms belonging to the colony in Annapolis revealed the following:

In Council Chamber

185 Musketts, with slings, which appear to be in good order
23 halberts
19 pikes
30 trumpets
70 broadswords
15 daggers
78 buff slings
50 sword blades

Above the Conference Chamber

85 black hilted swords; 42 bright ditto; 15 cutlasses; 35 pistols; 2 new drums; 1 old ditto, a little damaged; 200 new bayonets, with cartouch boxes, and bullet moulds; 90 buff belts; 29 old bayonets; 86 carbines and short muskets; 57 old muskets, and carbines; 104 ditto, mostly without locks, and not worth repairing; 9 pistols, the locks broke; 4 pair holsters; 7 broken drums; 3 chests matches; 30 blue cases for musketts; 1/4 C. wt. musket ball and great shott; 15 musketts in good order, being removed from the council chamber.

Under the Conference Chamber

382 muskets, very rusty, and many of the locks want repairing; 60 ditto mostly without locks; 35 musket barrels; 16 kegs musket ball, each 1/2 C. wt. 3 powder barrels, filled with ditto, 200 bayonets; 1500 gunflints.

—Report of Committee to Inspect Arms, June 9, 1768, Proceedings and Acts of the General Assembly of Maryland, 1766-1768, Browne, *Archives of Maryland*, XXIX, 363, 364.

VIRGINIA, 1775

The powder magazine at Williamsburg contained the following military goods:

19 halberds
157 trading guns
51 pewter basins

      8 camp kettles
    180 new muskets
    527 old muskets
   1200 cartouch boxes
   1500 cutlasses with scabbards
    170 pistol holsters
    150 old pistols (or thereabouts)
     50 mallets
      2 bundles match rope
    200 canteens
     35 small swords
      1 tent and tent poles
      1 pkg. of powder horns
    127 bayonets
    100 knapsacks

—Tuesday, June 13, 1775, *Journals of the House of Burgesses*, XIII, 223, 224.

UNITED STATES, 1775

On July 18, 1775, the Continental Congress recommended the following equipment for the militia of the various colonies:

That each solder be furnished with a good musket, that will carray an ounce ball, with a bayonet, steel ram-rod, worm, priming wire and brush fitted thereto, a cutting sword or tomahawk, a cartridge box, that will contain 23 rounds of cartridges, twelve flints and a knapsack.

—Ford, *Journals of the Continental Congress*, II, 188.

SOUTH CAROLINA, 1776

These instructions were given by the Council of Safety to an agent of the colony:

You are also to procure at Bermuda any quatity you can of good gunpowder and salt-petre, and good muskets, good six and four-pound cannon, with shot, match, and all necessary appurtenances, swiveled guns and shot, swiveled blunderbusses, and good pistols, cutlasses and half-pikes or lances, musket, pistol and blunderbuss ball, hand-grenades, good flints and cartridge paper.

—Henry Laurens to Elisha Sawyer, January 19, 1776, South Carolina, "Journal of the Council of Safety," III, 199-201.

VIRGINIA, 1776

Each trooper to be furnished with a carbine with bucket and strap, a pair of pistols and holsters, a tomahawk and a spear.

> —An ordinance to supply certain defects in a former ordinance of this convention for raising six troops of horse, May 1776, Henning. *Statutes*, IX, 142.

UNITED STATES, 1778

In March 1778 when the Continental Congress requested the various states to raise troops of cavalry, the Board of War prepared the following list of suggested arms and accoutrements:

List of Necessaries and Accoutrements for Each Horseman

1. A well tempered sword, the blade straight, and three feet long, with the back sharpened up six inches from the point; an open guard about the hilt; that will be light and yet defend the hand; with a scabbard of substantial leather without wood.

2. A carbine, fusee, or short blunderbuss; the barrel of the blunderbuss not to exceed two feet in length.

3. A pair of pistols and holsters.

4. A sword-belt—a belt for the carbine, with a running swivel that will slip to any part of the belt.

5. A cartridge-box to buckle round the waist, with twelve tin pipes for the cartridges.

6. A helmet of jacked leather, and effectually guarded by several rows of small chain, iron or steel hoops; or a hat with a steel or iron scull piece inside the crown.

7. A saddle; saddlecloth, breastplate, crupper, saddlestraps and pad.

8. Saddlebags connected by two broad straps, in the common fashion, and not a portmanteau.

9. A double reined bridle, with a curb and snaffle bit, and a halter.

10. A cloak sufficient to cover all the arms and accoutrements, and which is to serve also in the place of a blanket.

11. Boots and spurs.

> —George Clinton, *Public Papers of George Clinton*, edited by Hugh Hastings, 8 vols, New York, 1899-1904, II, 829, 830.

THE FRENCH WARS AND THE REVOLUTION

MASSACHUSETTS, 1779

The following order was directed to the militia:

You are hereby ordered and directed to complete yourself with Arms and Accoutrements, by the 12th instant, upon failure thereof you are liable to a fine of Three Pounds: and for every sixty days after, a Fine of Six Pounds.

Articles of Equipment

A good fire arm, with a steel or iron ramrod, and a spring to retain the same, a worm, priming iron and brush, and a bayonet fitted to your Gun, a scabbard and belt therefore, and a cutting sword or a tomahawk or hatchet, a Pouch containing a cartridge box, that will hold fifteen Rounds of cartridges at least, a hundred buckshot, a Jack Knife and Tow for wadding, six flints, one pound of powder, fourty leaden Balls fitted to your Gun, a Knapsack and Blanket a Canteen or wooden Bottle sufficient to hold one Quart.

—Gabriel, *Pageant*, VI, 187.

Bibliography

The following list should by no means be taken for a complete bibliography of the subject. Indeed it does not even reflect the total number of books consulted in the preparation of this volume. Rather it lists only those works which contained material of sufficient interest to cause them to be referred to in the text.

CONTEMPORARY SOURCES

"Acts, Orders and Resolutions of the General Assembly of Virginia, July 1, 1644," *Virginia Magazine of History and Biography*, XXIII (July 1915).

Adams, John and Abigail, *Familiar Letters of John Adams and his Wife, Abigail Adams During the Revolution*, edited by Charles Francis Adams, New York, 1876.

Annual Register, London, 1758-1783.

Arber, Edward, editor, *The Story of the Pilgrim Fathers 1606-1623 A.D.; As Told by Themselves, Their Friends, and Their Enemies,* London, 1897.

Barriffe, Lt. Col. William, *Militarie Discipline: or the Young Artillery-man,* London, 1643.

Bartlett, John R., editor, *Records of the Colony of Rhode Island and Providence Plantation in New England,* 10 vols., Providence, 1856-1865.

Biedma, Luys Hernandez de, *Relation of the Conquest of Florida,* 1544, Edward G. Bourne, editor, *Narratives of the Career of Hernando de Soto,* 2 vols., New York, 1904, II, 1-40.

Blakeslee, Samuel, "Narrative of Colonel Samuel Blakeslee," Buffalo Historical Society *Publications,* VIII (1905), 419-438.

Bland, Humphrey, *A Treatise of Military Discipline,* 4th edition, London, 1740.

Boone, Nicholas, *Military Discipline,* Boston, 1701.

Boston Gazette, Boston, 1756.

Bouton, Nathaniel, and others, editors, *New Hampshire State Papers,* 40 vols., Manchester, N. H., 1867-1941.

Bradford, William, *History of Plimoth Plantation,* Boston, 1899.

[Bradford, William, and Edward Winslow] *A Relation or Journal of the Beginning and Proceedings of the English Plantation,* Edward Arber, editor, *The Story of the Pilgrim Fathers, 1606-1623 A.D., As Told by Themselves, Their Friends, and Their Enemies,* London, 1897.

Brattle, William, *Sundry Rules and Directions for Drawing up a Regiment,* Boston, 1733.

Brown, Alexander, editor, *The Genesis of the United States,* 2 vols., Boston, 1890, 1897.

Brown, Alexander, *The First Republic in America,* Boston, 1898.

Browne, William H., and others, editors, *Archives of Maryland,* Baltimore, 1884-.

Cabeça de Vaca, Alvar Nuñez, *The Narrative of Cabeza de Vaca,* Frederick W. Hodges and Theodore H. Lewis, editors, *Spanish Explorers in the Southern United States, 1528-1543,* New York, 1907.

Cabrillo, Juan Rodriguez, *The Voyage of Juan Rodriguez Cabrillo, 1542-1543,* Herbert E. Bolton, editor, *Spanish Exploration in the South West,* New York, 1916.

Candles, Allen D., compiler, *The Revolutionary Records of the State of Georgia,* 3 vols., Atlanta, 1908.

Castañeda, Pedro de, *The Narrative of the Expedition of Coronado . . .,* Frederick W. Hodges and Theodore H. Lewis, editors, *Spanish Explorers in the Southern United States, 1528-1543,* New York, 1907.

Champlain, Samuel de, *The Second Voyage to New France in the Year 1610,* W. L. Grant, editor, *Voyages of Samuel De Champlain, 1604-1618,* New York, 1907.

Church, Thomas [and Benjamin Church], *The History of Philip's War, Commonly Called the Great Indian War of 1675 and 1676, Also of the French and Indian Wars at the Eastward, in 1689, 1690, 1692, 1696, and 1704,* Exeter, New Hampshire, 1829.

Clinton, George, *The Public Papers of George Clinton,* War of The Revolution Series, 8 vols., New York, 1899-1904.

Connor, Jeanette, editor, *Colonial Records of Spanish Florida,* 2 vols., Deland, Florida, 1925, 1930.

Davies, Edward, "England's Trainings," 1619, partially reprinted in Grose, *Military Antiquities,* II, 121-128.

Deane, Silas, *Deane Papers,* Charles Isham, editor, (Collections of the New York Historical Society, 1886-1890), 5 vols.

Dearborn, Henry, *Revolutionary War Journals of Henry Dearborn, 1775-1783,* Lloyd A. Brown and Howard H. Peckham, editors, Chicago, 1939.

Diderot, Dennis, *Encyclopédie ou Dictionnaire Raisonné des Sciences, des Arts et des Métiers,* 17 vols., Paris, 1751-1765.

Diderot, Dennis, *Recueil de Planches sur les Sciences, les Arts Libéraux, et les Arts Méchanique avec leur Explication,* 11 vols., Paris, 1762-1772.

Donkin, Robert, *Military Collections and Remarks,* New York, 1777.

Drake, Samuel, editor, *The Old Indian Chronicle,* Boston, 1836.

Duane, William, *A Military Dictionary,* Philadelphia, 1810.

Dundas, Col. David, *Principles of Military Movements Chiefly Applied to Infantry,* London, 1788.

Egle, William H., and others, editors, *Pennsylvania Archives,* 2nd series, 16 vols., Harrisburg, 1890.

Elvas, Gentleman of, *The Narrative of the Expedition of Hernando de Soto, by the Gentleman of Elvas*, Frederick W. Hodges and Theodore H. Lewis, editors, *Spanish Explorers in the Southern United States, 1528-1543*, New York, 1907.

[Elvas, Gentleman of], *Virginia Richly Valued*, translated by Richard Hackluyt, London, 1609, Peter Force, compiler, *Tracts and Other Papers*, 4 vols., Washington, 1836-1846, IV, no. 1. In some instances this translation has been considered better for quotation than the Elvas *Narrative* listed above.

Encyclopedia Britannica, 2nd edition, 11 vols., Edinburgh, 1778-1783.

Esquemeling, John, *Bucaniers of America*, London, 1684.

Force, Peter, compiler, *American Archives*, 4th series, 6 vols., Washington, 1837-1846; 5th series, 2 vols., Washington, 1848-1851.

Force, Peter, compiler, *Tracts and Other Papers*, 4 vols., Washington, 1836-1846.

Ford, Worthington C., editor, *Journals of the Continental Congress, 1774-1789*, 34 vols., Washington, 1904-1937.

Fortification and Military Discipline, London, 1688.

Garcilasco de la Vega, *The Florida of the Inca*, edited by Varner Austin, Texas, 1951.

Gaya, Louis de, *Gaya's Traité des Armes, 1678*, Charles ffoulkes, editor, London, 1911.

Gheyn, Jacques de, *Maniement d'Armes, d'Arquebuses, Mousquetz, et Piques*, Amsterdam, 1608.

Hackett, Charles Wilson, editor, *Historical Documents Relating to New Mexico, Nueva Vizcaya, and Approaches Thereto, to 1773*, 3 vols., Washington, 1923-1937.

Hammond, George P., and Agapito Rey, editors, *Narratives of the Coronado Expedition, 1540-1542*, Albuquerque, 1940.

Hammond, George P., and Agapito Rey, editors, *Don Juan de Oñate, Colonizer of New Mexico, 1595-1628*, 2 vols., Albuquerque, 1953.

Hanger, Col. George, *Colonel George Hanger to all Sportsmen*, London, 1814.

Hazard, Samuel, and others, editors, *Pennsylvania Archives*, 17 vols., Philadelphia, 1852-1892.

Henning, William G., *Statutes at Large, Being a Collection of all the Laws of Virginia*, 13 vols., various places and dates.

Hexham, Henry, *The First Part of the Principles of the Art Military*, Delft, 1642.

Hicks, James E., compiler, *Notes on United States Ordnance*, 2 vols., Mount Vernon, New York, 1940.

Historisch-genealogischer Calender oder Jahrbuch, Leipzig, 1784.

Hoadly, Charles J., editor, *The Public Records of the Colony of Connecticut*, 15 vols., Hartford, 1850-1890.

Hoadly, Charles J., editor, *Records of the Colony and Plantation of New Haven from 1638 to 1649*, Hartford, 1857.

Hoyt, Epaphras, *A Treatise on the Military Art*, Brattleborough, 1798.

Hubbard, William, *The History of the Indian Wars in New England from the First Settlement to the Termination of the War with King Philip, in 1677*, Samuel Drake, editor, 2 vols., Roxbury, Massachusetts, 1845.

Il Manoscritto Messicano 3738 Dette Il Codice Rios, Rome, 1900.

James, Charles, *A New and Enlarged Military Dictionary*, 3rd edition, 2 vols., London, 1810.

Juet, Robert, *The Third Voyage of Master Henry Hudson*, J. Franklin Jameson, editor, *Narratives of New Netherlands, 1609-1664*, New York, 1909.

Kimball, Gertrude S., editor, *The Correspondence of the Colonial Governors of Rhode Island, 1723-1775*, 2 vols., Boston, 1902, 1903.

Kingsbury, Susan M., editor, *The Records of the Virginia Company of London*, 4 vols., Washington, 1906-1935.

Lacroix, Irenée de, *Military and Political Hints*, Philadelphia, 1808.

Lambert, Richard, 6th Earl of Cavan, *A New System of Military Discipline, Founded upon Principle*, Philadelphia, 1776.

Lamont, M. de, and the Chevalier de la Valliere, *The Art of War*, Philadelphia, 1776.

Lane, Ralph, *Account of the Particularities of the Imployments of the Englishmen Left in Virginia, 1585-1586*, Henry S. Burrage, editor, *Early English and French Voyages Chiefly from Hakluyt, 1534-1608*, New York, 1906, 243-268.

Lee, Henry, *Memoirs of the War in the Southern Department*, New York, 1869.

Mackenzie, Frederick, *A British Fusilier in Revolutionary Boston*, Allen French, editor, Cambridge, 1926.

Mather, Cotton, *Magnalia Christi Americana*, 2 vols., Hartford, 1855.

Matthew, Thomas, *The Beginning, Progress, and Conclusion of Bacon's Rebellion, 1675-1676*, in Lyon Gardiner Tyler, editor, *Narratives of Early Virginia, 1606-1625*, New York, 1907, 15-41.

Narratives of Early Virginia, 1606-1625, New York, 1907, 15-41.

McIlwaine, H. R., editor, *Journals of the Council of the State of Virginia*, 2 vols., Richmond, 1931.

"Military Census of Middlesex County," November 23, 1687, *Virginia Magazine of History and Biography*, VIII, (October 1900), 189.

"Military Census of Virginia," *Virginia Magazine of History and Biography*, VII (April 1900), 364-367.

Minutes of the Provincial Court of Pennsylvania, 10 vols., Philadelphia, 1852.

Minutes of the Supreme Executive Council of Pennsylvania, 4 vols., Harrisburg, 1853.

Moore, Frank, compiler, *Diary of the American Revolution*, 2 vols., New York, 1860.

Myers, Albert C., editor, *Narratives of Early Pennsylvania, West New Jersey and Delaware, 1630-1707*, New York, 1912.

Nicola, Lewis, *A Treatise of Military Exercise Calculated for the Use of the Americans*, Philadelphia, 1776.

Niles, Samuel, *A Summary Historical Narrative of the Wars in New England with the French and Indians in the Several Parts of the Country*, Massachusetts Historical Society *Collections*, Boston, 3rd Series, VI (1837), 174-279; 4th Series, V (1861), 311-584.

Noble, John, editor, *Records of the Court of Assistants in the Colony of the Massachusetts Bay, 1630-1692*, 3 vols., Boston, 1904.

O'Callaghan, Edmund B., and others, editors, *Documents Relative to the Colonial History of New York*, 15 vols., Albany, 1853-1887.

Ogden, Matthias, *Journal of Major Matthias Ogden*, Morristown, New Jersey, 1928.

Orderly Book of the Siege of Yorktown from September 26th, 1781 to November 2nd, 1781, Philadelphia, 1865.

Orrery, Roger, Earl of, *A Treatise of the Art of War*, London, 1677.

Oviedo, Gonzalo Fernandez de, *A Narrative of the De Soto Expedition based on the diary of Rodrigo Ranjel*, Edward G. Bourne, editor, *Narratives of the Career of Hernando de Soto*, 2 vols., New York, 1904, II, 41-158.

Palmer, William P., and H. W. Flournoy, editors, *Calendar of Virginia State Papers and other Manuscripts,* 11 vols., Richmond, 1875-1893.

Papers of the Continental Congress, Manuscript Division of the Library of Congress.

Pargellis, Stanley, editor, *Military Affairs in North America, 1748-1765,* New York, 1936.

The Pennsylvania Packet or the General Advertizer, Philadelphia, 1777-1780.

Percy, George, "A Trewe Relacyon," *Tyler's Quarterly Historical and Geneological Magazine,* III (April 1922).

The Perfection of Military Discipline after the Newest Method as Practiced in England and Ireland &c., 4th edition, London, 1702.

Pickering, Timothy, Jr., *An Easy Plan of Discipline for a Militia,* Salem, 1775.

Plantagenet, Beauchamp, *A Description of the Province of New Albion,* in Peter Force, compiler, *Tracts and Other Papers,* 4 vols., Washington, 1836-1846, II, no. 7.

Political Magazine, Naval, Military, and Literary, 1781.

Pring, Martin, *Voyage from Bristoll,* in Henry S. Burrage, editor, *Early English and French Voyages Chiefly from Hakluyt, 1534-1608,* New York, 1906.

A Relation of Maryland, 1635, Clayton C. Hall, editor, *Narratives of Early Maryland, 1633-1684,* New York, 1910.

Roberts, Kenneth, compiler, *March to Quebec,* New York, 1940.

Saint Remy, Pierre Surirey de, *Memoires d'Artillerie,* 2nd edition, 2 vols., Paris, 1707.

Saunders, William L., editor, *The Colonial Records of North Carolina,* 10 vols., Raleigh, 1886-1890.

Shurtleff, Nathaniel B., editor, *Records of the Governor and Company of Massachusetts Bay in New England,* 5 vols., Boston, 1853, 1854.

Shurtleff, Nathaniel B., and David Pulsifer, editors, *Records of the Colony of New Plymouth In New England,* 12 vols., Boston 1855, 1861.

Simcoe, John G., *Simcoe's Military Journal,* New York, 1844.

Simes, Thomas, *The Military Medley,* London, 1768.

[Simmonds, William, editor,] *Proceedings of the English Colonies in Virginia,* Lyon Gardiner Tyler, editor, *Narratives of Early Virginia, 1606-1625,* New York, 1907, 119-204.

Smith, George, *An Universal Military Dictionary,* London, 1779.

Smith, Capt. John, *A True Relation . . . ,* Lyon Gardiner Tyler, editor, *Narratives of Early Virginia 1606-1625,* New York, 1907, 30-71.

South Carolina, "Journal of the Council of Safety, for the Province of South Carolina, 1775" in *Collections* of the South Carolina Historical Society, II, III, Charleston, 1858, 1859.

Strachey, William, *For the Colony in Virginea Britannia. Lavves Diuine, Morall and Martiall, &c.,* London, 1612, Peter Force, compiler, *Tracts and Other Papers,* 4 vols., Washington, 1836-1846, III, no. 2.

Strachey, William, *Historie of Travaile into Virginia,* Henry S. Burrage, editor, *Early English and French Voyages Chiefly from Hakluyt, 1534-1608,* New York, 1906, 415-419.

Tucker, St. George, "St. George Tucker's Journal of the Siege of Yorktown, 1781," edited by Edward M. Riley, *The William and Mary Quarterly,* Third Series, V, no. 3 (July 1948), 375-395.

Underhill, Captaine John, *Nevves From America, A.D. 1638,* David Harris Underhill, editor, n.p., 1902.

Villehuet, Bourdé de, *The Manoeuverer or Skilful Seaman,* translated by the Chevalier de Sauseuil, London, 1788.

Von Steuben, Baron Friedrich Wilhelm August Heinrich Ferdinand, *Regulations for the Order and Discipline of the Troops of the United States,* Portsmouth, 1794.

Wallhausen, Johann Jacobi von, *Kriegskunst zu Fuss,* Frankfurt, 1634.

Wallhausen, Johann Jacobi von, *Kriegskunst zu Pferd,* Frankfurt, 1620.

Ward, Robert, *Animadversions of Warre,* London, 1639.

Washington, George, *The Papers of George Washington,* Manuscript Division, Library of Congress.

Washington, George, *The Writings of George Washington,* John C. Fitzpatrick, editor, 39 vols., Washington, 1933-1944.

Wayne, Anthony, *Papers,* Revolutionary series, transcribed by Henry B. Dawson in 1860 from original manuscripts in the possession of the Wayne family, 10 bound folios, Morristown National Historical Park.

Whitehead, William, and others, editors, *New Jersey Archives,* 39 vols., Newark, 1880-1946.

Williams, Edward, *Virginia, More Especially the South Part Thereof, Richly and Truly Valued,* London, 1650, Peter Force, compiler, *Tracts and Other Papers,* 4 vols., Washington, 1836-1846, III, no. 11.

Windham, William, *A Plan of Discipline Composed for the Use of the Militia of the County of Norfolk,* London, 1759.

Winthrop, John, *The History of New England from 1630 to 1649,* James Savage, editor, 2 vols., Boston, 1853.

SECONDARY WORKS

Alm, J., *Blanka Vapen Och Skyddsvapen,* Stockholm, 1932.

Alm, J., *Eldhandvapen,* 2 vols., Stockholm, 1933, 1934.

Alm, J., "Europeiska Armborst," *Vaabenhistoriske Aarbøger,* Vb (1947), 105-255.

Ashdown, Charles H., *British and Foreign Arms and Armour,* London, 1909.

Aylward, J. D., *The Small-Sword In England,* London, 1945.

Bingham, Robert W., "The American Military Pike of '76," *Miscellany of Arms and Armor,* New York, 1928, 39, 40.

Bottet, Maurice, *L'Arme Blanche de Guerre Française Au XVIIIe Siècle,* Paris, 1910.

Bottet, Maurice, *Monographie de l'Arme a Feu Portative des Armèes Françaises,* Paris, n.d.

Boyd, Thomas, *Light-Horse Harry Lee,* New York, 1931.

Bright, James R., "The Rifle in Washington's Army," *The American Rifleman,* XCV, no. 8 (August 1947), 7-10.

Calver, Reginald P., and William L. Bolton, *History Written With Pick and Shovel,* New York, 1950.

Calvert, Albert F., *Spanish Arms and Armour,* London, 1907.

Castle, Edgerton, *Schools and Masters of Fence,* London, 1892.

Chapin, Howard M., and Charles D. Cook, "Colonial Firearms," *Antiques Magazine,* February and June, 1927, April, 1928.

Clephin, Robert C., *An Outline of the History and Development of Hand Firearms, from the Earliest Period to About the End of the Fifteenth Century,* reprint edition, Huntingdon, West Virginia, 1946.

Dean, Bashford, *Catalogue of European Court Swords and Hunting Swords,* New York, 1929.

Dean, Bashford, *Catalogue of European Daggers,* New York, 1929.

THE FRENCH WARS AND THE REVOLUTION

Dean, Bashford, *Handbook of Arms and Armor,* New York, 1915.

Dean, Bashford, *Helmets and Body Armor in Modern Warfare,* New Haven, 1920.

Dean, Bashford, "On American Polearms, Especially those in the Metropolitan Museum of Art," *Metropolitan Museum Studies,* I (1928), 32-48.

Deiss, Oberleutnant, "Blank-und Schutzwaffen Preussens vom 18. Jahrhundert ab," *Zeitschrift für Historische Waffenkunde,* Band V (1909-11), 324-330.

Dillin, John G. W., *The Kentucky Rifle,* 3rd edition, New York, 1946.

Doniol, Henri, *Historie de la Participation de la France à l'Établissement des États-Unis d'Amerique,* 6 vols., Paris, 1886.

Drummond, James, *Ancient Scottish Weapons,* Edinburgh and London, 1881.

Ellehauge, Martin, *Certain Phases in the Origin and Development of the Glaive,* Copenhagen, 1945.

Ellehauge, Martin, *The Spear Traced Through its Post-Roman Development,* Copenhagen, 1948.

Ffoulkes, Charles, *Arms and Armement,* London, 1945.

Ffoulkes, Charles, "Notes on the Bayonet," *Journal* of the Society for Army Historical Research, XVIII (1939), 190-198.

Ffoulkes, Charles, and E. C. Hopkinson, *Sword; Lance & Bayonet,* Cambridge, England, 1938.

Ffoulkes, Charles, and E. C. Hopkinson, "Swords of the British Army," in *Journal* of the Society for Army Historical Research, XII (1933), 152-158.

Franklin, Dwight, "Weapons of the Buccaneers and Pirates," *A Miscellany of Arms and Armor,* New York, 1928, 11-17.

Freytag, Gustav, "The Citizen and His Shooting Festivals," reprinted in *The Gun Collector,* no. 37, 587-612.

Gabriel, Ralph Henry, and others, editors, *The Pageant of America,* 15 vols., New Haven, 1925-1929.

Gardner, J. Starkie, *Armour in England,* London, 1897.

Gardner, J. Starkie, *Foreign Armour in England,* London, 1898.

Gardner, Robert E., *Five Centuries of Gunsmiths, Swordsmiths and Armourers, 1400-1900,* Columbus, Ohio, 1948.

George, John N., *English Guns and Rifles,* Plantersville, South Carolina, 1947.

George, John N., *English Pistols and Revolvers,* Onslow County, North Carolina, 1938.

Grancsay, Stephen V., *American Engraved Powder Horns,* New York, 1945.

Grancsay, Stephen V., "The Craft of the Early American Gunsmith," *Bulletin* of the Metropolitan Museum of Art, VI, no. 2 (October 1947), 54-61.

Grose, Francis, *Military Antiquities,* 2 vols., London, 1801.

Guillaume, Commandant, *Les Premières Armes à Feu de L'Infanterie,* Fribourg, n.d.

Harrison, G. Charter, Jr., "The Kentucky Rifle Credo," *The Gun Collector,* no. 38, 617-626.

Hicks, James E., *Notes on French Ordnance,* Mount Vernon, New York, 1938.

Hime, Henry W. L., *The Origin of Artillery,* London, 1915.

Hoopes, Thomas T., and William G. Renwick, *Three Essays on Firearms,* New York, 1927.

Hutton, Alfred, *The Sword and the Centuries,* London, 1901.

Illustrated Catalogue of United States Cartridge Company's Collection of Firearms, Lowell, Massachusetts, n.d.

Jackson, Herbert J., *European Hand Firearms of the Sixteenth, Seventeenth & Eighteenth Centuries,* London, 1923.

Johnston, Henry P., *The Storming of Stony Point,* New York, 1900.

Kauffman, Henry J., *Early American Gunsmiths, 1650-1850,* Harrisburg, Pennsylvania, 1952.

Kienbusch, Carl Otto v., "A Footnote on New England's Colonial Halberds," *Journal* of the American Military Institute, IV, no. 2 (1940), 121-124.

Laking, Sir Guy Francis, *A Record of European Armour and Arms Through Seven Centuries,* 5 vols., London, 1920-1922.

Lawson, Cecil C. P., *A History of the Uniform of the British Army,* 2 vols., London, 1940-1941.

Lefferts, Charles M., *Uniforms of the American, British, French, and German Armies in the War of the American Revolution, 1775-1783,* New York, 1926.

Lenk, Torsten, *Flintlåset, Dess Uppkomst och Utveckling,* Stockholm, 1939.

Lenk, Torsten, "Nordiska Snapplåsvapen," *Svenska Vapenhistoriska Sällskapets Skrifter,* Nya Serien II, (1952), 15-45.

Lowell, Edward J., *The Hessians and Other German Auxiliaries of Great Britain in the Revolutionary War,* New York, 1884.

Mann, Sir James G., and S. J. Camp, *European Arms and Armour,* Wallace Collection Catalogues, 3 vols., London, 1924-1945.

Manucy, Albert C., *Artillery Through the Ages,* Washington, 1949.

Mason, Louis B., *The Life and Times of Major John Mason,* New York, 1935.

Margerand, J., *Armement et Équipment de L'Infanterie Française du XVIe au XXe Siècle,* Paris, n.d.

Mayer, Joseph R., *Early Virginia Gunlocks,* Rochester Museum *Occasional Papers and Reprints,* Rochester, New York, 1939.

Mayer, Joseph R., *Flintlocks of the Iroquois, 1620-1687, Research Records* of the Rochester Museum of Arts and Sciences, no. 6, Rochester, New York, 1943.

Mayer, Joseph R., "Fragments of a Seventeenth Century Sword," *Bulletin* of the Society of American Sword Collectors, I, no. 4 (July 1947), 3.

Mayer, Joseph R., "A Theory About Snaphaunce Gun-Locks," *Journal* of the American Military Institute, III, no. 4 (Winter 1939), 258-263.

Metschl, John, *The Rudolph J. Nunnemacher Collection of Projectile Arms,* Bulletin no. 9 of the Milwaukee Public Museum, 2 vols., Milwaukee, 1928.

Miller, Robert L., "Fredericksburg Manufactory Muskets," *Military Collector & Historian,* III, no. 3 (September 1951), 63-65.

Payne-Gallwey, Sir Ralph, *The Crossbow,* London, 1903.

Pell, Stephen H. P., "American Pole Arms or Shafted Weapons," *Bulletin* of the Fort Ticonderoga Museum, V, no. 3 (July 1939), 66-103.

Pell, Stephen H. P., "The Gorget," *Bulletin* of the Fort Ticonderoga Museum, IV, no. 5 (September 1937), 126-141.

Peterson, Harold L., "The American Cavalry Saber of the Revolution," *Military Collector & Historian,* II, no. 3 (September 1950), 33-36.

Peterson, Harold L., "The American Cutlass," *Bulletin* of the Society of American Sword Collectors, III, no. 2 (October 1949), 8-15.

Peterson, Harold L., *American Silver Hilted Swords,* Washington, 1955.

Peterson, Harold L., *The American Sword, 1775-1945*, New Hope, 1954.

Peterson, Harold L., "The Military Equipment of the Plymouth and Bay Colonies, 1620-1690," *New England Quarterly*, XX, no. 2 (June 1947), 197-208.

Peterson, Harold L., "New Evidence on Colonial Firearms from Jamestown Excavations," *The Gun Collector*, June 1949, 313-316.

Peterson, Harold L., "The Private Soldiers' Ferguson Rifle," *Military Collector & Historian*, II, no. 4 (December 1950), 60-62.

Peterson, Harold L., *Silas Deane in France*, typescript of a Master of Arts thesis, University of Wisconsin, 1946.

Peterson, Harold L., "Did It Work?", *The American Rifleman*, February, 1955, 20-23.

Peterson, Harold L., "What is a Dog Lock," *The American Rifleman*, July, 1955, 42, 43.

Quinn, David B., "Preparations for the 1585 Virginia Voyage," *William and Mary Quarterly*, 3rd series, VI, no. 2 (April 1949), 208-236.

Satterlee, L. D., and Arcadi Gluckman, *American Gun Makers*, Buffalo, New York, 1945.

Sawyer, Charles W., *Firearms in American History, 1600 to 1800*, Boston, 1910.

Scoffern, J., *Projectile Weapons of War and Explosive Compounds*, London, 1858.

Sherlock, Herbert A., "Early British Grenade Launchers," *Military Collector & Historian*, III, no. 2 (June 1951), 44-46.

Stone, George C., *A Glossary of the Construction, Decoration and Use of Arms and Armor*, Portland, Maine, 1934.

Sumner, Percy, "Morier's Paintings of Grenadiers, 1751," *Journal* of the Society for Army Historical Research, XVIII (1939), 212-223.

Sumner, Percy, "Private, Light Troop, 11th Dragoons, c. 1760," *Journal* of the Society for Army Historical Research, XVIII (1939), 187.

Thierbach, Morritz, *Die Geschichtliche Entwickelung der Handfeuerwaffen*, Dresden, 1899.

Todd, Frederick P., "Major Patrick Campbell," *Military Collector & Historian*, III, no. 4 (December 1951), 88-90.

Tylden, Major G., "The Use of Firearms by Cavalry," *Journal* of the Society for Army Historical Research, XIX (1940), 15.

Valencia de Don Juan, El Conde de, *Catálogo Histórico-descriptivo de la Real Armería de Madrid*, Madrid, 1898.

Van Rensselaer, Stephen, *American Firearms*, Watkins Glen, New York, 1947.

Walton, R. H., *Early Civil War Firearms in the Curtis Museum, Alton*, Alton, Hampshire, 1948.

Woodward, Arthur, "The Metal Tomahawk," *Bulletin* of the Fort Ticonderoga Museum, VII, no. 3 (January 1946), 2-42.

Woodward, Arthur, "Some Notes on Gun Flints," *Military Collector & Historian*, III, no. 2 (June 1951), 29-36.

Wright, John W., "Some Notes on the Continental Army," *William and Mary College Quarterly*, Second Series, II, nos. 2 and 3 (April and July 1931).

Index

It should be noted that this index is for the main portion of the text only.
It does not cover the Preface, footnotes, Appendix or Bibliography.

[347]

INDEX